Engaged Buddhism

For my parents

'*a mountain keeps an echo deep inside itself
that's how I hold your voice*'

—Rumi

Engaged Buddhism
The Dalai Lama's Worldview

Bharati Puri

OXFORD
UNIVERSITY PRESS

OXFORD
UNIVERSITY PRESS

YMCA Library Building, Jai Singh Road, New Delhi 110 001

Oxford University Press is a department of the University of Oxford. It furthers the
University's objective of excellence in research, scholarship, and education
by publishing worldwide in

Oxford   New York

Auckland   Cape Town   Dar es Salaam   Hong Kong   Karachi
Kuala Lumpur   Madrid   Melbourne   Mexico City   Nairobi
New Delhi   Shanghai   Taipei   Toronto

With offices in

Argentina   Austria   Brazil   Chile   Czech Republic   France   Greece
Guatemala   Hungary   Italy   Japan   Poland   Portugal   Singapore
South Korea   Switzerland   Thailand   Turkey   Ukraine   Vietnam

Oxford is a registered trade mark of Oxford University Press
in the UK and in certain other countries

Published in India by Oxford University Press, New Delhi

ISBN 13: 978-0-19-567331-9
ISBN 10: 0-19-567331-X

Typeset in AGaramond 10.5/12.5
at Le Studio Graphique, Gurgaon 122 001
Printed in India at Ram Printograph, Delhi 110 051
Published by Manzar Khan, Oxford University Press
YMCA Library Building, Jai Singh Road, New Delhi 110 001

Contents

Acknowledgements

An insightful meeting with Professor Dawa T. Norbu sparked off the motivation to pursue this work which has eventually evolved into this book. I am very grateful to Professor Norbu for having encouraged my interest in studying culture and politics at the intersections of Philosophy and Ethics.

Among the many debts I have incurred during the formulation and completion of this work, is that owed to various institutions and libraries I could access as well as to the persons associated with them and I especially thank Mr Pema Yeshi and Mrs Norzum at Library of Tibetan Works and Archives in Dharamsala; Mr Jampa Samten at Shantarakshita Library of the Central Institute of Higher Tibetan Studies, Sarnath; Professor K. Angrup at the Tibet House Library, New Delhi and Mrs Tsewang Dolma at the Central Institute of Buddhist Studies Library, Choglamsar, Ladakh. I thank the following in Delhi: Nehru Memorial Museum and Library, Central Secretariat Library, Indira Gandhi National Centre for the Arts Library, British Council Library, American Center Library, Centre for the Study of Developing Societies (CSDS) Library, Institute for Chinese Studies Library at CSDS, Jawaharlal Nehru University Library, Devahuti Damodar Library of Indian Civilization, and Delhi University Library.

I am very grateful to Tenzin Geyche Tethong (Secretary to His Holiness The Dalai Lama), Tenzin Taklha (Deputy Secretary, Office of His Holiness the Dalai Lama) and Ven. Lhakdor (Director, Library of Tibetan Works and Archives) for my interview with His Holiness the Dalai Lama.

For the opportunities to research, interact, and lecture, I am grateful to: Professors Jeffrey Hopkins, William Magee, and Donald S. Lopez Jr. for their interest in this work; Professors G.P. Deshpande, Alka Acharya and Satya P. Gautam at Jawaharlal Nehru University as well as my teachers at

Panjab University, Chandigarh; Professors Suresh Sharma, Patricia Uberoi, Brij Tankha, Manoranjan Mohanty and colleagues at the Centre for the Study of Developing Societies; and my students and colleagues at the Indian Institute of Technology, Delhi. Luke Harding, Suzanne Goldenberg and Phoebe Taplin at *The Guardian*, South Asia Bureau for their enormous cooperation while I worked with them, and Mark Tully and Gillian Wright who have been extremely kind and helpful.

At OUP Delhi, Shashank Sinha and Aparajita Basu kept me going unswervingly and I am immensely grateful to them.

I thank my friends Manreet, Kelly, Sagar, Rashmi, Shankari, Surinder, Ravindranathan, Vishal, Prashant. I thank my uncle Dr Vishwa Chandra Ohri, Mini, Manu, and Rajiv for their love and encouragement.

One more person has taken as much interest in giving shape to this book—Raviprasad Narayanan—I thank him for being a patient partner in sustaining us in a number of ways through the tedium of working together.

To my parents Kanwal Puri and Krishan Chand Puri whom I owe this work and everything precious—for your voyage in life—my salutations!

Note to the Reader

In every chapter the complete reference to each citation is provided the first time it occurs in the endnotes. In occurrences thereafter, this note is referred to as 'nx', where x is the note number of first occurrence. For instance, in the examples below, the details of the references have appeared earlier in endnote numbers 4 and 5 respectively.

11. Weber, n. 4, p. 213.

Or

12. Sizemore and Swearer, n. 5, p. 223.

Introduction

Engaged Buddhist Ethic

Theory, Praxis, and the Dalai Lama's *Weltanschauung*

Buddhism, like other great systems, has at many points been developed and refined in accordance with the 'native genius' of a people who embrace it.[1] Standing testimony to this view is a movement which is still considered nascent and which is seeking to actualize Buddhism's traditional ideals of wisdom and compassion in the contemporary world.[2] This movement is called 'Engaged Buddhism.' Assumptions and claims that regard the central emphasis of Buddhism on the transmundane goal of *nirvana*, or in monastic withdrawal from the world and on individual extrication from the world[3], as Weber views Buddhism[4], come across as being antithetical to the social ethic of 'Engaged Buddhism,' which lays greater stress on world engagement rather than on world abandonment. It is the 'Middle Way' of the Buddha, which teaches that both extreme asceticism and extreme sensual indulgence are to be avoided; it has emphasized that even the lives and practices of monks who live austerely should not be excessively ascetic, and that the life of even the most lax Buddhist layperson ought not to be so pleasure-oriented as to become an object of attachment. It is in avoiding these two extremes, that the 'extent' of the 'Middle Way' is vast, wide, and very flexible.[5]

Extending the same logic, Buddhist social ethics, in keeping with the Buddhist doctrine of Pratityasamutpada (doctrine of dependent origination), shows that individual betterment and perfection on the one hand and social good on the other, are fundamentally interrelated and interdependent. A society, in which all individual members are self-sufficient or self-sustaining can be called happy and secure to a large extent. Further, a secure and peaceful society is favourable to individual, intellectual, and spiritual pursuits. The Buddhist standpoint ascertains that a minimal amount of responsibility for individual betterment and perfection is required of all individuals, while maintaining an appropriate degree of social responsibility. Even the most solitary monks have been in regular contact with—and are responsible for—the 'well-being' of a community, and studies show that it may not be entirely true to say that the Buddhist monastic order, for instance, stays entirely aloof from society. Therefore, even though it is acknowledged that Buddhism is a religion of renunciation and transcendental understanding, the 'challenge' to Buddhist praxis was—and is—to create, and to perpetuate an institutional framework that is 'of-the-world', yet at the same time 'out-of-the-world'. Scholars suggest that the community of monks and the monastery (*sangha*) are the vehicle for this.[6] Research reveals that apart from their individual spiritual quest, monks must also meet with villagers and share their spiritual attainment by teaching the Dharma. Monks perform this task for the good of lay society, not simply to return favours but out of their own virtue of compassion for the people:

Even in their earliest stages … Buddhist monastic communities developed symbiotic and reciprocal relationships with the laity. Monks and nuns became responsible for teaching the Middle Path and gained respect and patronage by their own exemplary moral conduct. Lay persons responded by providing food, clothing, and shelter for the monastic community and by regarding the ascetic life as a paradigm of the ethical-religious path.[7]

Therefore, those who see Buddhism to have no social or economic ethic in any recognizable sense,[8] engender as well as foster an ecliptic understanding of the social ethic of Buddhism. There is indeed an economic ethic in Buddhist theory as has been observed by some scholars[9] and studies explicitly argue that the monastic tradition is not really 'anti-economics' explaining how, historically, monasteries have even been centres of trade.[10]

Weber's thesis that the fundamental teachings of Buddhism cannot have an economic or social ethic in any recognizable sense argues that the doctrine of not self (*anatta*) must fundamentally undermine moral concern for the welfare of one's neighbour or one's community. Weber postulates that any kind of social ethic predicated upon the value of individual persons 'must be as remote as possible from a salvation doctrine which...could discern only the grand and pernicious basic illusion.'[11] He also claims that the central emphasis of Buddhism is on the transmundane goal of nirvana or monastic withdrawal from the world, and on individual self-extrication from the *samsara*, which can produce at best only an attenuated social ethic.[12] He regards Buddhism's entire lay ethic as an 'insufficiency ethic of the weak', lacking in normative specificity with regard to economic life.[13] In Weber's perception, the *karma* doctrine itself erodes any possible critical perspective on an existing economic order and because every individual's material circumstances—whether he be rich or poor—can be traced to his prior moral conduct in Buddhism, all social and economic status become 'deserved' and immune to criticisms.[14]

Contrary to such perceptions, commentators have observed that Buddhism has developed an important body of socio-ethical teachings and have sometimes traced these to the doctrinal positions that Weber and others are seen to undermine.[15] For instance, it has been observed that first, Buddhists have not usually interpreted the doctrine of 'not self' in such a way as to erode 'moral regard' for the other. On the contrary, this doctrine has been used to encourage 'selfless' compassion for others. In the economic domain, this teaching is meant to counter the sense of 'mineness' that stimulates greed and lust for material acquisition.[16] Second, it has been stressed that Buddhist social ethics would be badly misunderstood, if the ethics for the monastic community were to be severed from the rich body of teachings regarding the ideal political order and duties of the Buddhist righteous ruler, the *cakkavata*. It has been suggested that the monastic community ideally serves as the conscience for politics and economics in society.[17] Third, belief in karma in no way undercuts the possibility of specific normative regulations for the conduct of economic life, nor does it rule out a critique of existing economic arrangements in the light of an ideal moral vision of the economic order.[18] Further, those who critique Weber's view that Buddhism has an other-worldly ideal that devalues the existential world and its drives, argue that it is inaccurate to see Buddhism as having no positive role in bringing about changes in society, for while it has soteriological aims, it also has a genuine social ethic.

Critics of the Weberian thesis would regard his attempts at portraying the doctrine of karma as fatalistic, a misinterpretation of a seminal Buddhist concept.[19] 'Egolessness' does not undercut 'a healthy drive for personality integration, social reform or even nation-building', but should only reduce selfishness and avarice, thus aiding cooperation.[20] It is the logic of this very argument, that forms the bedrock for the existent social ethic in Pan-Buddhism and for the movement defined as Engaged Buddhism.

Buddhism has never existed in isolation,[21] and often changes within it can be connected to changes outside the *sangha*. Thus, it is contended that while socially Engaged Buddhism suggests that Buddhists are socially active and applying Buddhism to 'liberate society,' in many ways these leaders are instruments for helping the *sangha* to catch up with secular society and to 'liberate Buddhism.' Thus, it is argued that being socially engaged is not new to Buddhism, but the way that Buddhist leaders are engaging each other and are being engaged is new and deserves clarification.[22] According to a Buddhist scholar, Buddhism, viewed historically, may first have begun as an escape from the world and then turned into a re-visioning and re-engagement in the world when the one who experiences sees it with 'fresh eyes'[23].

Coined by the Vietnamese monk and social activist Thich Nhat Hanh in 1963 during the Vietnam war, the term 'Engaged Buddhism' has metamorphosed into a bigger movement. Drawing on traditional Buddhist ethical and social teachings, Engaged Buddhism seeks to apply them to social life as well as to social issues, thereby engaging them for social good.[24] Although Buddhism has always been socially engaged, considering that it draws its members and support from society, it is also true that on the reverse, many Buddhists join Buddhism to free themselves from society in retreat and contemplation. These 'forest recluses' and 'mountain meditators' have often won fame and admiration from society, 'partially in recognition of their capacity to transcend the social stresses that drive and divide ... ordinary lives.'[25] However, neither being socially engaged nor being a recluse is uniquely Buddhist. What is uniquely new to those contemporary Buddhists who are socially concerned is that they are 'adopting many new methods and styles: they are more international in scope, more educated in their training, more democratic and gender inclusive in their organizations, more aware of ecological destruction, more innovative institutionally and technologically, and more concerned than ever to move society toward non-violence, justice, truthfulness and peace'.[26] Today's Engaged Buddhists are addressing international issues ranging from the disposal of nuclear waste to human rights violations in Myanmar to a peaceful solution to the Tibet question.

Attributed to Thich Nhat Hanh, during the 1980s and 1990s other personages have been associated with this movement. The most internationally visible leader of this movement is the Dalai Lama. Other significant figures are Cheng Yen, Sulak Sivaraksa, Ahangamage T. Ariyaratna, Joanna Macy, Kenneth Kraft, among others.[27] All agree that for Buddhism to be an effective force for systemic institutional change, traditional Buddhist emphasis on individual, moral and spiritual transformation must be adjusted to address more forcefully the structures of oppression, exploitation, and environmental degradation while preserving the unique Buddhist emphasis on the practice of mindful awareness and a lifestyle of simplicity. Representing a radical departure from some earlier forms of Buddhist practice, the 'meaning' of these new Buddhist activities cannot be understood just in contrast with traditional forms of Buddhism since the new forms of socially Engaged Buddhism could not have arisen in traditional cultures. Thus there is a broad agreement that Buddhism could change because the cultural context changed.[28]

Interpreted thus, the spirit of Buddhism does not lie in clinging to old forms or outmoded ideas at the expense of 'personal authenticity and dignity.'[29] The Buddha is said to have been opposed to all those who had set views or closed systems of thought. He insisted that his followers should concentrate on the way leading to enlightenment. He did this because he realized that the adoption of definite views can lead to disputations with rival doctrines. In Mahayana Buddhism the goal of enlightenment may be reached by many means or *'upaya'* and, any way that relieves us of our spiritual blindness and leads to enlightenment is a permissible way. The Buddhist analogy between the teacher, who uses ideas and words in his instruction, and a raft that is of use only to cross the river[30], is an example of how Buddhism is malleable and relevant for every age.

It is with this *Weltanschauung* that the Dalai Lama considers, and examines ways in which Buddhism and social activism can complement each other. He says:

... Buddhism and social activism can contribute to each other. This is a timely and potentially faithful field of enquiry. *While the main emphasis of the Buddha's teaching is on inner development that is no reason for Buddhists not to participate in the society in which they live.* We are all dependent on others and so responsible to others. *The fundamental aim of Buddhist practice, to avoid harming others and if possible to help them, will not be fully achieved simply by thinking about it* [italics added]. The phenomenon of social activism is an attempt by like minded people to alleviate social problems through drawing attention to them and trying to change the attitudes of those in a position to affect them.[31]

The Dalai Lama contends that his philosophy of developing a 'good heart' is based on core Buddhist principles, but he maintains that it is also in accordance with the best principles of all religions.[32] In his talks with

Buddhist organizations, he often stresses the notion that compassion is basic to all Buddhist practice, and he further insists that direct engagement with other people and their problems is necessary in the development of genuine compassion. According to him, too many Buddhists withdraw from the world and cultivate their own minds, and although this is an important first step for many, he urges Buddhists to become involved in the world:

In the first stage, sometimes we need isolation while pursuing our own inner development; however, after you have some confidence, some strength, you must remain with, contact, and serve society in any field—health, education, politics or whatever. There are people who call themselves religious minded, trying to show this by dressing in a peculiar manner, maintaining a peculiar way of life, and isolating themselves from the rest of society. This is wrong. A scripture of mind-purification says, 'Transform your inner viewpoint, but leave your external appearance as it is.' This is important. Because the very purpose of practicing the Great Vehicle is service for others, you should not isolate yourself from society. In order to serve, in order to help, you must remain in society.[33]

He insists on the necessity to achieve a balance between contemplation and social activism, as both are essential components of a healthy spiritual life.[34] However, he issues a word of caution by suggesting that for most people no amount of contemplative activity can take the place of engagement in the world, while cautioning that activism alone tends to become sterile and can lead to negative emotions such as frustration, anger, and hatred.[35] A basic tenet of his teaching is that Buddhism is essentially activist. In his assessment Buddhism teaches people to renounce the world, but this does not mean physically separating oneself from worldly activities, but rather cultivating an attitude of *cognitive detachment* while still working for others. This is the proper attitude of a bodhisattva,[36] who is able to work within the world for the benefit of others without becoming dragged down by its negative elements.[37]

He makes simple practical suggestions, for instance one should engage in meditative practice early in the morning and then consciously remain mindful throughout the day of the motivation of practice, which is genuine compassion for all sentient beings. He also suggests that during the day one should regularly consider whether or not one's actions are of real benefit to others, and before going to sleep one should review the day's activities to evaluate what one has done for others. In his words:

We must promote compassion and love; this is our real duty. Government has too much business to have time for these things. As private persons we have more time to think along these lines—how to make a contribution to human society by promoting the development of compassion and a real sense of community.[38]

Clearly, the Dalai Lama shows that Weber, if he was not accurate in judging the value of Buddhism, is still inaccurate today, when Buddhism as presented by the Dalai Lama is evolving and moving to a stage where being engaged is the rule rather than the exception. Reflecting this is the claim that radical protest movements and pioneering thinkers are taking forth Buddhism into a creative engagement with modernism with various activist agendas.[39] In this movement the Dalai Lama has become a highly regarded international figure and has altered the image of Buddhism, which is sometimes interpreted only as a quietist and introverted spirituality.[40] Considered as the world's most renowned socially Engaged Buddhist, Tenzin Gyatso, the XIVth Dalai Lama says:

Each of us has responsibility for all mankind. It is time for us to think of other people as true brothers and sisters and to become concerned with their welfare, with lessening their suffering. Even if you cannot sacrifice your own benefit entirely, you should not forget the concerns of others. We should think more about the future and the benefit of all mankind.[41]

The Dalai Lama has become popular and this can be attributed to the hope he represents for new approaches to global problems by showing new ways in which an individual can relate to the world he lives in as also to other individuals by not leaving the world, but by staying within it.[42] According to the Dalai Lama, 'we need a new concept, *a lay spirituality* ... it could lead us to set up what we are all looking for, a *secular morality*.'[43] Thus the definition of Engaged Buddhism, can be sought in the Mahayana reform movement, which outlines three principles as foundational to Buddhism: to avoid all evil, to cultivate good, and to serve all beings.[44] In harmony with this when the Dalai Lama is asked what his goals are, he replies by quoting the Bodhicaryavatara of Santideva: 'For as long as space endures, and for as long as living beings remain, until then may I, too, abide to dispel the misery of the world.'[45]

Seen from this traditional point of view, emphasis on global responsibility to relieve suffering, has been intrinsic to Buddhism. It is the aim of the present study to see as to how this social responsibility—being carried out today—has some new features and how these features are seen in the Dalai Lama's thought, broadly charted out below:

(1) Like all Buddhist leaders, the Dalai Lama has a strong commitment to action in society. Complete reliance on meditation is rejected and considered inadequate by him. The Dalai Lama's observance that 'the sole reliance on prayer has created a "religious sentiment" that became an obstacle to human efforts to save Tibet,'[46] exemplifies this attitude. Therefore it is stated that 'unlike the old Buddhism, the new "international Buddhism" finds that meditation without action in society is not enough. However, the new Buddhism does not abandon meditation, but emphasizes "mindfulness in action." In contrast to the reforms of the 1960s that emphasized activism but not mindfulness, the creativity of this new Buddhism is based on inward calmness, mindfulness, and compassion that is (a) aware of the interdependence of self, others, and the environment, and (b) based on the impermanence of self and others, has compassion for others, that is free from ego.'[47]

(2) Buddhist morality is based upon 'right view', namely the quest for enlightenment. The Dalai Lama's 'secular morality' suggests that all humans need to: (a) restore a more balanced ecology (b) establish a more just economy (c) ensure more balanced relationships between the sexes (d) avoid absolutizing any ideology or doctrine, but be open to all ideas, and (e) be open to change based on consensus for the common.

(3) The Dalai Lama's influence has spread through various modes such as retreats, videos, the internet, international conferences, and magazines. Networking organizations dedicated to social justice, ecology, and human rights that exercise influence through the popular media and new interactive information technology (like on-line conferences relating to various issues on Buddhism) support the Dalai Lama's views that are of universal significance.

(4) With his inter-religious orientation, the Dalai Lama has attempted to break the boundaries of sectarianism of any sort.

(5) Understanding all life as being interconnected, it is the Dalai Lama's quest to restore the balance of nature, both within and around us. Like all Engaged Buddhists, he is committed to finding ways to make the economic system more sustainable.

(6) The Dalai Lama's belief that all social power and decisions should be shared and balanced among the sexes (although not completely sure-footed—keeping in view the separate *vinaya* rules for monks and nuns) is an attempt to see both the genders as equal. He has gone so far as to say that the next Dalai Lama could be a woman.

The outcome thus is that despite the fact that he is a Buddhist, the Dalai Lama is inclusive about all spiritual resources and accepts inter-faith dialogue as being extremely important. His thought is not reductionist or exclusive; like all Engaged Buddhist leaders of today, he is committed to working in this world to seek relief from suffering through compassion and enlightenment, here and now; the contemporary Buddhist reformers affirm the inherent goodness of the human heart. The Dalai Lama's attempt to empower ordinary people by emphasizing their Buddha nature, dignity, and inherent worth is a negation of the *karmic* debt that humans are meant to incur which according to traditional Buddhism is obstructive to salvation[48]. Like all the Buddhist leaders today, the Dalai Lama has sought to reform institutions in collaboration with education, democracy and the internet to ensure diversification, maximum participation, and fulfillment of one's potential. Recognizing that each form of life—whether biological or human—has integrity and value, no person or group is completely self-sufficient, no matter how powerful. The Dalai Lama insists that because of the phenomena of interdependence, everyone is partial and cannot survive for long without collaboration with others, while he still considers that each individual is precious and 'needed,' to balance and improve the whole. Engaged Buddhism lays stress on diversity as a source of enrichment rather than viewing it as a barrier or a failure. This includes respecting the diversity of religions. Thus, it would be suggested that 'today all religious scriptures need to balance ... but will become narrow and destructive without *engagement* [italics added] with a wider diversity of life.'[49]

The questions arise as to how, why, and what has enabled Buddhists to become socially engaged in new ways. It has been suggested that five conditions—an independent judiciary providing some protection from the state, a humanistic enlightenment movement that encourages independent intellectual inquiry, a modern communication system to support these individual developments, relative peace and a global economy have enabled new models, networks, and groups of Buddhists to emerge, and therefore have enabled Buddhists to become socially engaged. Thus the suggestion that socially Engaged Buddhism may be working to liberate society only because society has liberated Buddhism from its past restrictions. The result has been a transformation and liberation of Buddhism, as also the liberation of society. 'In classical terms, socially Engaged Buddhism is the mutual liberation of self and others, in a global and interactive context.'[50]

This book is an attempt to study the conceptual foundations of the Dalai Lama's thought. Very few studies within the vast literature on and by the Dalai Lama either establish or seek the conceptual foundations of his thought. The Dalai Lama's thought symbolizes a religious and ethical response to oppression. His ethical teachings have gained worldwide recognition primarily because his actions and writings reflect a concern for combining ancient religious traditions with a contemporary political/social/ religious cause. Also, his cause is not limited to the political situation of his own country but extends to the arena of international politics and human relations generally. In a sense, his voicing of the Tibetan question becomes the shared cause for those who defend justice wherever individual or group oppression exists. This is clearly reflected in his writings. His origins as a Buddhist leader in a particular area of the world provides a frame of reference for his focus on much wider considerations. Paramount among these considerations is the importance of cooperation, not competition or hostility, among world religions. A secondary feature is the recognition that all people living in the 'modern' world need to find a path that can combine spiritual values with the possibilities presented by the application of reason and scientific knowledge. It was the Dalai Lama's emphasis on such principles and the importance of using them to develop happiness and kindness that built his reputation as a champion of world peace. The Dalai Lama, by choosing to show the relevance of Buddhist moral precepts to every sphere of human activity—specifically the social, religious and political spheres, establishes them as ethical teachings and shows their relevance by asserting that they are rational principles, which, if followed, bring about social and individual betterment and well-being. It can be seen that the essential character of the Dalai Lama's thought is based on the logic that human life is a synthetic whole which cannot be insular. Basically a reformulation of Buddhism representing a distinct attitude towards politics and society, his thought links the seemingly separate segments—religious, moral, political, economic, social, individual, and collective as different but equally significant facets of human life.

The aim of this study will be to concentrate upon the Dalai Lama's concept of tolerance, compassion, right motivation, non-violence, eco-consciousness, universal responsibility, and interconnectedness with reference to his social, religious and political thought. The above-mentioned concepts are based upon metaphysical presuppositions and have important implications for his social, religious, and political thought.[51]

While articulating and carrying out an analysis of the Dalai Lama's thought, allusions to other thinkers and writers have been made in order to draw parallels. Such comparative analyses help in bringing out the significance of the eclectic dimensions of the Dalai Lama's thought. He has written a number of articles and books in which he has expounded his concepts and explained their implications and at times he has defended them against criticism and misconceptions. While employing a methodology that is eclectic and interdisciplinary, the aim has been to see the emergence of the Dalai Lama's *Weltanschauung.* The textual analysis of various works by the Dalai Lama is supported by an interview with him.

Notes

1. Dawa T. Norbu, 'What Tibet Has Done in 2100 Years', *Tibetan Review,* (Delhi), March 1973, p. 8.

Also see Donald S. Lopez Jr., *Modern Buddhism: Readings for the Unenlightened,* London: Penguin, 2002.

2. Philip Russell Brown, 'Socially Engaged Buddhism: A Buddhist Practice for the West', *http://www.buddhanet.net/filelib/genbud/eng_bud.txt.*

Fred Eppsteimer (ed.), *The Path of Compassion: Writings on Socially Engaged Buddhism,* Berkeley: Parallax Press, (1985) rev. ed., 1988, p. xii.

3. Since Max Weber, there has been an implicit (and sometimes explicit) understanding that Buddhism shuns the worldly arena. Max Weber, *The Religion of India: The Sociology of Hinduism and Buddhism*, New York: The Free Press, 1958. See, Eppsteimer, n. 2, p. ix.

4. Weber, ibid., pp. 204–30.

5. Russell F. Sizemore and Donald K. Swearer (eds), *Ethics, Wealth and Salvation: A Study of Buddhist Social Ethics,* Columbia: University of South Carolina Press, 1990, p. 30.

6. Melvyn C. Goldstein and Paljor Tsarong, 'Tibetan Buddhist Monasticism: Social, Psychological and Cultural Implications', *The Tibet Journal* (Dharamsala, Library of Tibetan Works and Archives), vol. 10, 1985, pp. 14–31. Goldstein has attempted to show in his study that Tibetan monasticism attempts to socialize recruits into an alternative set of norms, values, and standards for perceiving and evaluating the world, a cultural template in which love, desire, and wealth were renowned as the source of misery and suffering.

7. John Carman and Mark Juergensmeyer, *A Bibliographic Guide to the Comparative Study of Ethics,* Cambridge: Cambridge University Press, 1991, p. 72.

8. Sizemore and Swearer, n. 5, p. 222.

9. E.F. Schumacher, *Small Is Beautiful: A Study of Economics as if People Mattered*, London: Vintage, (1973), 1993, pp. 38–46.

10. M.N. Rajesh, 'Role of Gompa in Traditional Tibetan Society: A Thematic Study', Unpublished Doctoral Thesis, JNU, 1998.

11. a. Weber, n. 3, p. 213.

　b. Sizemore and Swearer, n. 5, p. 223.

12. Sizemore and Swearer, ibid.

13. a. Weber, n. 3, p. 215.

　b. Ibid. as cited in Sizemore and Swearer, n. 5, p. 223.

14. Sizemore and Swearer, n. 5, p. 223.

15. E. Sarkisyanz, *Buddhist Backgrounds of Burmese Revolution*, The Hague: Martinus Nijhoff, 1965, Chapters 6 and 7 and Stanley J. Tambiah, *World Conqueror and World Renouncer*, Cambridge, Mass.: Harvard University Press, 1976, Chapters 1–5 as cited in Sizemore and Swearer, n. 5, p. 233.

16. Sizemore and Swearer, n. 5, p. 223.

17. Ibid., p. 223.

18. Ibid., p. 224.

19. Padmasiri De Silva, *Value Orientations and Nation Building*, Colombo: Lake House Investment Ltd., 1976, pp. 6–7.

20. Ibid., p. 8.

21. David W. Chappell, 'Engaged Buddhists in a Global Society: Who is Being Liberated?' in Sulak Sivaraksa (hon. ed.), Pipob Udomittipong and Chris Walker (eds), *Socially Engaged Buddhism for the New Millennium: Essays in Honour of The Ven. Phra Dhammapitaka (Bhikku P.A. Payutto) On His 60th Birthday Anniversary*, Bangkok: Sathikoses-Nagapradipa Foundation & Foundation for Children, 12 May 2542 (1999), p. 76.

22. Ibid.

23. Herbert Guenther, 'Reflections on Vision and World-engagement', in Ramesh Chandra Tewari and Krishna Nath (eds), *Universal Responsibility: A Collection of Essays to Honour Tenzin Gyatso the XIVth Dalai Lama*, New Delhi: Foundation for Universal Responsibility of His Holiness The Dalai Lama and ANB Publishers Pvt. Ltd., 1996, p. 1.

24. Peter Harvey, *An Introduction to Buddhist Ethics*, Cambridge: Cambridge University Press, 2000, p. 112.

25. Chappell, n. 21, p. 76.

26. Ibid.

Also see Sunita Aron, 'Can Dalai Lama Do What Others Couldn't?' *Hindustan Times*, (New Delhi), 18 January 2004.

27. Donald K. Swearer, 'Buddhism and Ecology: Challenge and Promise', *Earth Ethics*, (Washington), vol. 10, no. 1, Fall 1998, p. 22.

Also see Lopez, n. 1.

28. Chappell, n. 21, p. 81.

29. S. Radhakrishnan, *Recovery of Faith*, New Delhi: HarperCollins Publishers India, 1997, p. 191.

30. Ibid., pp. 190–1.

31. Ken Jones, *The Social Face of Buddhism: An Approach to Political and Social Activism*, London: Wisdom Publications, 1989, p. 9.

32. The Fourteenth Dalai Lama His Holiness Tenzin Gyatso, *Kindness, Clarity and Insight*, Jeffrey Hopkins and Elizabeth Napper, (eds) trans. Jeffrey Hopkins, New York: Snow Lion Publications, 1984, pp. 9–17 and 45–50.

The same point of view is acknowledged by Powers. See John Powers, 'The Free Tibet Movement: A Selected Narrative', in Christopher S. Queen (ed.), *Engaged Buddhism in The West*, Boston: Wisdom Publications, 2000, p. 231.

33. Tenzin Gyatso, 'A Talk to Western Buddhists', in Sidney Piburn (ed. and compiler), *The Dalai Lama: A Policy of Kindness: An Anthology of Writings By and About the Dalai Lama*, Delhi: Motilal Banarsidass Publishers Pvt. Ltd., (1990), 1997, p. 82.

Also see Powers, n. 32, p. 231.

34. Ibid.

35. Ibid.

36. The Bodhisattva is a Buddhist practitioner who is committed to achieving Buddha-hood in order to benefit others. This is the ideal of Mahayana Buddhism. See Queen, n. 32, p. 243.

37. Powers, n. 32, p. 231.

38. The Fourteenth Dalai Lama His Holiness Tenzin Gyatso, n. 32, p. 64.

Also see Powers, n. 32, p. 232.

39. Ken Jones, *The Social Face of Buddhism*, London: Wisdom Publications, 1989, pp. 228, 242–52, 324.

40. Ibid., pp. 9–10.

41. Brown, n. 2.

42. Chappell, n. 21, p. 77.

In a significant development on the Ayodhya issue the Dalai Lama had proposed a solution to bring about a meaningful dialogue between Hindus and Muslims. See Aron, n. 26.

43. *Tricycle*, Fall 1995, 39a, as cited in Chappell, n. 21, p. 77.

44. Ibid.

45. *Tricycle*, Fall 1991, 20, as cited in Chappell, n. 21, p. 78.

46. *Tricycle*, Fall 1995, 5b, as cited in Chappell, n. 21, p. 78.

47. Chappell, n. 21, p. 78.

48. Ibid., pp. 79–80.

49. Ibid., p. 81.

50. Ibid., p. 84.

51. The writer had discussed these points in an interview with His Holiness the Dalai Lama, in the Office of His Holiness The Dalai Lama, McLeod Ganj, Dharamsala. See Appendix–I.

'It would be natural to compare him with Mahatma Gandhi, one of the century's greatest protagonists of peace, and the Dalai Lama likes to consider himself one of Gandhi's successor's...In a world in which suspicion and aggression have all too long characterized relations between people and nations, and where the only realistic policy has been reliance on the use of power, a new confession of faith is emerging, namely that the least realistic of all solutions to conflict is the consistent use of force....The world has shrunk. Increasingly people and nations have grown dependent on one another. No one can any longer act entirely in his own interests. It is therefore imperative that we should accept mutual responsibility for all political, economic and ecological problems. In this view, fewer and fewer people would venture to discuss The Dalai Lama's philosophy as utopian: on the contrary, one would be increasingly justified in asserting that his gospel of non-violence is the truly realistic one, with most promise for the future. And this applies not only to Tibet but to each and every conflict.' ['Statement of the Norwegian Nobel Committee: The 1989 Nobel Peace Prize,' In *The Nobel Peace Prize and The Dalai Lama,* compiled and edited by Sidney Piburn, New York: Snow Lion Publications, 1990, pp. 18, 22].

'Revolution, fighting, aggression .... From a Buddhist point of view it is rather difficult to judge violence. You must judge the motivation and the result. Combine these two, then we can judge the violence itself. So it depends on the particular circumstances.' ['An American Press Conference with the Dalai Lama,' *The Tibet Journal,* (Dharamsala: Library of Tibetan Works and Archives), vol. 5, no.1 and 2, Spring-Summer 1980, p. 65].

'If we seriously desire to eliminate wars and conflicts as also the deadly suffocating pollution of the atmosphere, first we will have to de-pollute our minds by making efforts to eliminate mental impurities and negativities and will have to discard misleading notions, theories and ideologies. One will have to question the foundational values of the present day civilization and think of saner alternatives. This may also require a search for the roots and origins of the sacred and the eternal.' [Ramesh Chandra Tewari and Krishna Nath (eds.), *Universal Responsibility: A Felicitation Volume in Honour of His Holiness the Fourteenth Dalai Lama, Tenzin Gyatso, on His Sixtieth Birthday,* New Delhi: Foundation for Universal Responsibility of His Holiness The Dalai Lama and A 'N' B Publishers, 1996, p. XIV].

1

Bodhisattva and Satyagrahi

Evolving Dynamics in the Dalai Lama's Formulation of Non-Violence

The Dalai Lama's consideration of human nature show it to be compassionate and gentle as also intrinsically non-violent, with a pre-existing sense of peace. He regards any violence as contrary to these intrinsic human qualities. Agreeing with Gandhi's approach to non-violence, he accepts that his own Buddhist conceptualization of non-violence is deeply influenced by Gandhi's thought. This chapter will make an attempt to outline the similarities between the thought of the Dalai Lama and the thought of Gandhi, specifically on non-violence, human nature, and conflict resolution, and will also show the Dalai Lama's point of departure from the Gandhian approach.

The Dalai Lama's point of departure from Gandhi is clearly couched—as also outlined—in his characteristically contemporary theorizing on conflict resolution. Therefore, this chapter will also attempt to look into the question of whether or not the Dalai Lama's thesis on non-violence can become a model for conflict resolution. To understand his original ideas on conflict resolution, the 'means' of conflict resolution as emergent in the Dalai Lama's thought will be highlighted, followed by a critique of the same.

Continuing this critique, two strands of dissimilar perceptions in the Dalai Lama seem to emerge. These perceptions pertain to the Tibet issue and thereby have implications for his thesis on non-violence. Hypothesized in the chapter are the observations drawn from within the Tibetan Diaspora, and the writings of various Tibetologists, as also from observations made by others, which mainly emphasize that even though the 'Earlier Dalai Lama' (term used by writer for pre-Strasbourg Dalai Lama thought [see

Appendix III for Strasbourg Proposal]) was intent on 'independence' for Tibet through non-violent means, the 'Later Dalai Lama' (term used by writer for post-Strasbourg Dalai Lama thought), which starts laying emphasis on 'autonomy', albeit through non-violent means again. An added observation is that the 'Earlier Dalai Lama' had conceded to violence to some extent and was not totally abhorrent towards it. The apparently mutually opposed 'positions' that are mentioned above (of the Earlier and the Later Dalai Lama) can be seen in tension with—although not as actually opposed to—each other; each 'position' picks out and elaborates upon different themes in a complex, multi-faceted moral picture, driven towards the same end, which is the Dalai Lama's unconditional commitment to non-violence.

Given below is a comparative study of the Dalai Lama and Gandhi.

Non-violence is the bedrock of the Dalai Lama's commitment to universal responsibility.[1] Buddhism is generally seen to be deeply associated with non-violence and peace, both strongly represented in its value system.[2] It is important in Buddhism to see humans as a part of the community of sentient beings in a conditioned world where suffering is endemic, and thus to kill or harm another being deliberately is to ignore the fragility and aspiration for happiness that one has in common with it.[3] Buddhism also suggests that it is by understanding the impermanent nature of phenomena that one can eschew violence.[4] However, it is to be noted that impermanence, as a concept, referred to in Buddhism is radically different from violence. 'Impermanence' stresses the phenomenon of transitoriness, which entails that nothing is permanent and therefore could, by its definitional logic, suggest the rectitude in violence. Even yet, the difference between the two can be drawn by understanding that whereas one is essentially based on the nature of the phenomenon, the latter calls for a change brought about by a human agency, and thereby becomes a violation of the 'natural' law of change. Therefore, it may be said that according to Buddhist opposition to violence, the ideal is to 'Let the law of impermanence, not lawlessness of violence, determine the life-span of all that lives: individuals, species, cultures, the earth as a whole.'[5] Thus it can be seen that the Buddhist law of impermanence supports non-violence.

Although the Dalai Lama acknowledges the deep influence of Buddhism on his thought, he also recognizes the influence of Mahatma Gandhi on his views on non-violence. He states that it was Gandhi who implemented this new and what he terms as 'noble' idea in politics.[6] Gandhi in turn has acknowledged the influence of Buddha on his thought. According to Albert Schweitzer: 'Gandhi continues what the Buddha began. In the Buddha the spirit of love set itself the task of creating different spiritual conditions in the world; in Gandhi it undertakes to transform *all* worldly conditions.'[7] In his writings, the Dalai Lama has attempted to show how non-violence and compassion, which are ancient Indian concepts, were revived by Mahatma Gandhi and put in practice in modern times, not only in politics, but in day-to-day life as well. Non-violence as an idea is original to Gandhi, primarily because it was he who gave to it a 'social' rather than 'mystical' use. Says Gandhi:

Wherever there is a clash of *ephemeral* [italics added] interests, men tend to resort to violence.[8]

Mahatma Gandhi recognized that, violence is born because men see themselves as being separate with exclusive individual concerns and as striving for personal benefits at any cost. For Gandhi

Ahimsa is important not just as a desirable virtue or merely as the means for the purification and ennobling of the soul but even more as the fundamental and perhaps the only way in which we can express our respect for the innate worth of any human being. It is an essential and universal obligation without which we would cease to be human.[9]

In consonance with Gandhi's thought, the Dalai Lama draws attention to the reality of man as a social animal and thus seeks to show and establish the interdependence between the two. He professes: 'We must realise that human happiness is interdependent. One's own successful or happy future is related to that of others.'[10] In this context, the Buddhist philosophy itself has laid stress on the 'heresy' of *attavada* or separateness: 'In the Buddhist tradition *himsa* and *asatya* alike proceed from *attavada*, the dire heresy of separateness. They equally constitute violence against the omnipresent truth, the subjection of a whole to a part or the pretence of the part to be the whole.'[11] Both the Dalai Lama and Gandhi have dealt with this 'heresy'. In the Dalai Lama, we find it juxtaposed against interdependence, a very important concept in his thought. In the context of non-violence and peace he would suggest that maintaining obsolete values and beliefs engenders a fragmented and self-centred spirit—if one continues to hold on to outdated goals and behaviour: 'Such an attitude by a large number of people would block the entire transition to an interdependent yet peaceful and cooperative global society.'[12] This idea of interdependence, which the Dalai Lama

relates to a number of disparate issues—from ecology to Tibet's policy of
isolationism which ultimately brought it trouble, has a far-reaching influence
on his thought: 'We must realize that human happiness is interdependent.
One's own successful or happy future is related to that of others...we need
others for our very existence. The practice of compassion and non-violence
is therefore in one's own self-interest.'[13]

Both Gandhi and the Dalai Lama draw distinctions between the positive
and negative meanings of *ahimsa*. For Gandhi:

In its negative form, it means not injuring any living being whether by body or
mind. I may not, therefore, hurt the person or any wrongdoer or bear any ill will to
him and so cause him mental suffering... This statement does not cover suffering
caused to the wrongdoer by natural acts of mine which do not proceed from ill will
... In its positive form, *Ahimsa* means the largest love, the greatest charity. If I am a
follower of *Ahimsa*, I must love my enemy or a stranger to me as I would to my
wrong doing father or son. The active *Ahimsa* necessarily includes truth and
fearlessness.[14]

This is acknowledged and affirmed in the Dalai Lama's thought. The point
at which both Gandhi and the Dalai Lama would converge is in their
cognizance that all human beings are alike. Says Gandhi, 'The basic principle
on which the practice of non-violence rests is that what holds good in respect
of oneself, equally applies to the whole universe. All mankind in essence are
alike, what is therefore possible for one is possible for everybody.'[15] The
Dalai Lama says:

Human beings by nature want happiness and do not want suffering...Basically, from
the viewpoint of real human value, we are all the same...we fabricate distinctions
based on colour, geographical location, and so forth, and then on the basis of a
feeling of separation, we sometimes quarrel with each other, sometimes criticize, and
sometimes fight. From a broader viewpoint, however, we are all brothers and sisters.[16]

Echoing the same thought while at the same time acknowledging the
influence of Gandhi on himself, the Dalai Lama says:

Mahatma Gandhi was a great human being with a deep understanding of human
nature. He made every effort to encourage the full development of the positive
aspects of human potential and to reduce or restrain the negative. I consider myself
to be one of the followers of Mahatma Gandhi.[17]

The Dalai Lama himself upholds human nature to be compassionate and
gentle.[18] The Dalai Lama realizes that sometimes people feel human beings
are not all that gentle and a fallacy that compassion and love are human

values only for the religious could emerge.[19] While acknowledging that these feelings can be strengthened by a religious attitude, the Dalai Lama draws a clear distinction between religious attitudes and intrinsic human qualities. He draws attention to the fact that even though many religions teach about compassion and love, it is also true that at birth no one has any religion. However, these qualities are there in 'human nature' by birth.[20] This, while it demonstrates how human beings are socialized to become 'religious,' is also a pointer to another reality, that having compassion and love may after all be different from being religious: 'Now, developing such attitudes as love and compassion, patience and tolerance, genuine understanding between human beings is not simply a religious matter, but a condition for survival. Sometimes I refer to it as a universal religion.'[21]

Thus he makes it clear that following the path of non-violence does not mean that one is following the path of religion. He says most people believe that following the path of compassion or non-violence is related to religion. These are, in fact, secular ethics and have nothing to do with religion. These are a must for the betterment of self, others and the whole world.[22] It has been suggested that if practitioners of the world's religions would take their own beliefs seriously they could—and would—largely eliminate war and violence, give new hope to those who survive under the shadow of disease and poverty, and create 'fullness of life' for all people.[23] Thus, the Dalai Lama clearly reiterates the Gandhian idea when he says:

... It is very important to consider oneself as one human being or one member of a big human family. Because every human is basically the same irrespective of culture, religion, country or race. It means that everyone wants and has the need for happiness and doesn't want suffering.[24]

The Dalai Lama further postulates that human nature is good, well disposed, and helpful with a pre-existing a sense of peace.[25] At the same time, he also recognizes that though human nature is good, it is also subject to an undeserved ignorance and wretchedness.[26] This is reminiscent of philosophers like Rousseau who claim the goodness and innocence of human nature. According to them, human nature is corrupted by life in society.[27] Buddhists have called this corruption 'contamination.'[28]

The Dalai Lama's argument for non-violence, which is based on the non-violent nature of human beings, holds true in the context of war as well. In fact, many disciplines like anthropology and neuroscience have been questioning the assumption that humans are intrinsically violent, to the degree of being 'killers'.[29] In the same vein, the Spanish UNESCO sponsored Seville Statement on Violence in 1986 concluded that violence is unnatural to human nature.[30]

Similarly, the Dalai Lama's view of human nature postulates gentle and compassionate elements in it. He discusses different philosophies and traditions and stresses the different meanings of love and compassion that they articulate.[31] The Buddhist interpretation of compassion is based on a clear acceptance or recognition that others, like oneself, want happiness and have the right to overcome suffering. It is on this basis that one develops some kind of concern about the welfare of others, irrespective of one's attitude to oneself. He calls this attitude 'compassion'. Genuine compassion according to him is unbiased and is based on reason. Genuine compassion is not pity or a feeling that others are somehow lower than oneself. Rather, with genuine compassion, one views others as being more important than oneself. Says the Dalai Lama: 'I began to think less of myself and more of others and became aware of compassion'.[32] He realized that 'the practice of compassion is not idealistic, but the most effective way to pursue the best interest of others as well as our own.'[33] He says that 'to experience genuine compassion is to develop a feeling of closeness to others combined with a sense of responsibility for their welfare.'[34] Most importantly, he suggests that non-violence is 'compassion in action',[35] which goes to show that for the Dalai Lama, non-violence is not a passive response to a situation, but entails a non-violent 'engaged' ethic.

By recognizing the active nature of non-violence, the Dalai Lama holds violence to be the result of short sightedness and lack of vision, arising out of the inability to put oneself in the position of an antagonist and to disarm or to convert him so that he ceases to regard himself as an irreconcilable enemy. However, non-violence does not mean abdicating moral responsibility, either for the Dalai Lama or for Gandhi. Clearly, non-violence for Gandhi does not come from remaining passive and employing peaceful means to pacify, but it consists in remaining fully prepared for maintaining living and dynamic moral and spiritual values. It has been suggested that Gandhi was ready to respond actively to several challenging situations and to make non-violence more meaningful and concrete.[36] Therefore, the non-violence Gandhi speaks of, clearly, does not abdicate moral responsibility. The following quote makes this clear:

While all violence is bad and must be condemned in the abstract, it is permissible for, it is even the duty of a believer in *ahimsa* to distinguish between the aggressor and the defender. Having done so, he will side with the defender in a non-violent manner, i.e., give his life in saving him.[37]

This example is very similar to the *Jataka Katha* which gives a description of the Buddha cutting off his head in order to scare the aggressor Angulimala.[38] Another example of the Buddha 'choosing' to sacrifice the life of a bandit, who has brought under threat the lives of a boatful of people, shows that the Buddha seemingly chose violence in certain conditions.[39] Various scholars have interpreted the concept of ahimsa in various ways and whereas some would concede to violence being legitimate situationally, others have entirely rejected it as per their reading of Buddhist texts. A scholar, who strongly condemns killing, says: 'Do not kill a living being, you should not kill or condone killing done by others. Having abandoned the use of violence, you should not use force against either the strong or the feeble.'[40] From this example it can be discerned that since the origin of Buddhism the theory of non-violence has never been presented without some restrictions. The example of Buddha *Sakyamuni* killing a bandit corroborates the difficulties that the term 'non-violence' can face in Buddhism.[41]

Contrary to the ambivalence that sometimes surfaces in his thought, the strongly emergent idea in the Dalai Lama's writings is of violence being unacceptable to him on the ethical plane. Yet just as it is for Gandhi, ahimsa for the Dalai Lama does not mean detachment or inactivity. In this context, the example is cited of Gandhi's having put one ailing calf to death. Says Gandhi:

my action in putting the ailing calf out of pain was a visible image of the purest *ahimsa*...If I had dealt with the calf as I did in order to assuage my own pain, it would not have been *ahimsa*, but it was *ahimsa* to assuage the calf's pain. Indeed *ahimsa* implies an inability to go on witnessing another's pain...it is bad logic to say that we must look on while others suffer...*ahimsa* is a most powerful emotion and gives rise to multitudinous forms of beneficence. If it becomes manifest even in one man in all its splendour, its light would be greater than the light of the sun.[42]

For Gandhi ahimsa entails the ability to treat all beings, as one's very self. This standpoint is repeatedly stressed in the Dalai Lama's thought. His exposition of human rights corroborates his stand on non-violence, which attempts to instill the realization of the sacred unity of all life and of the identity of all humans by virtue of the fact that 'dignity' is a common denominator to all human life. Therefore, it is the moral interdependence that is stressed in the thought of the Dalai Lama. Like Gandhi, he too takes into cognizance the innate virtue of ahimsa, not merely as a means for the purification and ennobling of the soul, but fundamentally as the only way in which we can express respect for the innate worth of any human being. It would be interesting to note the apparent ambivalence in the Dalai Lama's stance through some of his writings. Security concerns are important for the Dalai Lama and he says: 'Each nation has a right to its security but the non-violent approach is the best.'[43] In another argument he says: 'It is always right to protest against injustice.'[44] Again, although the Dalai Lama defies the notion that non-violence is a 'utopian' concept[45] and thinks that it is a strength.[46] He is willing to compromise where non-violence would no longer be a strength, especially where non-violence would entail a threat to one's life: 'If there is no other possibility, then I think it is the individual right, but without killing, you could do some harm on the leg or arm. If you have some choice, if no choice then ...'[47] (he does not complete the sentence). This is reminiscent of Gandhi's stand for which he was criticized, specifically in the case when he advocated the extermination of pests and the killing of a rabid dog and an ailing calf.

In support of these apparently violent actions, Gandhi says:

If I wish to be an agriculturist...I will have to use the minimum avoidable violence in order to protect my fields...If I do not wish to do so myself I will have to engage someone to do it for me. There is not much difference between the two. To allow crops to be eaten up by animals in the name of *ahimsa,* while there is a famine in the land, is certainly a sin. Evil and good are relative terms. What is good under certain conditions can become an evil or a sin under a different set of conditions.[48]

The Dalai Lama is also practical in his approach to certain things. For example, to the question 'What would you do with parasites in our stomach?', the Dalai Lama says: 'I think we have to follow doctor's advice.'[49] About the Khampas, whom he could not persuade to be non-violent, he says:

In spite of my beliefs, I very much admired their courage and their determination to carry on the grim battle they had started for our freedom, culture and religion. I asked them not be annoyed at the government proclamations, which described them as reactionaries and bandits ... By then, *I could not* [italics added] in honesty advise them to avoid violence. In order to fight, they had sacrificed their homes and all the comforts and benefits of a peaceful life. Now they could see no alternative but to go on fighting, and I had none to offer. I only asked them not to use violence except in defending their position in the mountains.[50]

Yet, while conceding that violence can be permitted theoretically, depending on the motive, he advocates restraint and caution, and in many instances, advocates 'compromise' as an alternative. He says: 'The nature of violence is very unpredictable ... In today's world, destruction of your neighbour is destruction of yourself.'[51]

Gandhi firmly says:

We are helpless mortals caught in the conflagration of *himsa*. Man cannot live for a moment without causing or unconsciously committing outward *himsa*. The saying that life lives on life has a deep meaning in it. Man cannot for a moment live without consciously or unconsciously committing outward *himsa*. The very fact of his living—eating, drinking and moving about—necessarily involves some *himsa*, destruction of life, be it ever so minute. A votary of *ahimsa* therefore remains true to his faith if the spring of all his actions is compassion, if he shuns to the best of his ability the destruction of the tiniest creature, tries to save it, and thus incessantly strives to be free from the deadly coil of *himsa*. He will be constantly growing in self-restraint and compassion, but he can never become entirely free from outward *himsa*.[52]

The greatest apostle of non-violence, it has been argued, also permitted violence, even if limited, for the sake of one's honour, justice, freedom and dignity. 'He upheld the resistance of the Poles against the Germans as non-violent.'[53] This is further corroborated in the following statement by Gandhi: 'Haven't I said to...women that, if in defense of their honour, they used their nails and teeth and even a dagger, I should regard their conduct non-violent...use your arms well if you must. Do not ill-use them.'[54]

It has been suggested that Gandhi may have been acutely aware of the limitations of his theory:

He knew that his ideal of a completely non-violent society was unrealizable and that violence was necessary, unavoidable or understandable when used in the pursuit of such values as individual and social life, justice, the assertion of human dignity and the development of courage or when provoked by unbearable oppression.[55]

It becomes pertinent at this point to examine the ideas regarding war held by both the Dalai Lama and by Gandhi.

Is War Legitimate Violence for the Dalai Lama and for Gandhi?

The Dalai Lama would agree with Erasmus, for whom war is directly opposed to every purpose for which, according to his vision, man has been created. Erasmus insisted that man is born not for destruction, but for love, friendship, and service to his fellow men.[56] Thus, hypothetically, the Dalai

Lama would agree with Erasmus that it is every man's duty to spare no pains to put an end to war. While adopting, a non-violent policy of reasoned argument the Dalai Lama with his astute political perception has persuaded one generation of young Tibetan refugees against adopting arms or engaging in violent protest.[57] However, this again does not mean that he is aligned to passivity, for he recognizes the reality of violence that could otherwise be considered legitimate.

It is in the context of war that the Dalai Lama brings out the distinction between the concepts of legitimate and illegitimate violence. He considers it an unfortunate truth that we are conditioned to regard warfare as exciting, and even glamorous. Murder is considered dreadful, yet no element of criminality is associated with war. On the contrary, it is seen as an opportunity for people to prove their competence and courage. He says: 'we speak of the heroes it produces, almost as if the greater the number killed, the more heroic the individual.'[58]

Both the Dalai Lama and Gandhi share the same thought on the military and its wrongful use. In Gandhi's words the glamour in armed intervention is 'the glamour of misused heroism and sacrifice in a bad cause.'[59] To which the Dalai Lama's view can be considered an extended argument: 'All forms of violence, especially war, are totally unacceptable as a means to settle disputes between and among nations, groups and persons.'[60] Even though the Dalai Lama speaks of deterrent violence,[61] he considers violent opposition both unethical and impractical at the same time.[62] However, it is nuclear intervention that he considers the worst.[63] He says: '... The worst thing is warfare. But even warfare with human affection and human compassion is much less destructive. The completely mechanized warfare that is without human feeling is worse.'[64] In arguments reminiscent of the British philosopher Bertrand Russell, who held a firm belief in the utter futility of nuclear war, and suggested that realities of thermonuclear war should be widely publicized,[65] the Dalai Lama continues to show the dismal results of nuclear intervention in his writings.

Referring to nuclear war the Dalai Lama asserts that the solution to nuclear weapons is compassion: '... the threat of nuclear weapons is extremely dangerous, but in order to stop this threat, ultimately the solution is compassion, realizing that other people are our human brothers and sisters.'[66] He also cognizes that in the event of a nuclear war, no one will win because no one will survive. Recognizing that nuclear destruction is still the greatest danger facing all living beings on this planet, he points out that as long as even a handful of weapons remain, the risk of destruction is never far.[67]

It has been suggested that if social progress is measured by the evolution of cooperation and of peaceful means for the resolution of conflicts, then international society still appears to be very primitive.[68] Characterized mainly by the stark necessities of a Hobbesian society, the international order is based not so much on the consensus of its participants as on the physical fact that states coexist and cannot escape from interaction.[69] Conversely, for the Dalai Lama whether a conflict lies in the field of politics, economy or religion, an altruistic approach is frequently the sole means of solving it.[70] He says:

Often, the very concepts we employ to mediate a dispute, are themselves the cause of the problem. At such times, when a solution seems impossible to reach, it is useful for all parties to recall the basic human nature, which unites them. Doing so will help break the impasses and perhaps, in the long run, make it easier for each to obtain their goal. Though no side may be fully satisfied, at the very least, if each makes concessions, the danger of further conflict will be eliminated. We all know that this form of compromise is the most effective way to solve problems. The question is, why do we not pursue it more often.'[71]

To this he himself replies: '... it stems from ignorance of our interdependent nature.[72]

Addressing the question on how conflicts occur, the Dalai Lama says that they occur because people become oblivious to the basic humanity that ties everyone together as a human family. In his own words: 'we tend to forget that despite the diversity of race, religion, ideology and so forth, people are the same in their basic wish for peace and happiness.'[73] It has been suggested that conflicts can be resolved by debates in which opponents try to convert each other.[74] According to the Dalai Lama, this would yield the best results, for the reason that disputes, which could often become violent, get resolved through debates. He refers to this process as 'dialogue'. By participating in a dialogue, opponents try to find areas of common interest, based upon common humanity, which would put the conflicting aims of the concerned parties into a proper perspective. More and more people are realizing today that the proper way of resolving differences is through dialogue, compromise, and negotiations, which the Dalai Lama understands as symbolic of human understanding and humility.[75] This, he says, is at variance with the period in the fifties and the sixties, when many people felt that the ultimate decision in any disagreement or conflict could only come through war, or weapons that were believed to deter violence.[76] Thus, dialogue, not war, becomes the keyword to solving conflicts in the Dalai Lama's thought. In this context, it may be said the Dalai Lama has been trying to find common interests, based upon a shared humanity, which could put into perspective the conflicting aims of Tibet and China.

One of the means for conflict resolution is demilitarization. According to the Dalai Lama, the greatest single danger facing the entire planet is the threat of nuclear destruction. Understanding the implications of such a catastrophe, he appeals to 'the leaders of the nuclear powers, the scientists and the technicians who can create these destructive weapons and to all at large, who can influence...them'[77] to follow the policy of dismantling and destroying all nuclear weapons. He cautions however, that the task of arms control and disarmament cannot be accomplished by confrontation and condemnation, as any hostile attitude can only serve to aggravate a situation. On the other hand, he favours what he terms as 'a true sense of respect' which gradually cools down what could otherwise become an explosive situation.[78] However, in the context of disarmament, the Dalai Lama is aware that this can occur only within the context of new political and economic relationships.[79] He suggests that it is worth examining the kind of peace process from which we would benefit most.

First we should work on eliminating nuclear weapons, next biological and chemical ones, then offensive arms, and finally, defensive ones. At the same time to safeguard peace, we should start developing in one or more global regions an international police force made up of an equal number of members from each nation under a collective command. Eventually this force would cover the whole world.[80]

He thus suggests that because the dual process of disarmament and the development of a joint force would be both multilateral and democratic, it would ensure the right of the majority to criticize or even intervene if any nation violated the basic rules. With all large armies eliminated and all conflicts such as border disputes subject to the control of the joint international force, large and small nations would be truly equal, resulting in a stable international order.[81]

Conflicts between nations are based on the same problems as those between individual human beings. Buddhists identify the most basic of these as greed (*lobha*), hatred (*dvésa*), and ignorance (*avijja/avidya*), disrespect for the precepts and intolerance.[82] Renowned philosopher Radhakrishnan suggests that hatred is never appeased by hatred in this world; it is appeased by love. He cites the *Dhammapada*: '"He abused me, he struck me, he overcame me, he robbed me"—in those who harbour such thoughts hatred will never cease.' and '"He abused me, he struck me, he overcame me, he robbed me" in those who do not harbour such thoughts hatred will cease.'[83] Since the first precept is non-harming (ahimsa) in Buddhist philosophy, Buddhists obviously disapprove of violence.[84] Thus, it is also said that the general tenor of Buddhism is one of pacifism and non-violence (ahimsa).[85] However, it has been suggested that it would not be accurate to say that Buddhists would find the idea of the world's destruction or the annihilation of mankind totally new:

Traditional Buddhist cosmology describes vast universes and worlds within them, all of which come and go in cycles of evolution and dissolution. All worlds are impermanent (*avicca*). They develop and change and eventually pass away. What is important within this great movement of evolution and dissolution is the growth of sentient beings towards the state beyond extinction; the unborn, changeless peace of *Nirvana*.[86]

Nirvana, which is considered the goal of Buddhist practice and the experimental core of the Buddha's teaching and is seen as the cessation of suffering, is commonly described as 'supreme bliss.' It has been admitted that an adequate description of the 'perfect peace' of nirvana is not possible.[87] What becomes clear is that nirvana, which can be seen as the state of cessation of all conflicts, is designed as a state in which, primarily at the mental or psychological level, problems or conflicts have been solved.[88] In this context, what is significant is that the Buddha's analysis and much later, Buddhist teaching, places considerable emphasis on the mental factors that give rise to anger, tension, conflict and violence. This emphasis is amply clear in the opening verse of the *Dhammapada*.[89]

It has been suggested that although there are important social and political implications of the Buddha's teachings, and although the primary emphasis is on the internal processes, motivations, and conduct of the individual, their wider implications cannot be ignored. An example is cited of the teachings on 'right livelihood' of the eight-fold path, which prohibits a layperson from trading in weapons, human beings, flesh, and intoxicants. Military services, hunting, and fishing are effectively ruled out for lay followers in the early texts. The ban on hunting and fishing has obvious implications for meat eating. The *Lankavatara Sutra* says: '... in this long

course of transmigration here, there is not one living being that, having
assumed the form of a living being, has not been...as something standing in
some relationship with you...nowhere in the *sutras* is meat permitted as
something enjoyable, nor is it referred to as proper among the foods
prescribed. ...'[90] *Lankavatara Sutra* also states that 'Meat-eating is a medicine'
but adds to this that 'again, it is like a child's flesh...follow the proper measure
and be averse [to meat and thus].'[91] Again it says: 'There is no meat to be
regarded as pure...'[92] The Dalai Lama explains:

> There are different opinions among Buddhists about meat but it was a necessity in
> Tibet. The climate was rigorous and although food was plentiful, it was limited in
> variety so it was impossible to stay healthy without eating meat...Tibetans would
> think it a sin to kill any animals, for any reason, but they would not think it sinful to
> go to the market and buy the meat of an animal, which was already dead. The
> butchers who slaughtered the animals were regarded as sinners and outcastes.[93]

However, most western vegetarians are not able to reconcile to this argument
but most Tibetans do feel that 'buying' meat is not bad karma.[94] Thus, it
has been stated, 'Buddhism like every other religion revitalizes its ethic
opposed to killing. For example, some Buddhists will eat meat so long as
they have not intended the animal's slaughter. Armed defense and even
warfare has been justified in that such violence is a response not an intent.'[95]

Some writers have emphasized moderation in killing for eating. For
example: 'Impermanence of phenomenon is a tenet of Buddha's teaching.
While teaching that we must accept transitoriness, he forbids wilful killing
in order to retain one's environment. On the other hand, in the context...of
war, we must not kill and destroy beyond the capacity of Mother Earth.'[96]
The point to be noted is that the emphasis here is not on not killing but on
not destroying 'beyond the capacity of Mother Earth.' The Buddha is said
to have condemned destruction and violence in general as futile, harmful,
and inconclusive, and also to have instructed monks to avoid contact with
military matters and military personnel.[97]

It is in the light of the Buddha's philosophy that the Dalai Lama's
thought is being seen here. The Dalai Lama is of the view that the best way
to global military disestablishment is by gradually dismantling the arms
industry.[98] This, he suggests, can be done by gradual disarmament, which
can be made possible by developing political will. In the same context, he
emphasizes the contribution of religion to peace and says: '... under the
present circumstances, we in the religious community have a special
responsibility to all humanity, a universal responsibility.'[99]

The Dalai Lama also endorses the view that in order to protect human rights in a global democratic future, worldwide demilitarization is called for. He feels that re-evaluating the concept of military establishments is important as it is not only during times of war that military establishments are destructive. In this context he is dismissive of weapons whether they are intended for offensive or for defensive purposes. He insists that they exist solely to destroy human beings. He therefore proposes that for genuine world peace it is essential to dismantle the military establishments that have been built.[100] It is here that he brings out a very relevant point, which is the crux for his arguments on non-violence, demilitarization, and conflict resolution. He says: '... while people talk about disarmament in the world at large, some kind of an internal disarmament is also necessary.'[101]

External disarmament is only possible when negative thoughts and emotions have been countered and 'positive' qualities have been cultivated.[102] It is the Dalai Lama's suggestion that in order to create inner peace (so as to enable inner disarmament), it is very important to practice compassion, love and understanding and to instill a sense of respect for human beings. According to the Dalai Lama, the obstacles to inner peace are anger, hatred, fear, and suspicion.[103]

Handling Conflict from the Perspective of the Essential Unity of all Forms of Life

The fundamental issue being tackled by the Dalai Lama is not the presence or the absence of conflict, but rather the nature of the response to conflict as is evident from the preceding section, describing demilitarization as an important means to conflict resolution. The Dalai Lama handles conflict from another perspective—of the essential unity of all life, described by him as interdependence. It can thus be said that:

From the perspective of essential unity, the recognition that there is conflict, makes it possible for a recognition of interdependence of those in conflict...[conflict] becomes a problem to be addressed—a brokenness to be healed—and at the same time an opportunity to realize our fundamental interdependence, and through this realization, to restore a sense of unity. This is why conflict always represents...an opportunity.[104]

It is obvious in the writings of the Dalai Lama that he too sees a conflicting situation as an opportunity to establish the idea of 'interdependence.' He says: 'If we are genuinely interested in the development of peaceful and friendly human society, with a rich variety of faiths and political and economic systems, there is no alternative to working together.'[105] He suggests further that: 'We are interdependent and can no longer exist in complete isolation. Unless we have real cooperation, harmony and common effort difficulties will be created. Since we must live together, it is better to do that with a positive attitude.'[106]

According to the Dalai Lama, whether a conflict lies in the field of politics, economics, or religion, an altruistic approach is frequently the sole means of resolving it. He sees the very concepts that are used to mediate a dispute, as the cause of the problem. At such times he suggests that when a resolution seems impossible, both sides should recall the basic human nature that unites them, thus helping in breaking the impasse and in the long run making it easier for everyone to attain their goal. Although neither side may be fully satisfied, if both sides make concessions at the very least the danger of further conflict will be averted. In his opinion this form of *compromise* is the most effective way of solving problems.[107]

Transformative Approach to Mediation: Dialogue as a Means to Resolve Conflicts

The term conflict resolution is used broadly to refer to any process that is used to end a conflict or dispute in a peaceful way (war seldom being considered to be a means of conflict resolution, even though it does resolve conflicts once it is over). Used in this way, conflict resolution refers to all judicial processes and alternative dispute resolution techniques— negotiation, mediation, arbitration, as well as consensus building, diplomacy, analytical problem solving, and peacemaking. It involves all non-violent means of solving interpersonal, inter-group, inter-organizational, or international problems. The term refers to a relatively stable resolution of a conflict which is deep-rooted. This is done by obtaining and identifying the underlying sources of that conflict (usually fundamental human needs or value differences) and then instituting socio-economic and/or political changes that allow the values or needs of all sides to be met simultaneously.[108]

A recent movement in conflict resolution studies introduces the transformative approach to mediation. This approach, which is significant for this study, sets the goal of changing not just situations, but the people themselves through mediation activities, which encourage empowerment and mutual recognition. This typically, is one approach adopted by the

Dalai Lama whereby he suggests that Tibetans should see the Chinese as 'humans' and not as tyrants. This approach of the Dalai Lama is linked to the perspective of essential unity mentioned earlier.[109] In the context of the Tibet issue, while describing a dialogue he had with Felix Green, a close friend of Zhou Enlai of China, the Dalai Lama reveals:

He tried to convince me that everything was okay in my country...after many hours of discussion, he finally changed his attitude on most points. In such cases, a good argument based on sincere motivation can produce a positive result, provided both parties strive to be 'objective'. It is very helpful to talk, talk, and talk, until a solution is found.[110]

The Dalai Lama asserts that tackling problems like militarization, development, ecology, and population, and the constant search for new sources of energy and new materials require more than piecemeal actions and short-term problem-solving. He understands that modern scientific development has, to an extent, helped in solving mankind's problems. However, he postulates that in tackling these global issues there is the need to cultivate not only the rational mind but also the other remarkable faculties of the human spirit: the power of love, compassion, and solidarity. Therefore, he exhorts: 'Generate genuine compassion.'[111]

On the contrary, if more and more force is used, then he ventures to say that there are greater chances that human conflicts would increase.[112] Therefore he suggests that instead of using force, listening to other's views, ideas and opinions is more beneficial. In the conflict management field, the term dialogue refers to a method of getting people who are involved in deep-rooted conflict, to sit down together with a facilitator, to talk and listen, with the goal of increasing mutual understanding and, in some cases, coming up with joint solutions to mutual problems. Dialogue is seen as contributing to conflict resolution, firstly, by demonstrating that people from opposing sides can learn from one another. Secondly, it encourages the formation of, and linkage with other dialogue groups, which spreads the goodwill further and enhances the sense of the participants' efficacy. Thirdly, dialogue groups can collect, reinvent, or generate creative ideas that might contribute to a solution, and they can then publicize these ideas to decision makers and their own populations. Fourthly, they can obtain access to influential or powerful people who might be able to implement their ideas.[113] The Dalai Lama cites the example of the new developments in South Africa and the Middle East, where the spirit of dialogue and non-violence have had pragmatic and positive consequences. Connecting this to the question of Tibet he suggests a new approach to solving human problems. He says that:

Hence your support is not only for the six million Tibetans but also to create a new pattern or a new model for struggle...if we fail in this, then it is a disaster. Conversely, if our struggle through non-violence with a compassionate feeling succeeds, we will be creating a new way to solve problems and conflicts and thereby serve the interests of the entire human community.[114]

It is with such a conviction that the Dalai Lama has led the Tibetan freedom struggle on a path of non-violence and has sought a mutually agreeable solution to the Tibetan issue for both Tibet as well as China through negotiation in a spirit of reconciliation and compromise. Hence, inspired by the Buddha's message of non-violence and compassion, Tibetans have sought to respect every form of life and abandoned war as an instrument of national policy. The Dalai Lama has time and again reiterated that this approach is the most beneficial and practical course for Tibetans in the long run.[115] In this sense, like Gandhi, the Dalai Lama would differ from Marx, who thought that violence is the midwife of history and that only in periods of violence does history show its true face to 'dispel the fog of hypocritical dialogue and moral pretensions.'[116]

A Critique of the Dalai Lama's Vision on Non-Violence and the Tibet Issue

The 'perennial put down of pacifists'[117] does not spare the Dalai Lama either. He has been criticized for being a pacifist and a man whose ideas are 'surreal': 'Let's get real ... when an invading army crosses the border, its armed might[,] not an essay by the Dalai Lama, that counts.'[118] However, he has maintained his stand on non-violence specifically in the Tibetan context, where, in understanding realpolitik he has always insisted that if Tibet took up arms against China, it would prove suicidal for the Tibetans:

If Tibet took arms (against China) followed the violent course, that's almost like suicide. I understand that there are desperate feelings, (but) I always believe that non-violence is something important. The best way to solve human conflict is through understanding, not fighting.[119]

It has been suggested that seeing the Dalai Lama's stand on non-violence as pacifist is a misreading of his non-violent struggle which is neither pacifist, nor passive. It has further been suggested that the 'intellectual shallowness', which would seek to change or alter philosophical alignments is radically different from the Dalai Lama's.[120] It is suggested the Dalai Lama has understood that non-violent resistance is for the strong-willed and the principled, who refuse to rely on the logic of stopping the enemy's bad violence with one's own good violence.[121] In an extremely optimistic vein, the Dalai Lama feels the 'inevitable transition' towards achieving aspirations can be made without resorting to violence.[122] In this context, he has emphasized again and again his admiration and firm belief in non-violent struggles across the world. He acknowledges that he is a firm believer in non-violence on moral as well as 'practical grounds.' 'Using violence against a strong power can be suicidal. For countries like ours, the only hope of survival is to wage a non-violent struggle founded on justice, truth, and unswerving determination.'[123] Speaking to Lithuanians he said:

you, the people of Lithuania, under the leadership of President Landsbergis, have set a new example for others, like my people, to be inspired by you. You have strengthened our belief that non-violence is the correct path and renewed our hope we too will one day regain our lost freedom through "peaceful means".[124]

(The Dalai Lama sometimes refers to 'peaceful means' and 'non-violent means' interchangeably).

The Dalai Lama's conviction that non-violence is the appropriate way to bring about constructive political change holds equally true about his views in the Chinese context as well. To illustrate this, he gives the example of the Tiananmen Movement in China, which he considers to be a significant event that brought to light the Chinese people's yearning for freedom, democracy, equality, and human rights, no less than any other people seeking those rights. The Dalai Lama says: '...those young people, despite being taught that "political power comes out of the barrel of a gun" pursued their aims without resorting to violence.'[125]

Thus, *hijrat*, which means voluntary migration or temporary withdrawal out of the boundaries of a state, which is said to have been adopted 'usefully' by the Tibetans,[126] was initiated by the Dalai Lama. He has thus earned the title of '*Satyagrahi*'. Gandhi advocated hijrat, or voluntary negotiation or temporary withdrawal out of the boundaries of a state, to the Bardoli peasants in 1928, but by 1931 he came to think that this traditional device of 'despairing' protest is not a necessary part of the protest form of satyagraha. According to Raghavan Iyer, satyagraha has been adopted usefully by some of the Doukhobors and by Hungarian and Tibetan refugees. However, he contends that it is misleading to call it a method of satyagraha except in the liberal sense and even then only if it is completely voluntary. At the same time, he emphasizes that in the case of the Dalai Lama, it would be accurate to say that he has adopted the method of satyagraha completely.[127] The Dalai Lama concedes that '...Tibetans, or foreign friends of Tibet, should note that the solution to the Tibetan problems must come only through non-violence and human contact.'[128] He justifies civil disobedience by the Tibetans as he believes it to be representative of an 'expression of deep sorrow through non-violence.'[129] He further states: 'Expressions such as prayers, hunger-strikes, demonstrations without violence are meaningful.'[130]

Even though the Dalai Lama has earned the title of Satyagrahi, it has been at the cost of great criticism as well as a perhaps greater risk of being misunderstood. Some Tibetan scholars have debated the effectiveness of satyagraha, or truth-force, as an option in the Tibetan struggle.[131] Samdhong Rimpoche believes that the time for negotiating has passed. He says:

We know that it may be a kind of suicide, but unless we do not take action in the near future, there will be no Tibet left to free. Our civilization will disappear forever...If we don't oppose the Chinese occupation, we effectively encourage their actions. In history, one generation will be blamed for standing by and doing nothing.[132]

Known to be one of the most radical figures among the Tibetan exiles, he believes that his non-violent 'brigades' can educate, energize and call to action Tibetans in occupied Tibet.[133]

The Dalai Lama has cosigned and endorsed the 'Universal Declaration of Non-violence.' This document states that 'all forms of violence, especially war, are totally unacceptable as a means to settle disputes between and among nations, groups and persons.' On the one hand, the credibility of the Dalai Lama as a theorist and a practitioner have been vouched for,[134] on the other, his message of peace has divided the exiled Tibetan community.[135] Questions posed to him ask why he would still choose to believe in the power of non-violence especially when only those who resort to 'violent' means seem to attract attention and are taken seriously by governments.[136] His standard reply can be seen in the following quote:

I know some Tibetans are thinking about violence. But I tell them that they are wrong. Violence is immoral...basically, I think violence is an inhuman act. It is unworthy of a human being. Instead, humans should cultivate the feeling of compassion that exists within each one of us. How can humans be so attracted to blood? I have always felt violence is unnatural. Furthermore, I feel that while it is certainly possible to achieve results by means of violence, that achievement will not be a lasting one. Very often, instead of eliminating our problem, violence creates more problems. Look at us: there are six million of us and over a thousand million of them. To plan on using violence would be stupid. When I explain this to young Tibetans, they sometime start to cry. They can't contain their emotions. But they must accept the facts. Whether they like it or not, that is the reality.[137]

It has also been postulated that there is a strategic reason behind the Dalai Lama's argument for non-violence. It has been put forth by him that apart from considering violence as contrary to human nature, another reason is that it would provide ammunition for the factions in Beijing that favour a harder line in Tibet and it would also weaken the position of Chinese moderates. This position has again been bitterly rejected by the radical fringe among the Tibetans in exile, who consider no solution acceptable other than full independence.[138] The Tibetan Youth Congress,[139] an organization that has thousands of members, openly advocated terrorism against the Chinese inside Tibet until 1989. In Tibet as well, many members of the Tibetan resistance argue against what they consider the Dalai Lama's overtures to the Chinese.[140] The Dalai Lama, on the other hand, insists that he cannot ever accept violence. He gives three reasons for this: (1) as a Buddhist monk, he does not consider violence to be good; (2) he believes strongly in the Gandhian way of non-violence and therefore cannot accept violence; (3) he does not consider violence to be a strength for the Tibetans, and says: 'Our strength is truth, justice, reason and human understanding.'[141] Hence he tries to counsel them to pursue a path of non-violence even though he understands their frustration at the lack of any positive development.[142]

If the Dalai Lama is considered a pacifist by some, it is because they are unable to comprehend that for him, just as it was for Gandhi, non-violence is not a resignation from all real fighting. Gandhi had declared that the non-violent way to freedom would be the shortest, even though it may appear to be the longest to our impatient nature.[143] The Dalai Lama, in consonance with this view has consistently taken a similar stand, and has adopted it as a policy vis-à-vis the Tibet problem. It has to be understood that Tibetans, who criticize the Dalai Lama on what they perceive to be an overstatement of ahimsa as a policy, do so due to their disillusionment with the results of non-violence for their particular problem, and not with non-violence as a policy. In a revealing interview, the Dalai Lama responded to the question of how he replies to young people who believe there is little to show for the Dalai Lama's advocacy of non-violence, while knowing that even in the movements led by Mahatma Gandhi and Martin Luther King Jr. some people always grew impatient.

I disagree with the radicals who say the Chinese only know force and do not know compassion and non-violence [italics added]. I agree with them about (how effective the) violent way would be. We have few guns and ammunition, but where can we get more? We can buy some on the open market, but then how can we send them to Tibet? Even if we have 100,000 rifles and sufficient ammunition, to the Chinese this is nothing....The result is more suppression, more oppression, some publicity and headlines in major newspapers for a week or two, and that will be all. It is easy to say we want to fight the Chinese, but in reality, the implementation is not easy. They often make comparison with the Palestinians, who have the support of many governments—some publicly, some behind the scenes. The Palestinians have the support of all Arabs. Their opponent Israel is very efficient, but otherwise very small. So we cannot compare our situation with theirs. That is what I tell them.[144]

In a significant echoing of the Gandhian stance, the Dalai Lama has drawn a clear distinction between the Chinese as people, and Chinese as those people whose acts are not conducive to the Tibetan people's cause. Gandhi says: 'enemy is...the evil which men do, not the human beings themselves.'[145] Such a stand makes it clear that for Gandhi as well as for the Dalai Lama, the absence of hatred is very important. That the effects of the Buddha's non-violence persist and are likely to grow with age[146]—this is an idea that is seminal to the Dalai Lama just as it is for Gandhi.[147] In a remarkably similar statement to Gandhi's, the Dalai Lama says: 'Oppose the action, but not the person.'[148]

It may be said that the later Dalai Lama emerges from 1978 onwards. This transition in his stance has been captured in the following observation made by Tsering Shakya:

The signals emanating from Dharamsala suggested that the Dalai Lama was willing to dispense with the demand for total independence and that he might be prepared to accept some form of federation with China. The Dalai Lama told the Indian Press that if the 'choice before him was independence (or federation), he would choose that which was more beneficial for the Tibetans.'* He began to redefine the essence of the Tibetan question. Whereas throughout the 1960s and early 1970s, he had called for a plebiscite to determine the status of Tibet, in his annual statement issued during the commemoration of the 10 March uprising of 1978, he seemed to imply that the issue rested on the welfare of the six million Tibetans. Two years later,

---

* *Tibetan Bulletin*, vol. XI, no. 2, 1979, p. 5.

he said that 'the core of the Tibetan issue is the welfare and ultimate happiness (of the six million Tibetans in Tibet).' The Dalai Lama has thus reduced the question to the issue of social and economic welfare. This was also the basis for Deng's new China, where the reforms were meant to bring prosperity and happiness to the Chinese people. Therefore, it appears that there was some degree of conformity between Deng and the Dalai Lama on the fundamental issue of discussion.[149]

Therefore, the Dalai Lama has scaled down his demand for an independent Tibet, which was typical of the earlier Dalai Lama who was open-minded about explaining and seeking dialogue. Even though the later Dalai Lama still seeks dialogue, the keywords in his thought are 'compromise' or 'negotiated settlement'. The later Dalai Lama is mobilizing western public opinion, whereas Tibetan popular opinion has taken the backseat. Typical to this era is the media facility that he has gained and it is through the mobilization of the western media that he now seeks third party intervention for negotiating with China.

In what can be seen as a strategic shift, he has now graduated from a more radical agenda to one of moderation. The later Dalai Lama still seeks dialogue[150] like before and emphasizes non-violence as a policy, but at the same time, he has evolved a two-pronged strategy by weaving non-violence as a policy and conflict resolution as an appeal for Tibetan autonomy, through which he has tried to create space for a situation of 'compromise' for both Tibet and China. Studies have suggested that the search continues for an autonomy that China can live with (and retain face), which does not threaten its core strategic interests, and yet delivers true self-government to Tibetans. Even though no such 'model' of autonomy exists yet, the search for it is shifting the stance of Tibetans in exile, encouraging them to acknowledge the 'humanity' of the Chinese.[151]

Thus, based on his belief that the only way to achieve his goal is through dialogue and peaceful human contact, the Dalai Lama has been trying to engage with the Chinese government in serious negotiations on the future status of Tibet.[152] In his words:

... it is ... a political reality that Tibet is now under Chinese rule. Therefore, in order to find a mutually acceptable solution, I have tried a "middle-way approach to solve the problem". My approach is also a response to Mr Deng Xiaoping's message that "anything except independence can be discussed".[153]

It is interesting to note that the Dalai Lama has, over a period of time, changed his political vocabulary. His demand for Tibetan independence altered (gradually) into autonomy, a shift whereby he is willing to negotiate for either autonomy or independence. To quote the Dalai Lama:

For our part, we seek to solve the Tibet issue in a spirit of reconciliation, compromise and understanding. Solving of the Tibet problem needs a soft landing, not a hard crash. Under any circumstances, the Tibetan movement must remain firmly committed to non-violent, peaceful means. We seek a sustainable relationship with China based on mutual respect and mutual benefit. We seek a long lasting good relationship with China. We seek no hostility toward China. If we choose to be separate, we should become good neighbours. A long lasting good relationship with China should always be the top priority of Tibet. When solving the Tibet problem, not only do we need to think about the fundamental interest of Tibet and the Tibetan people, we also seriously take into consideration China's strategic concerns, economic interests and Chinese people's national feelings. Chinese who are living and working in Tibet, their lives, property and their human rights will be protected. Eventually and peacefully a workable arrangement concerning their status will be made. My proposal made in Strasbourg,[154] France, 1988 outlined in principle these considerations.[155]

In a remarkable change of stance, the Dalai Lama has started negotiating, keeping China's interest in mind: 'If the problem is solved properly, it would not only help China's own transition, it could also help bring Tibetans into alliance with China's democratization process.'[156] He adds further: '... Continuing the current harsh policy in Tibet ... will increase the danger of violence. This is definitely not in the interest of Tibet or China.'[157]

❄

Thus, it can be seen that the Dalai Lama, like Gandhi, recognizes the practical limitations of non-violence but continues his attempts to reduce violence and replace it with non-violence. Even though Gandhi does not use the word 'conflict resolution', it is clear that the motivation behind words like 'solving problems' is based on such intent. Gandhi says:

It may be long before the law of love will be recognized in international affairs. The machinery of Government stands between minds and the hearts of one people from those of another. Yet...we could see how the world is moving steadily to realize that between nation and nation as between man and man, force has failed to solve problems.[158]

Influenced by Gandhi's thought, albeit with variations, and with strands of thought that are original to him and more akin to the Buddhist thought, the Dalai Lama has couched the message of Gandhi in the currently popular vocabulary with finesse, and hence contextualized it for the present era. In this sense, it would not be wrong to say that even though Gandhi remains the apostle of non-violence and non-violence a value and a creed forever, the Dalai Lama attempts to make it a powerful plea for tolerance, universal responsibility, and a compassionate and humane solution to contemporary human problems, which can be seen in his attempts at finding viable means of conflict resolution.

Stressing the need for a compassionate motivation and the need for knowledge of long-term consequences of actions, especially the negative effects of violence, the Dalai Lama calls for 'inner disarmament.' Moving beyond the concepts of 'we' and 'they'[159] and 'narrow minded nationalism in an interdependent world', he says that since one's own welfare is intertwined with that of others, a compromise is the only solution for the inevitable contradictions occurring in a diverse environment, and emphasizes that having or inculcating concern for others is a way to 'open one's horizon and gain strength.' It is thus suggested that through hope and determination the seemingly impossible goal of long-term global disarmament can be achieved: '...fewer and fewer people would venture to dismiss the Dalai Lama's philosophy as utopian: on the contrary, one would be increasingly justified in asserting that his gospel of non-violence is the truly realistic one ...'[160]

The Dalai Lama's non-violent stance as a device for conflict resolution may or may not succeed in being a solution to the Tibet problem; it is an issue that is a moot point and hence open to future developments. What however emerges as a full-bodied and conclusive point of view is that the Dalai Lama's non-violent stand has the seed for strengthening the Tibetans and their diaspora. The significant international support garnered by the Dalai Lama through immense media recognition corroborates this conjecture. The statement of the Norwegian Nobel Committee for the 1989 Nobel Peace Prize brings this out clearly:

In his efforts to promote peace the Dalai Lama has shown that what he aims to achieve is not a power base at the expense of others. He claims no more for his people than what everybody—no doubt the Chinese themselves—recognize as elementary human rights.[161]

Notes

1. *The Political Philosophy of His Holiness the XIV Dalai Lama: Selected Speeches and Writings*, A.A. Shiromany, (ed.) New Delhi: Tibetan Parliamentary and Policy Research Centre and Friedrich Naumann Stiftung, 1998, p. XXVI.

2. Peter Harvey, *An Introduction to Buddhist Ethics*, Cambridge: Cambridge University Press, 2000, p. 239.

3. Ibid., pp. 185–6.

4. Some scholars have attempted to explain environmental issues from the Buddhist perspective by drawing a parallel from the Buddhist concept of impermanence: Impermanence of Phenomenon is a tenet of Buddha's teaching. While teaching that we must accept transitoriness, he forbade willful killing. It was Buddha's injunction that in order to retain our environment, we must not kill and destroy beyond the capacity of Mother Earth. Doboom Tulku Lama, *The Buddhist Path to Enlightenment: Tibetan Buddhist Philosophy and Practice*, California: Point Loma Publications, 1996, pp. 162–3.

5. Ibid., p. 163.

6. 'Violence and Non-violence', in n. 1, p. 250.

7. Albert Schweitzer, *Indian Thought and Its Development*, London: Hodder & Stoughton, 1936, p. 231.

8. M.K. Gandhi, *Ashram Observances in Action*, (trans. from Gujarati by Valji Govindji Desai, Ahmedabad: Navjivan Publishing House, (1932) 1955, p. 45.

9. Raghavan Iyer, *The Moral and Political Thought of Mahatma Gandhi*, London: Concord Grove Press, 1983, p. 184.

10. His Holiness the Dalai Lama, *The Heart of Compassion: A Dalai Lama Reader*, Delhi: Full Circle, 1997, p. 68.

11. Iyer, n. 9, p. 226.

12. 'Statement of His Holiness the Dalai Lama on the 38th Anniversary of Tibetan National Uprising Day,' *Tibetan Bulletin*, (Department of Information and International Relations, Gangchen Kyishong, Dharamsala), March–April 1997, p. 5.

13. His Holiness the Dalai Lama, n. 10, p. 68.

14. M.K. Gandhi, *Letter in Modern Review*, October 1916, as cited in Iyer, n. 9, p. 180.

15. D.G. Tendulkar, *Mahatma: Life of Mohandas Karamchand Gandhi*, vol. 4, 1934–1938, Bombay: Vithalbhai K. Jhaveri and D.G. Tendulkar, July 1952, p. 353.

16. The Fourteenth Dalai Lama His Holiness Tenzin Gyatso, *Kindness, Clarity and Insight*, edited by Jeffrey Hopkins and Elizabeth Napper, trans. Jeffrey Hopkins, New York: Snow Lion Publications, 1984, p. 158.

17. 'The Path Without Violence,' *The Spirit of Tibet, Vision for Human Liberation: Selected Speeches and Writings of HH The XIV Dalai Lama*, edited by

A.A. Shiromany, New Delhi: Tibetan Parliamentary and Policy Research Centre in association with Vikas Publishing House Pvt. Ltd., 1996, p. 320.

18. The Dalai Lama, *The Power of Compassion: A Collection of Lectures by His Holiness The XIV Dalai Lama*, trans. by Geshe Thupten Jinpa, New Delhi: Harper Collins *Publishers India Pvt. Ltd.*, (1955) 1998, p. 58.

19. His Holiness the Dalai Lama, n. 10, p. 70.

20. Ibid.

21. Tenzin Gyatso, His Holiness the 14th Dalai Lama, 'What Can Religion Contribute to Mankind,' *Chöyang: The Voice of Tibetan Religion and Culture*, (Dharamsala: Council for Religious and Cultural Affairs), vol. 1, no. 2, 1987, p. 4.

22. 'The Dalai Lama: On Human Value,' *http://www.news.utoronto.ca/bin6/ thoughts/040510-36.asp.*

23. John Ferguson, 'Religion and Peace,' in Linus Pauling (Honorary Editor-in-Chief), Erwin Lazlo and Jong Youl Yoo (eds), *World Encyclopedia of Peace*, vol. 2, Oxford: Pergamon Press, 1986, p. 335.

24. His Holiness the XIV Dalai Lama, 'Universal Responsibility and the Inner Environment,' *On the Environment: Collected Statements*, Dharamsala: Department of Information and International Relations, Central Tibetan Administration of His Holiness the XIV Dalai Lama, 1995, p. 41.

25. The Dalai Lama and Jean-Claude Carrière, *The Power of Buddhism*, Dublin: Newleaf, 1988, p. 15.

26. Ibid., p. 28.

27. Ibid., pp. 15–16.

28. Ibid., p. 16.

29. Glenn D. Paige, 'Buddhism and Nonkilling Global Transformation,' in Sulak Sivaraksa (Hon. ed.), Pipob Udomittipong & Chris Walker (eds), *Socially Engaged Buddhism for the New Millennium: Essays in Honour of the Ven. Phra Dhammapitaka (Bhikkhu P.A. Payutto) on his 60th Birthday Anniversary*, Bangkok: Sathikoses-Nagapradipa Foundation and Foundation for Children, 12 May 2542 (1999), p. 255.

30. Elise Boulding (ed.), *New Agendas for Peace Research*, London: Lynne Riener, 1992, as cited in Paul Redetop, 'The Emerging Discipline of Conflict Resolution Studies,' *Peace Research*, (Manitoba, Canada), vol. 31, no. 1, February 1999, p. 82.

In the same vein, the Spanish UNESCO sponsored Seville Statement on Violence in 1986 conclusively said: 'It is scientifically incorrect to say that war or any other violent behavior is genetically programmed into human nature.' David Adams et al., 'Statement on Violence,' *Journal of Peace Research*, 26, (1989), pp. 120–1 as cited in Paige, n. 29, pp. 255–6.

31. The Dalai Lama, n. 18, p. 62.

32. His Holiness the Dalai Lama of Tibet, *My Land My People: Memoirs of His Holiness the Dalai Lama of Tibet*, Srishti Publishers and Distributors, (1962) 1997, p. 48.

33. 'Human Rights and Universal Responsibilities,' in n. 1, p. 93.

34. 'Importance of Compassion in Human Life,' in *The Spirit of Tibet, Universal Heritage: Selected Speeches and Writings of H.H. The Dalai Lama XIV*, edited by A.A. Shiromany, New Delhi: Tibetan Parliamentary and Policy Research Centre/ Allied Publishers Limited, 1995, p. 252.

35. The Dalai Lama, *The Four Noble Truths*, New Delhi: Harper Collins Publishers India, (1997) 1998, pp. 147–8.

36. H.M. Joshi, 'Violence—Gandhian Technique of Resisting Violence,' *Journal of Oriental Institute*, (Baroda: Oriental Institute), no.1–2, September–December 1993, p. 82.

37. Iyer, n. 9, p. 203.

38. Graeme MacQueen, 'Engaged Nonviolence,' in Sivaraksa et al., n. 29, p. 265.

39. 'Having embarked one day on a boat that was crossing a river and seeing a bandit who was threatening the lives of other passengers, he chose to sacrifice the life of the bandit.' The Dalai Lama and Carrière, n. 25, pp. 172–3.

40. H. Saddhatisa, *Buddhist Ethics,* Allen and Unwin, 1970, p. 88, as cited in Pauling et al., n. 23, p. 98.

41. The Dalai Lama and Carrière, n. 25, p. 172.

42. *The Diary of Mahadev Desai*, Valji Govindji Desai, (ed. and trans.) vol. I, *Yeravda-Pact Eve*, 1932, Ahmedabad: Navjivan Publishing House, 1953, pp. 110–11.

43. The Dalai Lama, 'Non-Violence and Democracy,' *Tibetan Bulletin*, January–February 1999, p. 20.

44. His Holiness the Dalai Lama of Tibet, n. 32, p. 230.

45. *Nobel Peace Prize Award Ceremony 1989: Speeches*, Dharamsala: Office of Information and International Affairs, n.d., p. 10.

46. John F. Kennedy, Jr., 'I am Optimistic: The Dalai Lama Speaks', *Tibetan Bulletin*, January–February 1998, p. 21.

47. His Holiness the XIV Dalai Lama, *Path for Spiritual Practice*, New Delhi: Tushita Mahayana Meditation Centre, 16 November 1997, p. 17.

48. M.K. Gandhi, 'Religion V. No Religion,' *Harijan: A Journal of Applied Gandhism*, vol. X, 1946, New York and London: Garland Publishing Inc., 1973, p. 172.

49. His Holiness the XIV Dalai Lama, n. 47, p. 17.

50. His Holiness the Dalai Lama of Tibet, n. 32, p. 209.

51. 'Dalai Lama Against Hatred Towards Chinese,' *Tibetan Review*, (Delhi), vol. XXV, no. 5, May 2000, p. 14.

52. Gandhi, M.K., *An Autobiography Or The Story of My Experiments With Truth*, (trans.) Mahadev Desai, Ahmedabad: Navjivan, (1927) 1956, p. 349.

53. Singh, Birinder Pal, *Problem of Violence: Themes in Literature*, Shimla: Indian Institute of Advanced Study, 1999, p. 176.

54. Ibid.

55. Bhikhu Parekh, *Colonialism, Tradition and Reform: An Analysis of Gandhi's Political Discourse*, Delhi: Sage, p. 137.

56. Paul Edwards (ed.), *The Encyclopedia of Philosophy*, vol. VI, New York: Cromwell Collier & Macmillan Inc., 1967, p. 65.

57. David Ennals and Frederick Hyde-Chambers, *Tibet in China: An International Alert Report*, (London), August 1988, p. 41.

58. Tenzin Gyatso His Holiness the Dalai Lama, *Ancient Wisdom, Modern World: Ethics for The New Millennium*, London: Abacus, (1999) 2000, p. 212.

59. 'A Revolutionary's Defence', *Young India*, vol. VII, no. 12 February 1925, M.K. Gandhi, (ed.) Ahmedabad: Navjivan Publishing House, 1981, p. 60.

60. His Holiness the Dalai Lama, *Speeches, Statements, Articles, Interviews: 1987 to June 1995*, Dharamsala: Department of Information and International Relations, Central Tibetan Administration, Gangchen Kyishong, 1995, p. 136.

61. His Holiness the XIV Dalai Lama, n. 24, p. 45.

62. His Holiness the Dalai Lama of Tibet, n. 32, p. 98.

63. The Dalai Lama, n. 18, p. 73.

64. Ibid.

65. Edwards, n. 56, p. 11.

66. H.H. the Dalai Lama, *Worlds in Harmony: Dialogues on Compassionate Action*, New Delhi: Full Circle, 1998, p. 73.

67. 'World Peace and the Environment', in n. 1, p. 127.

68. Joseph Frankel, *International Relations in a Changing World*, Oxford: Oxford University Press, (1979) 1981, p. 96.

69. Ibid., p. 171.

70. H.H. Tenzin Gyatso, the XIV Dalai Lama of Tibet in Conversation with Geeti Sen and Rajiv Mehrotra, 'Laughter and Compassion', *India International Centre Quarterly*, New Delhi, vol. 18, no. 4, Winter 1991, p. 112.

71. Ibid.

72. Ibid.

73. n. 67, p. 127.

74. Anatole Rapaport, *Fights, Games and Debates*, Michigan: Michigan University Press, 1960 as cited in Iyer, n. 9, p. 188.

75. In the wake of the massive destruction caused to human life in the twin towers of the World Trade Center in New York the Dalai Lama had commented that the: 'Use of force in retaliation might not be appropriate. Any problem within humanity should be solved in a humanitarian way.' Dalai Lama, 'Voices,' *Hindustan Times*, (New Delhi), 18 September 2001.

76. His Holiness the Dalai Lama, n. 13, p. 69.

77. 'True Meaning of Peace,' in n. 1, pp. 34–5.

78. His Holiness The XIV Dalai Lama, 'Spiritual Contributions to Social Progress,' *Tibetan Review*, vol. XIV, no. 2, p. 18.

79. His Holiness the Dalai Lama and Fabien Ouaki, *Imagine All the People: A Conversation with the Dalai Lama on Money, Politics and Life As It Could Be*, Boston: Wisdom Publications, 1999, p. 155.

80. Ibid.

81. Ibid.

82. Peggy Morgan and Clive Lawton (eds), *Ethical Issues in Six Religious Traditions*, Edinburgh: Edinburgh University Press, 1996, p. 88.

83. S. Radhakrishnan, *The Dhammapada: With Introductory Essays, Pali Text, English Translation and Notes*, Madras: Oxford University Press, (1950) 1984, p. 59.

84. Morgan and Lawton, n. 82, p. 88.

85. Ibid, p. 89.

86. Ibid., p. 90.

87. 'Buddhism', in Pauling et al., n. 23, p. 97.

88. Ibid., p. 98.

89. The opening verse of the *Dhammapada*: '(The mental) natures are the result of what we have thought, are chieftained by our thoughts, are made up of our thoughts. If a man speaks or acts with an evil thought, sorrow follows him (as a consequence) even as the wheel follows the foot of the drawer (i.e. the ox which draws the cart)' Radhakrishnan, n. 83, p. 58.

90. Daisetz Teitaro Suzuki, (trans. from the Sanskrit), *The Lankavatara Sutra: A Mahayana Text*, London: Routledge and Kegan Paul, (1932) 1978, pp. 213, 218.

For another perspective see Tsepak Rigzin and Francesca Hamilton, 'Buddhism and Meat Eating', *Tibetan Review*, vol. XVII, no. 9, September 1983, pp. 8, 10:

'Said the Buddha in the *Descent Into The Lanka Sutra*: "All meats known by seeing, by hearing, or by suspicion to have been killed "for oneself" must be fiercely deprecated." However, in the *Mahayana Sutra* known as "*For The Wise Ones*," the Buddha says again: "In order to fulfill the great purpose, to consume meat brings no faults" and again in the *Descent Into The Lanka Sutra*, he says: "If either one who will not eat what is not permitted, or a Bodhisattva be ill with such a disease as a danger to life or a hindrance to good then without remorse and without hesitation, he may think of these things as a remedy and eat them.'"

91. Suzuki, n. 90, p. 221.

92. Ibid., p. 220.

93. His Holiness the Dalai Lama of Tibet, n. 32, pp. 16–17.

94. Rigzin and Hamilton, n. 90, p. 9.

95. Robert T. Bobilin, 'Buddhism, Nationalism and Violence', in Sivaraksa et al., n. 29, p. 300.

96. Doboom Tulku Lama, n. 4, pp. 162–3.

97. Phys. T.W. Davids, *Dialogues of the Buddha*: Part I, London: Luzac, 1969, pp. 3–5, 13, 20, and I.B. Horner, *Early Buddhism and The Taking of Life*, Kandy, Sri Lanka: The Wheel Publication, no. 104, Buddhist Publication Society, 1967, p. 16. The Buddha has been described as a peacemaker and peacekeeper. An example is given where Buddha is shown to be intervening between the armies of the two states, the Sakyas and the Koliyas, where they are in conflict over irrigation rights.

On another occasion, he uses his psychic power to pacify and convert the murderer Angulimala. See K.L. Hazra, *Royal Patronage of Buddhism in Ancient India*, Delhi: D.K. Publications, 1984, p. 29.

98. Tenzin Gyatso His Holiness the Dalai Lama, n. 58, p. 217.

99. The Fourteenth Dalai Lama His Holiness Tenzin Gyatso, n. 16, p. 48.

100. Tenzin Gyatso His Holiness the Dalai Lama, n. 58, p. 214.

101. 'True Meaning of Peace', in n. 1, p. 32.

102. Tenzin Gyatso His Holiness the Dalai Lama, 2000, p. 215.

103. 'True Meaning of Peace', in n. 1, p. 32.

104. Redetop, n. 30, p. 78.

105. Vijay Kranti, *The Dalai Lama The Nobel Laureate Speaks: Based on First-Hand Interviews and Exclusive Photographs of HH Tenzin Gyatso, the 14th Dalai Lama of Tibet*, New Delhi: Centrasia Publishing Group, 1990, p. 193.

106. The Fourteenth Dalai Lama His Holiness Tenzin Gyatso, n. 99, p. 61.

107. His Holiness the Dalai Lama with Ouaki, n. 79, p. 143.

108. Heidi Burgess and Guy M. Burgess, *Encyclopedia of Conflict Resolution*, Santa Barbara, California: ABC-CLIO, Inc., 1997, pp. 76–7.

109. In this context, an argument put forth by Engaged Buddhists suggests that people in conflicts see each other as selfish and villainous, and stack up the injustice to be avenged. It has been suggested that this manner of thinking leads to unsolvable conflicts, which escalate to violence. 'We tend to think in a static, extreme manner ... we will divide things into plus minus, black or white, they or we. Always in this way, then that leads to confrontation. But...Buddha said don't approach the

static extremes: always think in terms of dynamic relationships. Apply to everything—mind, society, everything. The dynamic interconnectedness—this way always.' John McConnell, 'The "Realism" of Applying Dhamma to Situations of Conflict', in Sivaraksa et al., n. 29, p. 317.

110. His Holiness the Dalai Lama and Ouaki, n. 79, p. 17.

111. The Dalai Lama, n. 18, p. 64.

112. 'Keynote Address at Tibet Support Group Conference', in n. 1, p. 125.

113. Burgess and Burgess, pp. 97, 99.

114. 'Keynote Address at Tibet Support Group Conference', in n. 1, p. 125.

115. His Holiness the Dalai Lama in an interview with the writer on 27 August 2001 corroborated his stance again. See Appendix I for details of the interview.

116. Iyer, n. 9, p. 222.

117. Coleman McCarthy 'The Dalai Lama's Radical Non-violence' in n. 60, p. 137.

118. Ibid., p. 136.

119. Ibid.

120. 'During the Gulf War John Paul II aligned himself philosophically with George Bush'. It has further been said that: 'In Tibet, the Buddhist resisters who are staying faithful to the vision of their exiled leader are remaining well short of seeking "peace at any cost". They realize that the cost would be massively larger if he chose to fight the Chinese with guns. Leaders like the Pope who sanction the use of killing as means to solve disputes turn their position upside down. They accept war at any cost.' See McCarthy, n. 117, p. 137.

121. Ibid.

122. 'World Peace and the Environment', in n. 1, p. 126.

123. 'Speech at Lithuanian Parliament', in n. 1, p. 71.

124. Ibid., p. 71.

125. 'March 10 Statement 1996', n. 1, p. 450.

Also see the following text: 'H.H. the Dalai Lama's message on the 11th anniversary of the Tiananmen Square massacre', *Tibetan Review*, vol. XXXV, no. 7, July 2000, p. 16:

'As human rights activists and the Chinese who work for the promotion of fundamental freedoms and human rights in China commemorate the 11th anniversary of the crackdown on the Chinese student's protest on the Tiananmen Square in Beijing, I would like to add my support for their efforts and to honour the memory of those who were killed in the 1989 massacre.

I have always believed that as China becomes more integrated into the global economy, it will have to change not only to meet the changing aspirations of the

Chinese people but also to meet the demands of a dynamic economy which requires an open and transparent political system.

My main message to my Chinese brothers and sisters is not to lose hope. On my part, I am working not for Tibet's separation from China but towards a solution where Tibet's separate and distinct identity can co-exist and develop within the framework of an open and tolerant China. This I think will also accord with the wishes and aspirations of those Chinese students who so bravely gave up their lives on June 4, 1989.

—The Dalai Lama, June 3, 2000, Dharamsala.

126. Iyer, n. 9, p. 305.

127. Ibid.

128. 'Speech at Assembly of Tibetan People's Deputies', in n. 1, p. 275.

129. 'Interview to "World Press" October 7, 1987', in n. 1, p. 161.

130. 'Violence and Non-Violence', in n. 1, p. 253.

131. Oliver Dupuis, '"Pacifism is Not Non-violence": Activating the Tibetan Struggle Through Worldwide Satyagraha,' *Tibetan Review*, vol. XXXII, no. 7, July 1997, p. 19.

This argument of Oliver Dupuis is seconded by Mullens who highlights the place of 'tactical' non-violent action on behalf of Tibet and suggests that this should not be given up: 'Those who suggest that being non-violent means giving up such tactical non-violent action risk steering the struggle for Tibet into a condition of debilitating passivity. Passivity may offer no offence, but it doesn't qualify as genuine non-violence because it is not "from the heart".' See James G. Mullens, 'Action is Still Tibet's Best Strategy', *Tibetan Review*, vol. XXXII, no. 7, July 1997, p. 18.

Also see Tsering D. Wangkhang. 'Can 100,000 exiles decide for Six Million in Tibet?' *Tibetan Review*, vol. XXXII, no. 8, August 1997, p. 13; Edward Lazar (ed.), *Tibet, The Issue is Independence: Tibetans-In-Exile Address the Key Tibetan Issue the World Avoids*, New Delhi: Full Circle, 1998.

132. Godfrey Paul, '*Satyagraha* as an Option in Tibetan Struggle', *Tibetan Bulletin*, May–June 1996, p. 33.

133. Ibid., n. 60, p. 33.

134. McCarthy, n. 117, p. 136.

135. Pierre-Antoine Donnet, *Tibet: Survival in Question*, trans., Tica Broch, Delhi: Oxford University Press, 1994, p. 176.

136. Ibid., p. 177.

137. Ibid.

138. One of the arguments for independence is as follows: 'The only realistic course is to seek full independence for Tibet....We must take heart from the examples of... Indians and Africans, who waited centuries before they attained independence.

Why did they succeed after so long a struggle? Because they never gave up. Each generation passed the torch of liberty to the next until finally freedom was achieved.' Shakbapa Wangchuk Derek, 'Referendum: Independence is the Key to Tibet's Survival', *Tibetan Review*, vol. XXXII, no. 6, June 1997, p. 19.

139. Tseten Norbu, 'Where are The Conditions for Holding A Referendum', *Tibetan Review*, vol. XXXII, no. 10, October 1997, pp. 20–1.

140. Donnet, n. 135, p. 175.

141. 'Violence and Non-Violence', in n. 1, p. 253.

142. 'Address at the III World Parliamentarians' Convention on Tibet', in n. 1, p. 149.

143. M.K. Gandhi, 'War or Peace', *Young India*, vol. VIII, 20 May 1926, Ahmedabad: Navjivan Publishing House, 1981, p. 184.

144. Kennedy, n. 46, p. 21.

145. D.G. Tendulkar, vol. 8, n. 15, p. 339.

146. Therefore it has been argued that a tradition that originated 2500 years ago, remains compelling even today, primarily because Buddhism has shown that its definition of the human condition and its solutions to finite existence have enduring value, even so, to those in the contemporary world. Stephen D. Glazier (ed.), *Anthropology of Religion*, Westport, Connecticut: Greenwood Press, 1997, p. 349.

147. Tendulkar, vol. 4, n. 15.

148. n. 51, p. 14.

149. Tsering Shakya, *Dragon in the Land of Snows: A History of Modern Tibet Since 1947*, London: Pimlico, 1999, p. 375.

150. This is apparent in the Dalai Lama's initial remarks on being awarded the Nobel Peace Prize on October 5, 1989: 'The eventual success of all people seeking a more tolerant atmosphere must derive from a commitment to counter hatred and violence through patience. We must seek change through dialogue and trust.' Piburn Sidney (ed.), *The Nobel Peace Prize and The Dalai Lama*, New York: Snow Lion Publications, 1990, p. 13.

151. Gabriel Lafitte, 'Making Autonomy Work for Tibetans', in Sivaraksa et al., n. 29, p. 522.

152. His Holiness the Dalai Lama, 'Solving The Tibet Problem Needs a Soft Landing, Not a Hard Crash', *Tibetan Bulletin*, September–December 1995, p. 32.

153. Ibid.

154. On 23 October 1988 the Dalai Lama addressed the European Parliament (EP) in Strasbourg where he outlined what is known as his 'Strasbourg Proposal' in which he pointed out that he was willing to enter into negotiations with China, which did not include independence. 'Strasbourg Unrolls the Red Carpet for the Dalai Lama', *Tibetan Review*, vol. XXXI, no. 12, December 1996, pp. 10–11. See Appendix-III for Strasbourg Proposal.

155. His Holiness the Dalai Lama, n. 152, p. 33.

156. Ibid., p. 33.

157. Ibid.

158. M.K. Gandhi (ed.), *Young India*, Ahmedabad: Navjivan, June 1919, as cited in Iyer, p. 211.

159. See Appendix-I for details on the use of terms 'we' and 'they' according to the Dalai Lama.

160. Jeffrey Hopkins (ed.), *The Art of Peace: Nobel Peace Laureates Discuss Human Rights, Conflict and Reconciliation,* New York: Snow Lion Publications, 2000, p. 13.

161. 'Statement of the Norwegian Nobel Committee: The 1989 Nobel Peace Prize,' in n. 50, p. 22.

'Universal responsibility is the key to the human survival. It is the best guarantee for human rights and for world peace.' [His Holiness The Dalai Lama, Universal Responsibility: Key to Human Survival,' http://www.ahrchk.net/hrsolid/mainfile.php/1999vol09no03/829/?print=yes].

'The principle of *mutual love* admonishes men constantly to *come nearer* to each other, that of the *respect*, which they owe each other, to keep themselves at a distance from one another. And should one of these moral forces fail, 'then nothingness (immorality), with gaping throat, would drink the whole kingdom of (moral) beings like a drop of water ....' [Immanuel Kant, 'The Doctrine of Virtue' in *The Metaphysics of Morals*, 1797 (M.J. Gregor, trans. 1964), at 116, as cited in Henry J. Steiner and Philip Alston (Text and Materials), *International Human Rights in Context: Law, Politics, Morals*, Oxford: Clarendon Press, 1996 second reprint, p. 275].

'The broken myth is the situation ... in the world at large ... there is at present no endogenous theory capable of unifying contemporary societies and no imposed or imported ideology can be simply substituted for it. A mutual fecundation of cultures is a human imperative of our times.' [Henry J. Steiner and Philip Alston (Text and Materials). *International Human Rights in Context: Law, Politics, Morals*, Oxford: Clarendon Press, 1996 second reprint, p. 208].

2

Universal Responsibility in the Dalai Lama's Worldview

To merely say that there is widespread acceptance of the principle of human rights on the domestic and international plane is not to say that there is complete agreement about the nature of such rights or their substantive scope—in other words, there is little consensus on their definition. The basic questions, which are still to receive conclusive answers in this context, are the following: Are human rights to be viewed as divine, moral, or legal entitlements? Are they to be validated by intuition, custom, social contract theory, principles of distributive justice, or as prerequisites for happiness? Are they to be broad or limited in number or content? Are they to be understood as irrevocable or partially revocable? Therefore, the suggestion is that these issues are matters of ongoing debate and will remain so, as long as contending approaches to public order and scarcity of resources continue to exist.[1]

Also, the very meaning of human rights has become contested. Radically different definitions and interpretations of human rights are forwarded by those who advocate 'cultural relativism', and by those who are seen as struggling for universal human rights. Each position claims to be the correct articulation of the concept of human rights.[2] Even though the debates are fascinating, they are also interminable.[3]

The Dalai Lama is considered to be one of the foremost arbiters of human rights in the 'modern' world. He bases his argument for human rights on the Buddhist notions of human dignity and compassion, and conceptualizes them in a Kantian manner by postulating the reciprocity of 'human rights' and 'universal responsibilities'. Even though his human rights thesis may not be considered rigorous in terms of the arguments it has to offer, it cannot be denied that it attempts to offer a normative understanding of the issue.

I

A short comparative study of the Kantian and Buddhist interpretations of 'human rights', and the Dalai Lama's interpretation of the Buddhist view on the same, would help in delineating the normative underpinnings of the Dalai Lama's thought on the issue of human rights. According to Kant:

It is every man's duty to be beneficent—that is, to promote, according to his means, the happiness of others who are in need, and this without hope of gaining anything by it. For every man who finds himself in need wishes to be helped by other men. But if he lets his maxim of not willing to help others in turn when they are in need become public, i.e., makes this a universal permissive law, then everyone would likewise deny him assistance when he needs it, or at least would be entitled to. *Hence the maxim of self-interest contradicts itself when it is made universal law—that is, it is contrary to duty. Consequently the maxim of common interest—of beneficence toward the needy—is a universal duty of man* [italics added], and indeed for this reason: that men are to be considered fellow-men—that is, rational beings with needs, united by nature in one dwelling place for the purpose of helping one another.[4]

Kant says further:

Every man has a rightful claim to *respect* from his fellow men and is *reciprocally* obligated to show respect to every other man. Humanity itself is a dignity; for man cannot be used merely as a means by any man (either by others or by himself) but must always be treated at the same time as an end....[5]

This idea of 'reciprocity' as found in the Buddhist theory reflects the idea of human rights. Arguing from the Buddhist point of view, scholars who accept the concept of 'rights' as implicit in classical Buddhism contend that the modern concept of rights is implicit in the normative understanding of what is 'due' among and between individuals. They assert that:

Under Dharma, husbands and wives, kings and subjects, teachers and students, all have *reciprocal obligations* [italics added] which can be analyzed into rights and duties. We must qualify this conclusion, however, by noting that the requirements of Dharma are almost always expressed in the form of duties rather than rights. In other words, Dharma states what is due in the form 'A husband should support his wife' as opposed to 'Wives have a right to be maintained by their husbands.' Until rights as personal entitlements are recognized as discrete but integral parts of what is due under Dharma, the modern concept of rights cannot be said to be present.[6]

Such an understanding is also present in the Dalai Lama's conceptualization of human rights, which he sums up as 'human rights and universal responsibility'. It may be suggested in the light of the Dalai Lama's thought that 'universal rights'—as stipulated by the UN Declaration of Human Rights—are to be understood as 'universal duties' 'incumbent on any person *not* to treat other humans in certain negative ways.'[7]

Therefore, seen from the point of view of etymology, even though it has been accepted that Buddhism does not usually talk in terms of 'rights'—a term that, incidentally, has a long intellectual history in the Western philosophical tradition[8]—this does not imply that Buddhists cannot agree with the substance of what is expressed in the language of 'human rights'. As Harvey says:

Buddhists are sometimes unhappy using the language of 'rights' as they may associate it with people 'demanding their rights' in an aggressive, self-centred way, and may question whether talk of 'inalienable rights' implies some unchanging, essential self that 'has' these, which is out of accord with Buddhism's teaching on the nature of selfhood. Nevertheless, as duties imply duties, Buddhists are happier talking directly about duties themselves: about 'universal duties', or to use a phrase much used by the Dalai Lama, 'universal responsibilities' rather than 'universal rights'.[9]

As a corroborative exercise, an analysis dealing with the following issues: responsibility, universal responsibility, and the relation between universal responsibility and human rights, as they emerge in the Dalai Lama's worldview and as analysed by others, is given below.

II

Philosophical Foundation of 'Responsibility'

The word 'responsibility' comes from the verb 'respond', which means to answer or reply. Responsibility should therefore mean answerability. It has been argued that a reference to the term responsibility is expressive of—and concerned with—every individual in the society, as also with society itself.[10] Thus, it is in accordance with the *Dhammapada* which points out that the 'concept of one world' is theoretically realized when we accept the relationship between one individual and another:

न हि वेरेण वेराणि समन्तीध कुदाचन ।
अवेरेण हि सम्मन्ती एस धम्मो सनन्तनो ॥

This concept of non-enmity can be explained in the following way:

So, although the world may become large or small, ultimately it is the relation between two individuals only. As soon as the second man is visualized, the concept of the world also arises. The second man, therefore, includes in him all the rest of individuals in the world.[11]

It is due to this ontological assumption that this relation is suggested to be the formative principle of society even if one does not come into contact with every individual in society.[12]

As a concept, 'universal responsibility' resonates in many great ethical traditions, ancient and modern.[13] The Indian formulation of *vasudhaiva kutumbakam*, which literally means 'to regard the whole world as one's family', the Kantian insistence on the universalization of the maxims of moral will, as well as many utilitarian philosophers' concern with the 'common good' reveal that, as a concept, universal responsibility has earlier been accorded a wide range of ethical reflection, which accounts for its broad contemporary appeal. For such a broad concept, an affirmative formal definition stating its net content signals some difficulties.[14] It has been suggested that one way of understanding universal responsibility specifies a prohibition as in ahimsa, or to avoid all avoidable harm. This explanation of universal responsibility is seen to represent either an impossible or a quixotic moral path. Thus, the question arises whether this conception is consistent with the actuality of a world which is witness to conflicts, absence of resources and the limits of our knowledge and skill.[15] Second, is the idea of universal responsibility a moral platitude? Both questions can find cues to their answers in the argument in this chapter. For the Dalai Lama, a genuine sense of universal responsibility as advocated by him can never rise from the individualism bred by an economic worldview or overarching ideologies.[16] By emphasizing universal responsibility, the Dalai Lama attempts to articulate a 'moral vision'[17] in which 'universal connectedness' is emphasized. This unity implies according to the Dalai Lama, a universal feeling of responsibility for all people.[18] First employed by the Dalai Lama, this term has been put to more than just linguistic uses and today has become a rallying point for movements as well as the foundational principle for institutions.[19] Thus, it has been emphasized that:

... from the point of view of awareness, universal responsibility is not even a principle; it is an inherent aspect of everyone's deepest sense of being. Humans are as much a part of nature as rivers...And brilliant, effective actions to help others can arise, not alone from thoughts, plans and conceptual networks, but with fearless interdependence with the greater whole.'[20]

Therefore, it is stated, 'the principle of universal responsibility is what every person fundamentally *is*; we, by birth embody it.'[21]

Exploring the psychological roots of universal responsibility, the Dalai Lama postulates empathy as the foundation of the altruistic impulse, which leads one to take responsibility for those in distress or need. This has been corroborated by psychologists who agree that the 'tap roots of universal responsibility as seen in...psychology, in the development of children's sense of connectedness with others, of empathy, and of compassion ... [lie in the] intimate contact of mother and baby.[22] Adherents to such a view-point argue that this connectedness manifests itself in adulthood as empathetic and compassionate responses, and that only a mind that is empathetic and compassionate strengthens the roots of ethical judgement and gives rise to a genuine sense of universal responsibility.[23]

For the Dalai Lama the logic of 'human rights' lies in human nature itself. Even though he argues that human rights are based in human nature, he suggests that it is in the interrelatedness of person and of persons with nature that human rights are found. For the Dalai Lama human beings, like everything else, are in a relational process described in the 'doctrine of dependent origination.'[24] He postulates that since no one exists independently, we should all respect each other's rights. Human rights in the Dalai Lama's thought are closely bound to the Buddhist foundation of human dignity, which derives from the capacity of human nature to reach perfection. The Buddha is the living embodiment of human perfection, and it is in the profound wisdom and compassion that he exemplifies, and which are qualities all human beings can cultivate, that human dignity is to be found.[25] The Dalai Lama draws from this source when he suggests that Buddhahood is within the reach of all human beings. This is conceded by others, who comment from the pan-Buddhist point of view and suggest that Buddhist thought is in accord with the Universal Declaration of Human Rights, which facilitates the advancement of human beings towards the Buddhist goal.[26] According to the Dalai Lama human dignity in Buddhism lies in the infinite potential of human nature for participating in goodness. The writings of the Dalai Lama attempt to show that human rights and human dignity are in accord with human goodness. He sees basic rights and freedom as integrally related to human well being and self-realization. He also recognizes the fundamental sameness of all human beings in the Buddhist worldview.[27]

The Dalai Lama asserts that since the 'potential' for awakening and perfection is present in every human being, it becomes both a matter of right as well as a matter of personal effort to realize it.

Seen in the light of human nature and its fulfillment, the Dalai Lama's contention that freedom of religion is important in the Buddhist vision for both, individual and social good, makes it obvious that where there is no right to life, liberty and security of a person, (the example he cites is Tibet), the opportunity for realization of human good is greatly reduced. The Dalai Lama therefore contends that human rights give definite space to religious choice.

For the Dalai Lama the connection between human rights and responsibility is a clear example of his Engaged Buddhist ethic where individualism does not debunk social responsibility. This is the 'ideal' that emerges in his thought, and it can be said that the ideals of human rights and universal responsibility hold the key to his social thought. From his point of view every individual is important, as is the society in which the individual lives. Elaborated below are the chief tenets in his thought that aim to establish the link between human rights and universal responsibility.

The Dalai Lama argues that all human beings desire to be happy and wish to avoid suffering.[28] He therefore, considers the rights of every human being as being precious and important. He cites the Buddhist belief that every sentient being has a mind whose fundamental nature is essentially pure and unpolluted by mental distortions and therefore, capable of eventually achieving perfection. He asserts that because every sentient being has such potential, all beings are equal. From this vantage point he suggests that everyone has the right to be happy and to overcome suffering.[29]

In his analysis, the principal vows observed by fully ordained monks are explicitly concerned with a deep respect for the rights of others. In his words: 'I often describe the essence of Buddhism as being something like this: if you can, help other sentient beings, if you cannot, at least refrain from harming them. This reveals a deep respect for others, for life itself, and concern for others welfare.'[30] He gives reasons, the former being utilitarian, for respecting the rights of others as can be seen below:

(a) Practising Compassion and Love when we are Strong and Capable: Utilitarian Standpoint—Giving the example of infancy and old age, he draws attention to the age-old truth that both at the beginning of our life and also in old age, we appreciate the help of others. Thence he draws the conclusion that it would be better to practice compassion and love towards others when we are strong and capable.

(b) Respect for Others and Concern for their Rights: Drawing our attention to the reciprocity of feelings, the Dalai Lama explains that we gather genuine friends only when we express sincere human feelings, when we express respect for others and a concern for their rights. He understands that this is not a philosophical issue and that we are all witness to the truism of this in our daily lives. He suggests that the practice of compassion is conducive to one's own happiness and satisfaction. Once the altruistic attitude is developed, it automatically generates concern for the suffering of others. Thus he says, 'We will simultaneously develop a determination to do something to protect the rights of others and to be concerned with their fate.'[31]

III

The Dalai Lama on the Contentious Issue of the 'Universality' of 'Human Rights'

The Dalai Lama asserts that human rights are of universal interest because it is the inherent nature of all human beings to yearn for freedom, equality, and dignity, and that they have a right to achieve these. Having been born into this world as part of one great human family, ultimately all human beings are the same, whether they are rich or poor, educated or uneducated, whether they belong to one nation or another, to one religion or another, and adhere to one ideology or another.[32]

The argument forwarded by cultural relativists against contenders of universal human rights is that this concept is the product of Western individualism and that it attempts to impose international human rights on other cultures as a form of imperialism. They advocate the 'Asian' view of human rights.[33] Some Western commentators also agree with this view. Samuel Huntington offers the argument that the Western ideas of individualism, liberalism, constitutionalism, human rights, equality, liberty, the rule of law, democracy, free markets, the separation of church and state, often have little resonance in Islamic, Confucian, Japanese, Hindu, Buddhist, or Orthodox cultures. Western efforts to propagate such ideas produce instead a reaction against 'human rights imperialism' and 'a reaffirmation of indigenous values....'[34] It has been argued by some that such a relativist thesis is unconvincing for a number of reasons.

It assumes that there is a single set of Western, Islamic or Asian cultural values respectively. This is patently untrue ... Huntington's list—Confucian, Japanese, Hindu, Buddhist—is itself a refutation of the popular catchall of "Asian" values. There are many traditions and beliefs, some of them hostile to each other even within each of these.[35]

If an attempt is made to focus on the 'Asian' view of human rights subscribed to by some, chiefly China, it would suggest that the standards laid down in the Universal Declaration of Human Rights are basically advocated by the West. Hence the further suggestion would be that these 'universal' human rights cannot be applied to Asia and other parts of the Third World because of differences in cultural, social, and economic development.[36] Opposing such a view, the Dalai Lama holds that fundamental human rights are as important to the people of Asia as they are to those in Europe and the Americas.[37] This is because all human beings, whatever their race, religion, sex, or political status, are basically the same by virtue of the fact that they share common human needs and concerns.[38] For this reason, he stresses not only the logical need to respect human rights worldwide, but more importantly, the definition of these rights.[39] The Dalai Lama emphasizes that all human beings yearn for freedom, equality, and dignity. Since the Universal Declaration of Human Rights upholds these, for the Dalai Lama, it is the best definition of human rights.

Another major difference that the Asian view of human rights draws out is that universal human rights do not take into consideration the equitable economic development of the third world. The Dalai Lama has a different perspective on this. He holds that although trade and economy are related to human rights, yet 'respecting' human rights does not lead to lack of economic development. However, he does not clearly instantiate this in any of his writings, nor does he give any clarification for holding this view. In the same vein, he also suggests that in the case of human rights violations, economic pressure is the best strategy that can be adopted. In his own words:

I believe economics and human rights are interlinked...when China did not heed to world appeals on human rights, there was no alternative but to apply economic pressure. The US should have put economic pressure on China.[40]

This angle of the Dalai Lama's thought is revelatory as it shows his astute vision of political economy; the Dalai Lama recognizes what others have:

the current trend in the world is to stress economic gains rather than national glory.[41] Therefore, his view that China ought to be pressurized on the economic front can be seen as one offshoot of this vision. Contrary to the Asian view of human rights, that economic development can suffer due to human rights protection, the Dalai Lama—turning the argument around—suggests that sometimes with economic coercion human rights may be protected.

Taking a stand against discrimination of people from different races, women, or the weaker sections of society, the Dalai Lama contends that existent diversity and tradition are no justifications for the violation of rights. He says: 'the universal principles of equality of all human beings must take precedence.'[42] In his view, it is the authoritarian and totalitarian regimes that are opposed to the universality of human rights. Such regimes, he emphasizes, consider the fundamental human rights of their citizens an internal matter of the state—which he believes is incorrect. In this context he says: 'No government can claim discretionary authority to take away the inalienable rights of individuals and peoples.'[43] This kind of stance raises the question whether the Dalai Lama's agenda on human rights is anarchist. This is especially obvious when one takes note of his exhortations demanding protest against such 'atrocities' as state repression. In fact he posits that it is one's right as well as one's duty to do so: 'It is not only our right as members of the global human family to protest when our brothers and sisters are being treated brutally, but it is our duty to do whatever we can to help them.'[44] For the Dalai Lama, the demand for one's rights makes it imperative to also have serious consideration for one's responsibilities. He says, 'When we demand the rights and freedom we so cherish, we should also be aware of our responsibilities.'[45] The recognition of the fact that others have an equal right to peace and happiness like oneself, entails the responsibility of helping them, or in the least, of not harming them. Keeping this in view, the Dalai Lama says: 'We need to develop a concern for the problems of others, whether they be individuals or [an] entire people'.[46]

It is important to note that in the context of a discourse on human rights in the Dalai Lama's thought (especially where he uses terms like 'concern' etc.) the concept of globalization becomes important. He insists that individuals and nations can no longer resolve many of their problems by themselves. Keeping in view this interdependence, the Dalai Lama introduces the concept of universal responsibility. This concept basically entails a 'growing' awareness in people and signifies the responsibility that individuals share vis-à-vis one another and the responsibility they have to the planet they share.[47] Such a process is especially influenced by the Buddhist doctrine of Pratityasamutpada. Pratityasamutpada or the doctrine of Dependent Origination is considered to be the foundation of the Buddha's teachings.[48] Nagarjuna and Shantaraksita, both well-known commentators on Buddhism, suggest that Pratityasamutpada leads to the 'cessation of plurality'.[49] The Dalai Lama couches the concept of dependent origination in simple language and postulates that since no one exists independently, a mutual respect for rights is essential. One must remember that the Dalai Lama's considerations of human beings living in relationships with one another and the responsibility this 'interdependence' entails, is an argument with normative underpinnings, although they can be considered an appeal of sorts. Here he makes an interesting link between interdependence and the Tibetan question. His remark—that the popular democratic movements throughout the world have 'forced' totalitarian regimes and dictators out of power[50]—is notable. At certain points, he sees parallels in the ouster of totalitarian governments with the 'Chinese people's yearning for democracy.'[51] He then introduces the phenomenon of increasing interdependence as a veiled message for China, drawing attention to Tibet's tenacity in spite of its misery. In his words: 'the world is increasingly interdependent and the question of Tibet must be viewed in the context of world events.'[52] He exhorts the international community to take up the responsibility for encouraging such change. He concludes decisively that

dramatic and successful people's movements in Asia, Latin America and particularly in the East European countries are a clear indication that society cannot continue to be governed by dictatorial and totalitarian regimes. Sooner or later, humanity's innate desire for freedom and democracy asserts itself and ultimately triumphs.[53]

Although the Dalai Lama acknowledges that no system of government is perfect, he holds that democracy comes closest to essential human nature.[54] Laying to rest doubts about the possible anachronism in the western notion of human rights, he argues that Buddhism and democracy are compatible, and democracy is a prerequisite of human rights. His argument is based on the logic that they are both rooted in the same understanding of the equality and potential of the individual.[55] This establishes three things: one, speaking about human rights, based on Buddhist principles, is not an anachronism, two, both Buddhism and democracy have their roots in human dignity, and three, while their approach recognizes the individual, they do not sacrifice the sense of universal responsibility.

Democracy has been viewed from two perspectives: on the one hand, many nations define the most important aspect of democracy as respect for individual, civil, and political rights, on the other hand, many underdeveloped countries see the rights of society, particularly the right to economic development, overriding those of the individual. The Dalai Lama attempts to bridge the gap between these differing perspectives. In his words:

In reality I believe that economic advancement and respect for individual rights are closely linked. A society cannot fully maximize its economic advantage without granting its people individual, civil and political rights. At the same time, these freedoms are diminished if the basic necessities of life are not met.[56]

Another perspective, which is subscribed to by some Asian leaders, is that democracy, and the freedom that is supposed to come with it, are exclusive products of the Western civilization. It is their argument that while Asian cultures emphasize 'order', 'duty', and 'stability', western democracies emphasize individual rights and liberties, which basically undermine the values of the former. They also suggest that Asians have fundamentally different needs as far as personal and social fulfillments are concerned. The Dalai Lama does not share the Asian viewpoint. Arguing that all human beings sharing the same basic aspirations—that of wanting happiness and eschewing suffering—the Dalai Lama rejects the Asian view of human rights.

The Buddhist perspective adopted by the Dalai Lama compares modern democracy with fundamental Buddhist concepts. In Buddhism human dignity flows from the capacity of human nature to reach perfection, as demonstrated by the historical Buddha. Therefore it is suggested that the Buddha is the living embodiment of human perfection, and that dignity is exemplified by his profound wisdom and compassion, which are qualities that all human beings can cultivate.[57] Reiterating this idea, the Dalai Lama blends his perceptions on human rights and democracy. According to him:

at the heart of Buddhism lies the idea that the potential for awakening and perfection is present in every human being and it is a matter of personal effort to realize that potential. The Buddha proclaimed that each individual is the master of his or her own destiny, highlighting the ability that each person has for achieving enlightenment. In this sense, there is the recognition of a fundamental sameness of all human beings in the Buddhist world-view.[58]

Modern democracy is based on the principle that all human beings are essentially equal and that each has an equal right to life, liberty, and happiness, regardless of economic condition, education, or religion. The Dalai Lama suggests that each human being is equal to every other by virtue of being human.[59]

Comparing the decision-making procedure between them, the Dalai Lama highlights the recognition of the role of consensus, both in the Buddhist tradition as well as in democracy. He cites the example of the monastic establishment where any major decisions affecting the lives of individual monks are based on a collective discourse. Corroborating this, the Dalai Lama posits that the Vinaya rules of discipline that govern the behaviour and life of the monastic community are in keeping with democratic traditions. He says: 'In theory, at least, even the teachings of Buddha can be altered under certain circumstances by a congregation of a certain number of ordained monks.'[60] Keeping such flexibility in mind, the Dalai Lama compares all the important stipulations found in the Universal Declaration with the pan-Asian tradition of Buddhism. By doing so he also registers his plea against the human rights violations suffered by Tibetans. In this context, he postulates that it is not enough, as communist systems have assumed, that the human desire for freedom and dignity ends with good shelter and clothing because in the ultimate analysis, human nature needs liberty.[61]

The Dalai Lama concedes in all his writings that each human being can seek to live in a society where everyone is allowed free expression and can strive to be the best he/she can be.[62] However, he adds a very important point, which is in fact the crux of his human rights worldview:

To pursue one's own fulfillment at the expense of others would lead to chaos and anarchy. So what is required is a system whereby the pursuits of the individual are balanced with the wider well-being of the community at large.[63]

He postulates that this balancing feature is 'responsibility.' This responsibility, when it refers to a compassionate concern for mankind at large, is named 'universal responsibility'. He defines it as the developing of the 'sense' to work, not merely for one's individual self, family, or nation, but for the benefit of all mankind.[64]

Perhaps unique to the Dalai Lama thought is the vision that democracy should have a human approach which 'recognizes the importance of the individual' without sacrificing 'the Universal Sense of Responsibility'. He states that this is the typical Buddhist approach, which focuses on the individual without losing sight of the necessary corollary, which is the purpose of a meaningful individual life and can only be acheived by serving others.[65] The Buddhist stand reiterates that human dignity is to be found in the profound 'compassion' taught by the Buddha.[66] The Dalai Lama, in an tautological argument, states that it is important to reassess the rights and responsibilities of individuals, peoples, and nations, in globalization and interdependence.[67] Emphasizing common human needs and concerns, the Dalai Lama states that it is only due to a lack of understanding, (especially of the interconnectedness of all phenomena) that people inflict suffering on others. Violations of human rights is an example of such inflicted suffering,[68] which also includes the economic aspect of such violations defined as the inequitable distribution of the world's resources.[69]

Therefore, the Dalai Lama finds a logical and cohesive connection between rights and responsibilities in coming to grips with the interdependence that is an emerging concern of rapid globalization. He suggests that belief in interdependence ensures that the rights of others are recognized above one's own. He contends the more we become interdependent, the more it is in our interest to ensure the well being of others.[70] One of the principal factors that creates a hindrance in a complete appreciation of interdependence is an undue emphasis on material development,[71] and hence he suggests that the parameters of human progress and development are indicated by the concern against the violations of human rights in any part of the world.[72] Subtly, the Dalai Lama again brings in the concept of universal responsibility by suggesting that this concept is symbolic of the deeper concern for present and future generations.[73] Therefore, he would suggest that as nations and individuals are becoming 'increasingly interdependent' due to globalization, there is no choice but to have a sense of universal responsibility.[74] The Dalai Lama suggests that a keen awareness of the interdependence phenomenon is only possible with the help of compassion. How has the Dalai Lama viewed the concept of compassion? For him 'the practice of compassion is not idealistic, but the most effective way to pursue the best interest of others as well as our own'.[75] He says that to experience genuine compassion is to develop a feeling of closeness to others, combined with a sense of responsibility for their welfare.[76] Enumerating the Buddhist belief of freedom, equality and compassion for all as being fundamental to human rights,[77] the Dalai Lama recognizes that the notion of developing unconditional compassion is daunting, although he stresses that it can be accomplished by recognizing oneself clearly in others.[78] In fact, the Dalai Lama has consistently argued that the most important 'moral quality' individuals need to cultivate is compassion.[79]

Linking Human Rights and Compassion

Linking human rights and compassion, the Dalai Lama gives a Buddhist interpretation. He contends that genuine compassion is based on a clear acceptance or recognition that others, like oneself, desire happiness and have the right to overcome suffering.[80] On the basis of such a worldview one develops some kind of concern about the welfare of others, irrespective of one's attitude to them. He calls this concern compassion. Making a distinction between compassion and attachment, he states that whereas attachment is narrow-minded and biased, genuine compassion is healthier and unbiased.[81] He makes another distinction between compassion and religion, saying that compassion is about good human qualities and in this sense, is not linked to the religious attitude, which he broadly calls religion.[82] Referring to it as an aspect of human nature, he says:

I argue that if you study the structure of human body, you will see that it is akin to those species of mammals whose way of life is more gentle or peaceful. Sometime I half joke that our hands are arranged in such a manner that they are good for hugging rather than hitting ... that means that our basic physical structure creates a compassionate or gentle kind of nature.[83]

However, he does suggest that religion can play an important role in the cultivation of a compassionate society based on mutual respect, tolerance, and human well-being. It is in such a context that he makes the suggestion that religious practitioners, especially religious leaders have the responsibility of working in harmony with the common aim of 'converting the hearts' of people.[84] He asserts that to develop a feeling of closeness to others combined with a sense of responsibility for their welfare is to experience genuine compassion.[85]

A comparison of the Dalai Lama's worldview with philosophers like Locke and Kant shows that there is a clear attempt in the latter's thought to demarcate and defend the rights of the individual (only) against hegemonic powers that could transgress individual liberty. For instance, Kant attempted to protect the domain of thought, postulating the right to freedom of thought and expression as a fundamental right. 'What is enlightenment?'[86] asks Kant. To the German philosopher: 'Enlightenment is man's release from his self-incurred tutelage. Tutelage is man's inability to make use of his understanding without direction from another ... "Have courage to use your reason!" That is the motto of enlightenment'. Similarly for Locke, non-interference with one's use of one's property and conduct in one's home, symbolize fundamental rights.[87]

Relevant to the current discussion is that both Kant and Locke restrict duties to the public sphere while establishing the sanctity of the private. The most important thing about a discourse on human rights grounded in compassion is that it has the capacity to address moral life in what the liberal regards as the private domain.[88] The Dalai Lama's discourse on human rights is grounded in compassion.[89] According to him, true happiness does not come from a limited concern for one's own well-being, or that of those one feels close to, but from developing love and compassion for all sentient beings. Here love means wishing that all sentient beings find happiness, and compassion means wishing they should all be free of suffering. Developing this attitude gives rise to a sense of openness and trust that provides the basis for peace.[90] Linking human rights and peace, the Dalai Lama says: 'Human rights and true peace—which is more than the absence of war—are closely linked. So long as human rights are violated, there can be no foundation for peace'.[91] Therefore, Tsong Khapa says, 'The character of the great ones is limited to the benefit and happiness of others.'[92] Schopenhauer explains this as a situation in which 'distinction' between individuals ceases.[93] For the Dalai Lama, to begin with compassion is to have the good of others in one's heart, or as one's motive for action. For him the compassionate action is motivated by not merely one's family or friends, in other words, people for whom one has an attachment, but for those one does not know and even for ones enemies. This is especially contrary to Hume's position. According to Hume:

...'tis rare to meet with one, in whom all kind affections, taken together, do not over-balance all the selfish...there are few that do not bestow the largest part of their fortunes on the pleasure of their wives, and the education of their children, reserving the smallest portion for their own proper use and entertainment. (*Treatise*, 487)[94]

Such a thought is countered by the Dalai Lama when he stresses that love and compassion are the foundations of human existence.[95] He conceptualizes the marked differences between compassion and attachment. For him the Humean idea of 'selfish' interaction would be a case of action motivated by attachment rather than falling into the category of compassionate action. The Dalai Lama's explanation follows:

...parents' attitude towards their children contains a mixture of desire and attachment with compassion. The love and compassion between husband and wife...are on a superficial level. As soon as the attitude of one partner changes, the attitude of the other becomes opposite to what it was. That kind of love and compassion is more of the nature of attachment. Attachment means some kind of feeling of closeness projected by one .... As soon as the mental attitude changes, that picture completely changes.[96]

Hume's argument is that the farther in relation to us a person or a sentient being, the less natural compassion we feel for his or her suffering and the easier it is to be indifferent or even hostile. Evolving in a different way, the Dalai Lama's thought would dismiss the Humean logic by arguing that if such a phenomenon were to be, it would lead to a very unsatisfactory state of affairs. To look at another argument that Hume gives:

But tho' this generally must be acknowledg'd to do the honour of human nature, we may at the same time remark that so noble an affection, instead of fitting men for large societies, is almost as contrary to them, as the most narrow selfishness. For while each person loves himself better than any other single person, and in his love to others bears the greatest affection to his relation and acquaintance, this must necessarily produce an opposition of passions, and a consequent opposition of actions.[97]

Ironically, this thought would run against the self-interest of those concerned. The Dalai Lama would suggest that such an interaction would keep us in a state of perpetual hostility. Since the Dalai Lama considers compassion to be a natural quality of human nature,[98] the Humean definition is too narrow for his stance. In fact he tries to give a social face to compassion and extends it from the individual to the society at large, and in consonance with Schopenhauer, holds that differences between individuals are not real. Schopenhauer postulates the apparent difference between persons:

According to experience, the difference between my own person and another's appear to be absolute. The difference and time that separates me from him separates me also from his weal and woe.[99]

Again he says:

My true inner being exists in every living thing as distinctly as it makes itself known in my self-consciousness only to me...It is this that bursts through as compassion on which all genuine...virtue therefore depends.[100]

According to the Dalai Lama:

Different philosophies and traditions have different interpretations of the meaning of love and compassion....The Buddhist interpretation is that genuine compassion is based on a clear acceptance or recognition that others, like oneself, want happiness and have the right to overcome suffering. On that basis one develops some kind of concern about the welfare of others, irrespective of one's attitude to oneself. That is compassion.[101]

The Dalai Lama postulates that it is possible to have compassion without any physical proximity to the situation or person one feels compassionate towards. Giving the instance of Somalia he says when we see people starving even on television we automatically feel sad, regardless of whether that sadness can lead to some kind of active help.[102] This sense of solidarity with other human beings, who have obvious similarities, helps in building one's ability to feel a sense of solidarity at the universal level. Although this insight is originally attributed to Hume, recent moral theorists have also developed and defended it with great force.[103] This insight is encountered in Tibetan Buddhist philosophy, where visualizing each sentient being as one's mother becomes a 'means' to extend natural sympathy into universal compassion. It is said that '...cultivation of sentient beings as kinsfolk is for generating gratitude. Now, the ultimate kin is the mother. Therefore, the three, mother-contemplative repetition, mindfulness of kindness, and show of return of gratitude...generate compassion.'[104]

The Dalai Lama interprets it in a slightly different way. For him to generate genuine compassion, first of all, one must go through the training of equanimity. This provides one with an unbiased approach to others, whether they are people one likes, dislikes, or is indifferent to. This kind of approach has an obvious cue to the Dalai Lama's worldview on Human Rights and extending the debate further, it would be relevant to understand the root, namely the element of compassion, emerging from Tibetan Buddhism, on which the Dalai Lama has based his own view.[105] In this context, the question is why one should make all persons one is neutral to, such as also ones enemies, equal to one's mother? This, the Dalai Lama suggests, is to enable one to 'reflect on the fundamental equality between ...[oneself] and all other sentient being.'[106]

It can conclusively be said that the imaginative cognition of the other's suffering has a precursor—compassion. The Dalai Lama uses the assertion of rights as part of a rhetorical demonstration of the humanity of those on whose behalf these rights are asserted. His thought also suggests that 'right' can be used as a tool to fight against those who show a paucity of compassionate regard for the oppressed.

Thus, the Dalai Lama's critique of the 'Asian' view of human rights and his advocacy of a consensus seeking approach towards a 'universal' and 'globally applicable' definition of human rights is based on an argument that stresses the essential equality of all human beings. Linking human nature with its natural quality, 'compassion', the Dalai Lama grounds his discourse of human rights in 'compassion.' Attempting to give a social face to it, the Dalai Lama extends 'compassion' from the individual to the society by giving clear examples of the interdependence and interrelatedness between the society and the individual. His thought suggests a mutual reciprocity of rights as well as responsibilities. This, in effect, is the keystone to understanding the Dalai Lama's thought on human rights.

The Dalai Lama has argued for the need for universal human rights. Even though this idea has many advocates, it is also a contentious issue. Scholars agree with the Dalai Lama that human rights are not merely rights but are also duties, and that both rights as well as duties are interdependent.[107] They, however, suggest that at present there is no endogenous theory capable of unifying contemporary societies and no imposed or imported ideology, which can be simply substituted for it. Therefore, some scholars have suggested the need for 'a mutual fecundation of cultures.'[108] On the other hand, they also suggest that for a concept to become universally valid, it is imperative for it to fulfill at least the condition that it should be the universal point of reference for any problem regarding human dignity. Thus, their critique asserts that 'the culture which has given birth to the concept of human rights should also be called upon to become a universal culture.'[109]

Even when scholars discount that the concept of human rights is a peculiarly Western notion, they still assert that the world should not renounce declaring or enforcing human rights. It is suggested that human rights are imperative and that a 'technological' civilization without human rights amounts to the most inhuman situation imaginable. But they suggest that room should be made for other traditions to develop and formulate their own 'homoeomorphic' views corresponding to—or opposing—the Western theory of human rights. They argue that it is an urgent task, and that otherwise it will be impossible for non-Western cultures to survive, let alone offer viable alternatives. It is here that the role of a cross-cultural philosophical approach becomes important, in which the Dalai Lama's thought can be seen as an emergent key approach. Further, it is the view of these scholars that 'human pluralism' should be recognized in principle and practiced as well. They also hold the view that an intermediate space should be found for criticism that strives for 'mutual fecundation' and enrichment. And thus, Pannikar observes 'Perhaps such an interchange may help bring forth a new myth and eventually a more humane civilization. The dialogical dialogue appears as an unavoidable method.'[110] It may be said here, that the Dalai Lama has been constantly emphasizing the paramount need for 'dialogue'.

It would therefore be wrong to say that a cross-cultural critique invalidates the declaration of human rights. In fact it is seen as offering new perspectives for an internal criticism and sets the limits of validity of human rights, offering at the same time both the possibility of enlarging its realm, and of a mutual fecundation with other conceptions of man and reality.[111] Arguments also claim the universal validity for human rights in the formulated sense, as that of the Declaration of Human Rights, [as implying] the belief that most peoples of the world today are engaged in much the same way as the Western nations in a process of transition from more or less mythical *gemeinschaften*[112] (feudal principalities, self governing cities, guilds, local communities, tribal institutions ...) to a "rationally" and "contractually" organized "modernity" as known to the Western industrialized world. It is their contention that no one can predict the evolution (or eventual disintegration) of those traditional societies, which have started from different material and cultural bases and whose reactions to modern Western civilization may therefore follow hitherto unknown lives.'[113] Even though the Dalai Lama's argument for the legitimacy of human rights is significant for the Tibetan problem and is a legitimate protest against the 'violation of human rights' considerations in the Dalai Lama's thought, this sort of argument can still hold what Pannikar terms as the dangers of the 'Trojan Horse'.[114]

However, accepted simply as a plea for the dignity of humankind, the Dalai Lama's thought on human rights is obviously an ideal which he intends to make into a necessary foundation for every human society.[115] In fact in a significant way, the Dalai Lama gives a realistic response to the emergent situation of globalization and to the 'mutual fecundation' thesis to which Pannikar refers. This is corroborated in the Dalai Lama's words:

The world is becoming increasingly interdependent, and that is why I firmly believe in the need to develop a sense of universal responsibility. We need to think in global terms because the effect of one nation's actions are felt far beyond its borders ... Respect for fundamental human rights should not remain an ideal to be achieved but a requisite foundation for every human society.[116]

Notes

1. Henry J. Steiner and Philip Alston, *International Human Rights in Context: Low, Politics, Morals*, Oxford: Clarendon Press, 1996 second reprint, pp. 169–70.

2. Ibid., p. 170.

3. 'The Human Rights Law Survey', *The Economist*, (London), 5 December 1998, p. 8.

4. Immanuel Kant, 'The Doctrine for Virtue', in *The Metaphysics of Morals*, 1997, (M.J. Gregor, trans. 1964), as cited in Steiner and Alston, n. 1, p. 276.

5. Ibid., p. 277.

6. Damien Keown, *Contemporary Buddhist Ethics*, Richmond, Surrey: Curzon Press, 2000, p. 63.

7. Peter Harvey, *An Introduction to Buddhist Ethics*, Cambridge: Cambridge University Press, 2000, p. 119.

8. Richard Dagger, 'Rights' in Terence Bull *et al.* (eds), *Political Innovation and Conceptual Change*, Cambridge: Cambridge University Press, 1989, p. 297, as cited in Keown, n. 6, pp. 59–60.

9. Harvey, n. 7, p. 119. Also see *The Dalai Lama, A Policy of Kindness: An Anthology of Writings By and About the Dalai Lama*, edited and compiled by Sidney Piburn, Ithaca, NY: Snow Lion, 1990, pp. 111–15.

10. S.S. Barlingay, 'Responsibility, Universality and Religion', in Ramesh Chandra Tewari and Krishna Nath (eds), *Universal Responsibility: A Collection of Essays to Honour Tenzin Gyatso the XIVth Dalai Lama*, New Delhi: Foundation for Universal Responsibility of His Holiness The Dalai Lama and ANB Publishers Pvt. Ltd., 1996, p. 121.

11. Ibid., pp. 122, 123.

12. Ibid., p. 121.

13. Mathew Kapstein, 'Three Questions About Universal Responsibility', in Tewari and Nath, n. 10, p. 209.

14. Ibid.

15. Ibid., p. 211.

16. Tewari and Nath, n. 10, p. xvii.

17. Kapstein, n. 13, p. 213.

18. Tewari and Nath, n. 10, p. xii.

19. (a) Ibid., p. xxiii.

(b) An example can be given of 'The Foundation for Universal Responsibility of His Holiness The Dalai Lama' at New Delhi: 'The Foundation is not there to promote any one individual, political ideology or cause. It is rather to build bridges of cooperation and understanding.' Geeti Sen and Rajiv Mehrotra, 'Laughter and

Compassion: His Holiness Tenzin Gyatso The XIVth Dalai Lama of Tibet in Conversation with Geeti Sen and Rajiv Mehrotra', *India International Centre Quarterly*, (New Delhi), vol. 18, no. 4, p. 127.

20. Eleanor Rosch, 'Portraits of the Mind in Cognitive Science and Meditation,' In Tewari and Nath, n. 10, p. 162.

21. Ibid., p. 163.

22. Daniel Goleman, 'Universal Responsibility and the Roots of Empathy and Compassion,' in Tewari and Nath (eds), n. 10, p. 143.

23. Tewari and Nath, pp. xx–xxi.

24. The theory of causal efficiency (*artha-kriya-karitva*) which is based on the doctrine of Pratityasmutpada shows how each preceding link is causally efficient to produce the succeeding link and thus the capacity to produce an effect becomes the criterion of existence. See Chandradhar Sharma, *A Critical Survey of Indian Philosophy*, Delhi: Motilal Banarsidass Publishers, 1987, pp. 72–5.

25. *Encyclopedia of Applied Ethics*, vol. I, San Diego: Academic Press, 1998, p. 394.

26. L.P.N. Pereira, *Buddhism and Human Rights: A Buddhist Commentary on the Universal Declaration of Human Rights*, Colombo: Karunaratne and Sons, 1991, p. 24.

27. His Holiness The Dalai Lama, 'Asian Values and Democracy', *Tibetan Bulletin*, (Dharamsala: Department of Information and International Relations, Central Tibetan Administration), vol. 3, no.1, January–February, 1999, p. 19.

28. Tenzin Gyatso His Holiness The Dalai Lama, *Ancient Wisdom, Modern World: Ethics for the New Millennium*, London: Abacus, (1999) 2000, pp. 4–5.

29. His Holiness the Dalai Lama, 'Universal Responsibility: Key to Human Survival,' *http://www.ahrck.net/hrsolid/mainfile.php/1999vol09no03/829/?print=yes*.

30. Ibid.

31. Ibid.

32. Ibid.

33. 'Asian countries' have propagated ten points justifying why human rights should not be raised or linked with trade and aid: Sovereignty and Human Rights, Internal matters, Development, Food, Individual vs. Society, Order, Historical and religious background, Socio-genic and Cultural specific, Higher morality and Trade and Aid. Lopsang Sengay Taksham, 'Human Rights and Universality: Asian Excuses and Contradictions', *Tibetan Review*, (Delhi), vol. XXX, no. 2, February 1995, pp. 12–16.

34. Samuel P. Huntington, 'The Clash of Civilizations?' *Foreign Affairs*, (New York), vol. 72, 1993, pp. 40–1. The argument was explored further in Samuel P. Huntington. *The Clash of Civilizations and the Remaking of the World Order*, New Delhi: Penguin, 1997, pp. 40–1; also see pp. 22–49.

35. 'Controversies and Cultures', *The Economist*, 5 December , 1998, p. 10.

36. The Dalai Lama, 'Human Rights and Universal Responsibilities,' in *Speeches, Statements, Articles, Interviews, 1987 to June 1995*, Dharamsala: The Department of Information and International Relations, Gangchen Kyishong, 1995, pp. 205–6.

Advocates of 'Asian Values' sometimes say that the Asians place the 'common good' before the individual, whereas the West accords priority to the individual. Mahathir Mohamad has listed the six most important societal values of the East Asians on the basis of a survey by David Hitchcock. They could be enumerated as the following: (1) an orderly society; (2) societal harmony; (3) the accountability of public officials, (4) openness to new ideas, (5) freedom of expression, and (6) respect for authority. Mahathir Mohamad, 'Let's Have Mutual Cultural Enrichment', *New Straits Times*, (Singapore), March 16, 1995, pp. 10–11. Also see, Michael Freeman, 'Human Rights, Asian Values, and the Clash of Civilization', *Issues and Studies*, (Taipei: Institute of International Relations, National Chengchi University), 34, no. 10, September 1998, p. 62. Freeman suggests that the comparable values held by Americans are: (1) freedom of expression, (2) personal freedom, (3) the right of the individual, (4) open debate, (5) thinking for oneself, (6) the accountability of pubic officials. Mohamad concludes it is apparent that East Asians give priority to order-supporting values whereas Americans privilege rights-related values. Michael Freeman, 'Human Rights, Democracy and "Asian Values"', *The Pacific Review*, vol. 9, no. 3, 1996, 352–66. Also see David I. Hitchcock, *Asian Values and the United States: How Much Conflict*, Washington D.C.: Centre for Strategic and International Studies, 1994. Also see *http://www.anu.edu.au/asianstudies/values.html*.

37. (a) His Holiness The Dalai Lama, n. 36, p. 205.

(b) His Holiness The Dalai Lama, n. 27, p. 20.

(c) The Dalai Lama, *Speech Delivered to New York Lawyers Alliance for World Security and Council of Foreign Relations*, New York City, April 27, 1994.

38. 'Human Rights and Universal Responsibility, Vienna, Austria, June 15, 1993', in Shiromany, New Delhi: Tibetan Parliamentary and Policy Research Centre and Friedrich-Naumann-Stiftung, 1998, p. 89.

39. Ibid., p. 90. Also see His Holiness The Dalai Lama, n. 36, p. 205.

40. 'Interview to The Economic Times,' in n. 38, p. 195.

41. Dawa Norbu, 'Tibetan Buffer Good for Both India and China', *Demilitarization of the Tibetan Plateau*, Dharamsala: The Department of Information and International Relations, 2000, p. 23.

42. His Holiness The Dalai Lama, n. 36, p. 206.

43. 'Speech on Human Rights and Responsibilities', in n. 38, p. 39.

44. n. 38, p. 92.

45. His Holiness The Dalai Lama, n. 36, p. 205.

46. n. 43, p. 38.

47. His Holiness The Dalai Lama, n. 36, p. 204.

48. Chandradhar Sharma, *A Critical Survey of Indian Philosophy*, Delhi: Motilal Banarsidass Publishers, 1987, pp. 72–5 (For clarification of the concept of Pratityasamutpada see Ch. 3, n. 6).

49. Ibid., p. 72.

50. The Dalai Lama, 'Tibet's Case For Self-Determination', *Tibetan Bulletin*, May–June 1991, p. 8.

51. Ibid., p. 9.

52. Ibid., p. 8.

53. Ibid., p. 9.

54. His Holiness The Dalai Lama, n. 27, p. 19.

55. Ibid., p. 19.

56. Ibid.

57. n. 25, p. 394.

58. His Holiness The Dalai Lama, n. 27, p. 19.

59. Ibid.

60. Ibid.

61. The Dalai Lama, 'Human Rights and Universal Responsibility,' *http://www.tibet.com/DL/Vienna.html*.

62. His Holiness The Dalai Lama, n. 27, p. 19.

63. Ibid., p. 19.

64. 'No Substitute for Love', in n. 38, p. 79.

65. His Holiness The Dalai Lama, n. 27, p. 19.

66. n. 25, p. 394.

67. 'Speech On India's Role on Tibet', in n. 38, p. 89.

68. Ibid.

69. n. 38, p. 92.

70. His Holiness The Dalai Lama, n. 36, p. 208.

71. Ibid.

72. The Dalai Lama, 'I Believe', *Tibetan Bulletin*, vol. 3, no. 1, January–February, 1999, p. 29.

73. Ibid.

74. *Nobel Peace Prize Award Ceremony 1989: Speeches*, Dharamsala: Office of Information and International Relations, n.d., p. 18.

75. n. 38, p. 93.

76. 'Importance of Compassion in Human Life,' *The Spirit of Tibet: Universal Heritage, Selected Speeches and Writings of His Holiness the XIV Dalai Lama*, edited

by A.A. Shiromany, New Delhi: Tibetan Parliamentary and Policy Research Centre and Allied Publishers Ltd., 1995, p. 252.

77. 'Address to the U.S. Congress, US Capitol Rotunda,' April 18, 1999, in n. 38, p. 64.

78. Tenzin Gyatso His Holiness The Dalai Lama, n. 28, pp. 134–5.

79. (a) Jay L. Garfield, 'Human Rights and Compassion: Towards a Unified Moral Framework,' in Tewari and Nath, n. 10, p. 197.

(b) Tenzin Gyatso the Fourteenth Dalai Lama, *The Global Community and the Need for Universal Responsibility*, Boston: Wisdom Publications, 1992.

(c) The Fourteenth Dalai Lama His Holiness Tenzin Gyatso, *Kindness, Clarity and Insight*, edited by Jeffrey Hopkins and Elizabeth Napper, trans. Jeffrey Hopkins, New York, Ithaca: Snow Lion Publishers, 1984.

80. 'No Substitute for Love,' in n. 38, p. 81.

81. The Dalai Lama, *The Power of Compassion: A Collection of Lectures by His Holiness The XIV Dalai Lama*, trans. Geshe Thupten Jinpa, New Delhi: Harper Collins Publishers, India, 1995, pp. 62–3.

82. The Dalai Lama and Jean-Claude Carrière, *The Power of Buddhism*, Dublin: Newleaf, 1994, pp. 83, 86.

83. The Dalai Lama, n. 81, pp. 58–9.

84. 'Speech at Lithuanian Parliament, October 1, 1991', in n. 38, p. 73.

85. 'Importance of Compassion in Human Life,' in n. 76, p. 252.

86. Immanuel Kant, 'On History', as cited in Jay L. Garfield, 'Human Rights and Compassion: Towards a Unified Moral Framework', in Tewari and Nath, n. 10, p. 179.

87. Ibid.

88. Annette Baier, *Moral Prejudices*, Cambridge: Harvard University Press, 1994, p. 25. Also see Joan Tronto, *Moral Boundaries: A Political Argument for an Ethic of Care*, New York: Routledge, 1993.

89. Tenzin Gyatso the Fourteenth Dalai Lama, n. 79b.

It has been acknowledged (See Garfield, in Tewari and Nath, n. 10, p. 184) that there is a similarity in the arguments proposed by Baier (1994) and Tronto (1993).

90. *The Dalai Lama: A Policy of Kindness*, edited and compiled by Sidney Piburn, Delhi: Motilal Banarsidass, 1990, p. 103.

91. n. 38, p. 37.

92. Alex Wayman, *The Ethics of Tibet*, Albany: State University of New York Press, 1991, p. 26.

93. A. Schopenhauer, *On the Basis of Morality*, (trans. EFJ Payne), Indianapolis: Bobbs-Merrill, 1965, p. 144.

94. David Hume, *A Treatise of Human Nature,* L.A. Selby-Bigge (ed.), Oxford: Clarendon Press, 1978, Treatise, 487.

95. 'The Nobel Evening Address', in n. 76, p. 142.

96. Ibid., p. 143.

97. Hume, n. 94.

98. n. 95, p. 144.

99. Schopenhauer, n. 93, p. 205.

100. Ibid., p. 210.

101. The Dalai Lama, n. 81, pp. 62–3.

102. Ibid., p. 67.

103. (a) Annette Baier, *A Progress on Sentiments: Reflections on Hume's Treatise,* Cambridge: Harvard University Press, 1992.

(b) Tronto, n. 88.

104. Wayman, n. 92, p. 43.

105. The line of the Dalai Lamas is essentially rooted in Lama Drom Tonpa,[a] the 11th century disciple of Jowo Je Atiśa. The order of Tibetan Buddhism formed by Atiśa and Lama Drom, which became known as the Kadam Tradition, is now extinct; but historically it remains one of the most important schools to have appeared in Tibet, for it became a major foundation-stone for three of Tibet's four major orders of today, and has greatly influenced even the fourth.

Foremost of all Kadam doctrines was the transmission known as Lo-jong (Tib. *bLo-sByong*), or 'mental transformation'. Atiśa imparted this to Drom Tonpa, and eventually it came to the line of the Dalai Lamas. This doctrine, with its emphasis on compassion and the altruistic mind, was greatly treasured by each Dalai Lama, and was also widely taught by them. The third Dalai Lama used it to civilise the fierce Timut Mongols after he introduced them to Buddhism in 1578, and the Fifth used it to tame the border peoples of Western China in 1653.[b]

The Lo-jong tradition was particularly well-suited to the office of the Dalai Lamas. The first Tibetan to receive the lineage was Lama Drom Tonpa, the most important predecessor of the Dalai Lama line. Second, because the tradition places compassion and the altruistic mind as its spearhead (the Dalai Lamas are incarnations of Avalokiteśvara, the Bodhisattva of Compassion), it was ideal. Third, after the Dalai Lamas became Tibet's spiritual and temporal head it was significant that the Kadam Lo-jong tradition was the one element of Tibetan Buddhism most widely accepted and practised by all sects in the country.

A characteristic of the Lo-jong method conducive to its wide acceptance is its essentially humanistic rather than religious approach to the problems of Being. The practice involved primarily the transformation of afflicted emotions common to all men. There was very little in it even to mark it specifically as Buddhist, other than the occasional reference to the objects of Refuge. In both the European and American tours His Holiness the Fourteenth Dalai Lama dedicated many of his talks to giving commentaries to *The Eight Verses far Training the Mind* (Tib. *bLo-sByong tshigs-brGyad-ma*), a poem embodying the Lo-jong teachings in eight four-line verses.[c] When his subject was not formally Lo-jong, it was recognisably a Lo-jong topic as applied to the American situation. Because Lo-jong is applicable to men of almost any religion and does not convey its message in exclusively Buddhist terms, the approach was extremely well received.

The directness in his communication with the American people was much commented upon in the press. This same directness is a quality visible not only in the written works of the previous Dalai Lama, but also in the life of Lama Drom Tonpa. Once when Lama Drom was out walking he met a man who was circumambulating a stupa. 'Whatever are you doing?' Drom asked him. 'Walking around a stupa is a positive action', was the retort. 'Better to practise religion', Drom told him. Later Drom saw the man reading a scripture. 'Reading a holy book is good, but the practice of religion is better', he told him. The man decided to meditate, thinking that this must be what Drom meant. 'Meditation is good, but the practice of religion is better', Drom advised. 'Then what is practice?' asked the man. Drom replied, 'Make all practices one with your mind.'

The First Dalai Lama... was actually a Kadampa Lama by ordination. He gave much of his life to studying and teaching the Lo-jong tradition. When the time of his passing arrived, he sat leaning against a pillar in the main chapel of Tashilhunpo Monastery and told his disciples, 'Remember the spiritual advice I have given you and use it to develop your minds for the sake of all living beings. Especially, live, meditate and speak in accordance with the intent of the Enlightened Ones. This alone will fulfill my aspirations.' Having given this last Lo-jong precept, he entered into meditation and ceased breathing.

During the U.S. tour His Holiness repeatedly stressed the value and social importance of developing a viable system of humanitarian ethics that would solve many of the social problems confronting America today. His message was always fresh and alive, for it came in response to a particular people and for the unique conditions of late twentieth century America. *Yet the ethics themselves were not new. They were the same Lo-jong precepts that Lama Drom Tonpa and the early Dalai Lama cultivated in the Tibetan, Mongolian and Chinese peoples over the centuries* [italics added].

The collected works of Gyalwa Gendun Drub, the First Dalai Lama, contains a work entitled 'A Brief Commentary to Atiśa's *Spiritual Transformation in the Mahayana Tradition*.'[d] This work was not written by the First Dalai Lama; it is the edited notes of an oral talk on Atiśa's *Spiritual Transformation in the Mahayana Tradition* given by him in the mid-fifteenth century to a mixed audience of Tibetans. The seventh chapter of this work contains his elucidation of the ethical advice for spiritual practioners of Lo-jong. The precepts themselves were collected by Atiśa and orally given to Lama Drom, not to be written down for three further generations when Geshe Chekawa (Tib. *dGe-bShed Chad kha-ba*) listed them in his *Mind Transformation in Seven Points*. [e]

[a] That Lama Drom Tonpa was an early incarnation is clearly stated by the Seventh Dalai Lama himself in his *Radiating the Light of Goodness* (*Tib.dGe-legs-nyin-mor-byed-pai-sNang-ba*), Fol. 10b.

[b] Sir Charles Bell, *The Religion of Tibet*, pp. 95–110, Oxford Press, 1931.

[c] *Eight Verses of Training the Mind*, trans. Gonsar Tulku, New Delhi: Statesman Press, 1970.

[d] Tib. *Theg-chen-kyi-sLob-sPyong-khrid-yig-cung-zad-bsDud-pa*.

[e] See Rabten and Dargye, *Advice From A Spiritual Friend*, pp. 79–86, New Delhi: Publications For Wisdom Culture, 1977.

Glenn H. Mullin, 'The U.S. Tour: A Traditional Perspective,' *The Tibet Journal*, Dharamsala, Library of Tibetan Works and Archives, vol. V, nos 1&2, Spring/Summer 1980, pp. 69–71; 77.

106. The Dalai Lama, n. 81, pp. 64–6.

107. Steiner and Alston, n. 1, p. 208.

108. Ibid., p. 208.

109. Ibid.

110. R. Pannikar, 'Is The Notion of Human Rights a Western Concept', *120 Diogenes 75*, 1982 as cited in Steiner and Alston, n. 1, p. 209.

111. Ibid., p. 207.

112. *Gemeinsam* in German means together, mutual, joint, common. Therefore, Gemeinschaft means community. *Gemeinschaften* is the plural of community. See, *Langenscheidt's German-English, English-German Dictionary*, New York: Pocket Books, (1952) 1970, p. 120.

113. Pannikar, n. 110, p. 205.

114. The *Oxford Dictionary* meaning of Trojan Horse in this context is the following: 'Something intended to undermine or secretly overthrow an enemy or opponent; ORIGIN from the hollow wooden statue of a horse in which ancient Greeks are said to have concealed themselves in order to enter Troy.'

115. His Holiness the Dalai Lama, n. 29.

116. Ibid.

'The urge to build, to transform nature, to make something out of nothing is universal. But to conserve, to protect, to care for the past is something we have to learn.' [Romesh Gunesekara, *Reef*, London: Granta Books in Association with Penguin Books, 1994, p. 188].

3

'A Clean Environment is a
Human Right Like Any Other'

Interlinking Eco Justice, Social Justice,
and Environmental Protection

The *raison d'être* of the Dalai Lama's thought is very similar to Deep Ecology which encourages respect for the environment because nature and its inhabitants have inherent value and not because human beings depend on nature. Seeing human beings as masters of the planet, who ought to dominate, control, and exploit nature, is considered by Deep Ecologists to be arrogant and ultimately self-destructive.[1] It is in the spirit of such thoughts that the Dalai Lama's articulations on the environment, attempt to promote respect and non-violence toward the environment.

The very core of Buddhist thought revolves around compassion, respect and tolerance not only for every human being but also for all other creatures who share this planet. This is exemplified in a *Metta-Suttam* prayer:

Just as a mother would protect her only child at the risk of her own life, even so, let him cultivate a boundless heart towards all beings. Let his thoughts of boundless love pervade the whole world: above, below, and across without any obstruction, without any hatred, without any enmity.[2]

Regard for the survival of all species as an undeniable right brings out deep appreciation of nature in the early Buddhists:

Whatever living beings there be, feeble or strong, tall, stout or medium, short, small or large, without exception; seen or unseen, those dwelling far or near, those who are born or those who are to be born, may all beings be happy![3]

In an attempt to link eco-justice with social justice the Dalai Lama shows that in the context of the environmental protection, both right aspiration

and right conduct are required, and that an unmindful neglect of these
principles of right living may lead to chaos resulting in environmental crisis.
Reflected in his writings is the message that all life is interconnected, a
foundation for the Buddhist ethics of nature.

Based on his categorizing of human nature as non-violent, the Dalai
Lama visualizes that 'we should not only maintain non-violent relations
with our fellow human beings, but...we should extend a similar attitude
towards the environment'[4] as well. It has been suggested that the Buddhist
perspective on the environment is based on an individual's relationship with
the world and on his/her transforming of the world s/he lives in. The idea
of non-violence becomes significant in the context of interrelatedness of all
phenomena as it brings about the understanding that since nothing can exist
independently, the harmful destruction of human beings, animals, and the
environment amounts to violating this interrelatedness. Therefore, he says:

> We need to see how things live, and how they are interrelated. It is in this context
> that Buddhism expounds on the wholeness of all things in interrelationship. In the
> doctrine of Dependent Origination, the *Pratityasamutpada*, it is stated that nothing
> is created or can exist apart from this network of inter-relationships. Things do not
> exist independently. Also, this network is not a static process but one of dynamic
> motion with infinite potential in the infinite universe.[5]

The Buddhist perspective on the environment is a quest for harmonizing
an individual's relationship with the world and his/her attempt at sensitively
transforming the world s/he lives in. It emphasizes the need to see how
things live and how they are inter-related. In this context it emphasizes the
'wholeness' of all things in inter-relationship. In the doctrine of dependent
origination,[6] it is stated that nothing is created or can exist apart from this
network of inter-relationships. It emphasizes that things do not exist
independently.[7] The world is inter-related to the extent that when we
generate wholesome or unwholesome energies, it affects others and
everything in it either for good or ill. The Buddha often spoke of being
aware of one's thought, word, and deed and guarding against transmitting
any impure or harmful energies to others. By doing this, all mankind can
live happily in the world, and animals and plants are said to benefit as
well.[8] On reflecting upon the importance of Buddha's teachings on
dependent origination and causal relations, the Dalai Lama studies the
human-environmental crisis.

In the Dalai Lama's thought, the Buddha's teachings on dependent
origination and causal relations are important and should be studied closely.

It has been suggested that such a study is crucial in order to understand the entire problem of the human-environmental crisis and the crisis now facing all the other types of environments.[9] Due to this, Buddhism emphasizes the need to comprehend the nature of change in the universe and its characteristic impermanence and suffering. 'Ignorance' disables the understanding of the inter-relationship of things and their impermanence. Developing a false, and harmful attachment to the idea of 'I' or 'we' is a harbinger of ignorance.

This kind of concept creates boundaries and separation from the rest of the world as also much selfishness. When we have these kind of views then our energies are exerted to preserve our existence and procure personal possessions. Therefore as Buddhists, our main task is to eliminate ignorance and attachment and self-assertion. If we are free from these harmful mental defilements then we will be aware of and awaken to the oneness of the universe and will learn how to live within the wholeness of inter-related balance. Also we will see clearly as to how we are conditioning the entire universe and how much we are responsible to the inter-related world and how much we can contribute to its well-being or destruction.[10]

This perception becomes the crux of the Dalai Lama's environmental thought.

Environmental protection is one of the issues being addressed head-on by Engaged Buddhists today. The Dalai Lama is considered the most 'visible' leader in this movement internationally.[11] It has been suggested that for a contemporary Engaged Buddhist like the Dalai Lama, a sense of 'universal responsibility' lies at the very heart of the ecological ethic. In consonance with this thought a scholar writes: 'The world grows smaller and smaller, more and more interdependent...today more than ever before life must be characterized by a sense of universal responsibility, not only...human to human but also human to other forms of life.'[12] What Albert Schweitzer says, partly under the influence of Gandhi and Hindu thought, is reminiscent of the Dalai Lama's engagement with environmental concerns. The following excerpt makes that clear:

A man is ethical only when life, as such, is sacred to him, that of plants and animals as that of his fellowmen, and when he devotes himself helpfully to all life that is in need of help. Only the universal ethic of the feeling of responsibility in an ever-widening sphere for all that lives—only that ethic can be founded in thought. The ethic of the relation of man to man is not something apart by itself: it is only a particular relation which results from the universal one.[13]

To interpret the Dalai Lama's specific perspective on issues related to the environment the following theoretical framework, conceptualized on the methodology given by Donald K. Swearer,[14] provides a methodological basis for analysing and categorizing, and subsequently clarifies the Dalai Lama's eco-Buddhist concerns gleaned from his often-dispersed writings:

Existential Level

Existentially, Buddhists affirm that all sentient beings share the fundamental conditions of birth, old age, suffering, and death. This existential realization of the universality of suffering lies at the core of the Buddha's teaching.[15] The Buddha's resolve to share this existential insight into the cause and cessation of suffering is regarded by tradition as an act of universal compassion. Thus Buddhist environmentalists assert that the mindful awareness of the universality of suffering produces compassion and empathy for all forms of life, particularly for all sentient species. The *Dhammapada's* ethical injunction—not to do evil and to do good—is a moral principle that advocates the non-violent alleviation of suffering. It is out of concern for the living environment that Buddhist environmentalists extend loving kindness and compassion beyond people and animals to include plants and the earth itself.[16]

With Albert Schweitzer, and partly under the influence of Gandhi, ethics came to mean more than relations between humans. He introduced the idea that a man is ethical only when life as such is sacred to him, including those of plants and animals.

Only the universal ethic of the feeling of responsibility in an ever-widening sphere for all that lives—only that ethic can be founded in thought. The ethic of the relation of man to man is not something apart by itself: it is only a particular relation which results from the universal one ...

And therefore he suggests

While the unthinking modern world—and life—affirmation stumbles about its ideals won by discovery and invention, the thinking world—and life—affirmation sets up the spiritual and ethical perfecting of humankind as the highest ideal, and an ideal from which alone all other ideals of progress get their real value.[17]

In a similar vein, the Dalai Lama says that just as it is important to maintain gentle, peaceful relations with our fellow beings, similarly it is important to extend the same kind of attitude towards the natural environment. This goes to show that in describing man's place in the environment the Dalai Lama believes that one should not treat man or the environment as independent of each other. This is also a major premise upon which all concerns for the environment begin.[18] The Dalai Lama says: '...there is a very close inter-dependence, or inter-relationship, between the environment and the inhabitants.'[19]

He explains this with the help of Buddhist philosophy:

...according to Buddhist teachings, the innermost subtle consciousness is the sole sort of creator, itself consisting of five elements, very subtle forms of elements. These subtle elements serve as conditions for producing the internal elements, which form sentient beings, and that in turn causes the existence or evolution of the external elements. So, there is a very close inter-dependence ... between the environment and the inhabitants.[20]

Out of concern for the total living environment, like all Buddhist environmentalists, the Dalai Lama extends 'loving kindness' and compassion beyond people and animals, to include plants and the earth itself.

Moral Level

It is the concept of karma and rebirth (samsara) that integrates the existential sense of a shared common condition of all sentient life forms with the moral dimension of the Buddhist cosmology. Rebirth maps commonalities and differences among species on the basis of moral grounds. Even though this continuum constitutes a moral hierarchy, differences among life forms and individuals are considered relative and not absolute. Thus, *Lankavatara Sutra* says that '... wherever there is the evolution of living beings, let people cherish the thought of kinship with them....'[21] It suggests that being connected with the process of taking birth, one is kin to all wild and domestic animals, birds, and beings born from the womb, and essentially brings about the realization that all life forms share both a common problematic and a promise. With thorough understanding of one's existence among all, the avoidance of cruelty to other living creatures, no exploitation of nature beyond the limit of one's survival, and with right aspiration and conduct—most environmental problems of today can be solved. The teachings of Buddhism have concentrated on the theory of karma and the theory of cause and effect. They demonstrate that unmindful neglect of these principles of right living can result in an environmental crisis.[22]

'Although the Buddhist doctrines of karma and rebirth link together all forms of sentient existence in a moral continuum, Buddhist ethics focus on human agency and its consequences...humans have been the primary agents in creating the present ecological crisis and will bear the major responsibility in solving it.'[23] Even though it is philosophically important that Buddhism includes plants and animals in its soteriological schemes, human beings are considered responsible for the ecological crisis. This point subsequently develops in the Dalai Lama's perception on the human need to maintain genuine and peaceful relations with the environment. More importantly, even though change is an important 'inherent' element in nature, Buddhists believe that natural processes are directly affected by human morality. This aspect comes through succinctly in the following words: '...although change is inherent in nature, humanity's moral deterioration accelerates and shapes the changes bringing about circumstances which are adverse to human well-being and happiness.'[24] It is suggested that within the Buddha's enlightenment vision (nirvana) all the major dimensions of the Buddhist worldview are found. The Buddha finally fathomed the nature of suffering and the path to its cessation as formulated in the Four Noble Truths and the law of interdependent co-arising:

Buddha's enlightenment evolved in a specific sequence: from an understanding of the particular (his personal karmic history) then to the general (the karmic history of humankind), and finally to the suffering. Subsequently this principle is further generalized on a 'universal law of causality' which emphasizes that 'on the arising of this, that arises; on the cessation of that, that ceases.[25]

Cosmological Level

Swearer's conceptualization further elucidates how Buddhist environmentalists like the Dalai Lama find in the causal principle of interdependence an ecological vision that integrates all aspects of the ecosphere—particular individuals and general species—in terms of the principle of mutual codependence. Within the cosmological model individual entities are, by their very nature, 'relational', thereby undermining the autonomous self over and against the 'other', be it a human being, animal, or vegetable. Buddhist environmentalists see their worldview to be a rejection of hierarchical dominance of one human being over another or of the human over nature, and thus, as the basis of an ethic of empathetic compassion that respects biodiversity. To quote the Thai monk Buddhadasa Bhikku, who says:

The entire cosmos is a cooperative. The sun, the moon and the stars live together as a cooperative. The same is true for humans and animals, trees and the earth. When we realize that the earth is a mutual, interdependent, cooperative enterprise...then we can build a noble environment. If our lives are not based on this truth, then we shall perish.' A Western Buddhist observing that the Buddhist worldview or dharma not only refers to the teachings of the Buddha but also to all things in nature, characterizes Buddhism as a 'religious ecology'.[26]

Ontological Level

Swearer suggests that it is in the later schools of Buddhist thought that the cosmological vision of an interdependent causality evolved into a more substantive sense of ontological unity. Metaphorically, the image of Indra's net, found in the Hua Yen (J. Kegon) tradition's *Avatamsaka Sutra*, is important in Buddhist ecological discussions. The image of the universe as a vast web of many-sided jewels, each constituted by reflections of all the other jewels in the web and with each jewel being the image of the entire universe, symbolizes the world as a universe of bioregional ecological communities.[27]

Buddhist environmentalists argue that ontological notions such as the Buddha nature or *dharma* nature provide a basis for unifying all existent entities in a common sacred universe, even though the tradition privileges human life vis-à-vis spiritual realization. For T'ien-t'ai monks in eighth-century China, the belief in a universal Buddha nature blurred the distinction between sentient and non-sentient life forms and logically led to the view that plants, trees, and the earth could also achieve enlightenment. According to Swearer:

Kukai (774–835), the founder of the Japanese Shingon School and Dogen (1200–1253), the founder of the Soto Zen sect, described universal Buddha-nature in naturalistic terms, 'If plants and trees were devoid of Buddhahood, waves would then be without humidity' (Kukai); 'The sutras [i.e., the *dharma*] are the entire universe, mountains and rivers and the great wide earth, plants and trees' (Dogen). Buddhist environmentalists cite Dogen's view, as support, for the preservation of species biodiversity.[28]

To state clearly and precisely these different levels mentioned above, as they emerge and take shape in the Dalai Lama's thought, is a problematic task, primarily because in his thought the cosmological, ontological, and moral dimensions are intricately interspersed. Even though the distinctions rise to the surface of his arguments, to not see the perfect flow with which his thought moves from one level to another would reduce its richness. Therefore, these various levels have been clubbed together to give an accurate picture of his environmental concerns. Despite using a methodology of categorizing, it is still difficult to see the Dalai Lama's thought on environment in a neat, compartmentalized form.

Human Need to Maintain Gentle and Peaceful Relations with the Environment

The Existential Framework

It is seen that the Dalai Lama's conception of universal responsibility accords with man's subjective intentions to always prefer good to evil, creation to destruction, and to be just, generous, and compassionate. He theorizes on human nature with the presumption of its essential goodness. At various places, he describes human nature as compassionate and gentle[29] as well as good, well disposed, helpful,[30] and non-violent.[31] Thus, by stressing an essentially good human nature, the Dalai Lama tries to prove its non-violent nature by citing the example of human physiology. He maintains that human beings are intended to be non-violent, so much so that even human physiology is not intended for violence.[32] According to him, this shows the basic gentleness in human nature. Drawing inspiration in this regard from Mahatma Gandhi, the Dalai Lama acknowledges Gandhi as having a deep understanding of human nature. He appreciates Gandhi by saying: 'He made every effort to encourage the full development of the positive aspects of the human potential and to reduce or restrain the negative.'[33] Following this cue, the Dalai Lama postulates that every destructive action goes against basic human nature. He draws attention to the fact that this can be tested to be true, as all human beings dislike destruction. On the other hand, human nature desires constructive and fruitful growth as well as a sense of tranquility. He explains this aspect through a simple instance: '... when spring comes, the grass and trees come alive and everything is fresh. People feel happy. In autumn, one leaf falls, then another, then all the beautiful flowers die until we are surrounded by bare naked plants. We do not feel so joyful.'[34] Comparing the human need to maintain gentle and peaceful relations with one's fellow beings, the Dalai Lama says that human beings have a 'need' to be concerned about the environment. He speaks in the normative tone to say: '...I feel that we should not only maintain gentle, peaceful relations with our fellow human beings, but also that it is very important to extend the same kind of attitude toward the natural environment. Morally speaking, we should be concerned for our whole environment.'[35]

However, the question arises that despite being willing to accept human nature as good, we do witness humans beings acting in a depraved manner—be it towards one another or to their environment. Analysing these as wrong uses of human intelligence, the Dalai Lama hints at the importance of the motivation guiding the 'human mind'.[36] Commenting on this, the Dalai Lama states that the human mind is the key factor in solving any problem. Be it a problem of economics, international relations, science, technology, medicine, or ecology, the answer has to be sought within. In order to forge a change outside, a mental change has to be brought about. He elucidates this with a simple example: '... if we want a beautiful garden, we must first have a blueprint in imagination, a vision. Then the idea can be implemented and the external garden can materialize.'[37] Therefore, if there is an internal balance within human beings, they can manifest the latent capacity in themselves to have a non-violent attitude towards nature. Only then can they succeed in protecting, conserving, and preserving the natural environment. He suggests that by having a compassionate attitude human beings can develop a genuine sense of universal responsibility.

In the Dalai Lama's thesis, religions help to form cultures, worldviews, and ethics, and thus may assist in shaping solutions to environmental problems. Therefore, he says, religion is an important voice in environmental discussions. His thought clearly states that religious life and the earth's ecology are inextricably linked and organically related. He articulates this thought with the understanding that if human beings are interested in developing a more diverse and comprehensive context for understanding human-earth relations, then the perspectives of religious traditions can be of invaluable help. This has been argued by others, of which the following is an illustrative example: 'If we wish to understand ecology...in order to meet our current and future environmental challenges, we must also understand religions. Without the "photosynthesis", so to say, which occurs within the religious imagination there would be no human life on earth as we know it'.[38] Even though many religious leaders have recognized that their religions stood watch during a period of environmental degradation and that their traditions are not above reproach, it cannot be denied that deeply rooted religious values that bear positively on the environmental challenge do exist.[39]

The Dalai Lama emphasizes that Tibetan concerns about the environment are not based on Buddhism to the exclusion of other things.[40] To corroborate this, he comments on Tibetan concern for the environment, which draws from the Tibetan way of life and not just from Buddhism. He cites the example of Buddhism in Japan or Thailand where the culture and attitude, he says, are different from Tibet. Citing the Tibetan geography as an example, he says that Tibetans have experienced very little anxiety because Tibet is neither small nor heavily populated. This gives the Tibetans the advantage of having distant neighbours, which according to the Dalai Lama, makes them feel less oppressed. He connects this aspect to the implications for world peace and the practice of non-violence. To him it is not only the Tibetan religion that gives Tibetans the capacity to be peaceful by nature—their 'unique environment' is also a major contributing factor. He emphasizes: 'People are always looking for answers in our unique religion, forgetting that our environment is just as unusual'.[41]

However, some studies illustrate very clearly that more than anything, it was the traditional respect and concern for nature that lay behind Tibetan environmental concerns. Much of this traditional concern was based on religious beliefs and these in turn played a part in the formulation of social values and state policy. Thus in 1944, the Regent of Tibet renewed a traditional decree, stating:

The village heads, officials and governors of all districts of Tibet are commanded to prevent the killings of all animals, except hyenas and wolves. The fish and otters of the water, the animals of the hills and forests, the birds of the air, all animals endowed with the gift of life, whether great or small, must be protected and saved....Everyone must obey the essence of the five principles of hunting and environmental protection laws first proclaimed in the Earth-Dog Year (1896).[42]

Such observations suggest that Tibetans have always lived in total harmony with nature, seeking to learn and understand its masses and rhythms. In this respect, Buddhism has also played an important role. There are scholars who have found strong links between Buddhism and respect for nature.

Dharma, the Buddhist word for truth and the teachings, is also the word for nature. This is because they are the same. Nature is the manifestation of truth and of teachings. When we destroy nature we destroy the truth and the teaching. When we protect nature, we protect the truth and the teaching.[43]

Thus rather than divide the world into the realms of the 'human' and 'nature', the classical Buddhist perspective has seen a more appropriate division between sentient beings, of which humans are only one type, and the non-sentient environment or the 'receptacle-world'. While there are differences of views regarding this, the key quality is sentience. Thus the relatively special place of human beings in the Buddhist cosmos means that they can be seen at a 'higher level' of existence than animals. However, this is not seen as a justification for dominating and exploiting animals.[44] Therefore, it is only by seeing human beings and nature as inseparable that one can realize how human beings should act and live so as to be in a less destructive and self-undermining relationship with 'nature.' According to the Engaged Buddhist Thich Nhat Hanh:

... we classify other animals and living beings as nature, acting as if we ourselves are not part of it. Then we pose the question "How should we deal with Nature?" We should deal with nature the way we should deal with ourselves! We should not harm ourselves; we should not harm nature ... Human beings and nature are inseparable.[45]

The successful implementation of such concern for the environment in Tibet has been corroborated by visitors.[46] In fact it has been observed that monks and nuns, farmers, nomads, and other lay Tibetans had their own prescribed practices and conventions which show concern for the environment. Richardson in his book has tried to show how the majority of Tibetans made efforts to live as much as possible with nature, and not against it.[47] However, the Dalai Lama with his vision, which has space for tradition and civilization, does not always show his solidarity with the stereotypical 'Tibetan concern for nature'. If protecting the environment is by itself inherently good in his visionary landscape, 'progress' does not necessarily entail an inherent potential for destruction of preserved traditions either.

It is against such a context that the Dalai Lama systematically criticizes Tibetans for not having been progressive, and emphasizes how neglecting technological and economic development in Tibet was a crucial mistake:

As the Dalai Lama freely admits, there was a lot wrong with the old Tibet. The innate conservatism of Tibetans, combined with a reaction against the dramatic events of the early years of the century, meant that they had tried to resist almost all of the changes which were inevitable if Tibet was to survive into the twentieth and twenty-first centuries.[48]

He contends that material development without spiritual development can also cause serious problems and he disagrees over what 'progress' really means. He makes the observation that during the course of his extensive travelling he sees two sights—one of people revelling in pleasure and the other of people suffering. To this observation he adds: 'The advancement of science and technology seems to have achieved little more than linear, numerical improvement; development often means little more than more mansions in more cities. As a result, the ecological balance—the very basis of our life on earth—has been greatly affected.'[49] He adds: 'Progress has meant hardly anything more than great numbers of opulent houses in more cities...there is often a big gap between outward appearance and inner reality'.[50]

Making a pertinent observation about those who live in materially developed countries, he says: 'In their absorption they lose the dream of happiness which riches were to have provided.'[51] Hence he brings to the fore his observation that material progress alone cannot give lasting pleasure or satisfaction:

We have, in my view, created a society in which people find it harder and harder to show one another basic affection. In place of the sense of community and belonging, which we find such a reassuring feature of less wealthy (and generally rural) societies, we find a high degree of loneliness and alienation. Despite the fact that millions live in proximity to one another, it seems that many people, especially among the old, have no one to talk to but their pets. Modern industrial society often strikes me as being like a huge self-propelled machine. Instead of human beings in charge, each individual is a tiny insignificant component with no choice but to move when the machine moves.[52]

He says it seems the more we progress materially, the more we live under constant fear. Commenting on scientific and technological marvels, he says they will not possibly bring ultimate and permanent pleasure to human beings: 'for material progress always stimulates desire for even further progress, so that such pleasure as it brings is only ephemeral.'[53] Thus, he contrasts the ancient man's reverence of nature to the 'modern' man's desire to control it and pronounces that the ancient man was more aware of the importance of nature than his 'modern' counterpart.[54] In understanding man's motivation to control nature, the Dalai Lama draws out important implications for peace and non-violence. In a message on the United Nations Environmental Programme's World Environment Day, the Dalai Lama says: 'Peace and the survival of life on earth as we know it are threatened by human activities which lack a commitment to humanitarian values. Destruction of nature and natural resources results from ignorance, greed, and lack of respect for the earth's living things.'[55] His words are corroborated by the Buddhist scholar Doboom Tulku Lama, who argues that because in ancient times human ability was limited and people were relatively unaware of the importance of nature, they respected it. However, the contemporary situation is different. In recognition of this the Dalai Lama says: 'Now sometimes it seems people forget about the importance of nature. Sometimes we get some kind of wrong belief that we human beings can control nature with the help of technology.'[56] He suggests '...in the spirit of reconciliation, I advocate a sharing of interests so that *genuine progress* is possible. Compromise is the only way.'[57] Similarly, in the light of ecological problems, the Dalai Lama cannot help noticing that man's achievements have often been won at great moral and material cost while yesterday's successes have been nullified by their negative consequences today. His observation synchronizes with another observation that asserts that the paradox of development arises from the mistaken identification of 'culturally perceived' poverty with 'real material poverty,' and the mistaken identification of the growth of commodity production as providing better human sustenance.[58]

The Dalai Lama's Five Point Peace Plan[59] was presented in 1987. Two of the points cited in this are the following: the transformation of Tibet into a zone of peace (including non-violence to animals) and the restoration and protection of Tibet's natural environment, both clearly affirming the Dalai Lama's environmental concern.[60] However, he couches his arguments in a secular vocabulary, making their tone less of a religious diktat and more akin to a secular, practical, or utilitarian concern.

The Dalai Lama's Buddhist concern with the environment becomes clear again when he places the two ideas of consumerism and contentment in perspective. With the instance of the Buddhist principle of contentment, he concludes that Tibetans avoid consuming indiscriminately. Tibetans, he says, have always considered themselves a part of their environment. They believe in the relationship of the 'contained' and the 'container.' Drawing this inspiration from the scriptures, he says: 'The world is the container— our house—and we are the contained—the contents of the container. From these simple facts we deduce a special relationship because without the container, the contents cannot be contained. Without the contents, the container contains nothing, it is meaningless.'[61] This relation of 'container' and 'contained' is very important in order to illustrate the interdependence of all phenomena, especially in the context of the relation between human agency and the environment.

Contrary to what appears at the surface, the Dalai Lama categorically states that just as too much 'consumption' or consumerism is not good, similarly too much 'contentment' is also not good. In assessing the two he says: 'in principle, contentment is a goal, but pure contentment becomes almost like suicide.' Bringing up the Tibetan cause, he says that in certain ways Tibetans had too much contentment 'and we lost our country'. By suggesting that a callous, negligent attitude towards nature only brings disaster[62] the Dalai Lama draws attention to the symbiotic relation that all reality shares.

The Dalai Lama discusses Tibet as an example and says that in Tibet mountains are considered to be the abodes of deities. He takes the example of Amnye Machen, a mountain in northeastern Tibet, which is regarded as the home of Machen Pomra, one of the deities of Amdo. Since the people of Amdo consider Machen Pomra their special friend, many of them go around the foot of the mountain on pilgrimage. In this way they show their reverence for the mountain. The Dalai Lama also gives an environmental explanation for the 'Mani Stones'. Tibetan travellers have a tradition of adding stones to the cairns at the top of hills or passes. While placing the stones they shout 'Lha-gyal-lo' in Tibetan, which means 'Victory to the Gods.' Later 'Mani Stones', which are stones carved with prayers and other scriptures, are also added along with prayer flags. This traditional sense of respect for the environment also symbolizes a deep seated concern in the Tibetan community to protect it. Besides the 'practical' uses of nature both spiritually as well as materially—in the specific example of the mountains—which serve the purpose of meditation (spiritual use), gathering of plants and herbs for Tibetan medicines (material use) and pastures for animals of nomads[63] (material use and very crucial to Tibetan economy)—all reveal ecological implications as well. The Dalai Lama says that such traditions should be carried on: 'In Tibet, previously there was a good tradition of instituting laws to safeguard hills and valleys for unprotected and unsupported wild animals and birds and for the protection of various defenceless creatures. We should maintain the continuity of this tradition.'[64]

By suggesting the continuity of this tradition and by emphasizing the importance of environmental protection, the Dalai Lama acknowledges the normative underpinnings of his thought on environment. However, he makes it apparent that he would rather acknowledge the same in terms of a utilitarian intent and spirit, and thus he makes the observation that environmental protection is not merely '...a moral question but also a question of our own survival.'[65] He extends the logic of basic human interaction to human interaction with nature and suggests that even from a 'selfish' viewpoint one needs other people. The Dalai Lama says that the law of nature too is similar. Just as it is beneficial to be concerned about other people and to share their suffering, similarly, if we look after the environment, it too will respond to us in a positive way. He postulates that it is better to be 'wisely selfish' rather than 'narrow-mindedly selfish'[66]— which is again a very utilitarian stand. Simultaneously, the Dalai Lama also says that concern for the environment does not necessarily entail a compassionate attitude. Even though Buddhists express compassion for all sentient beings, this compassion does not necessarily have to be extended to every rock or tree or house. In his worldview, more than compassion, it is 'concern' for the environment that is important.[67]

In accordance with Buddhist teachings, the Dalai Lama maintains that there is a very close interdependence between the natural environment and sentient beings living in it.[68] The notion of interdependence has been a part of Buddhist thought from time immemorial,[69] and the Dalai Lama teaches that one aspect of life connects with every other.[70] He demonstrates its contemporary use, not merely as a concept, but as a theoretical construct that has a practical bearing. He says

...nation to nation, continent to continent, we are heavily dependent on each other. For instance, thousands upon thousands of new cars are moving in the streets of New York, Washington, or in Los Angles, but without oil they cannot move. Though at the moment human beings are carried by cars, if that fuel is finished, the humans will have to carry these big cars. Prosperity depends on other factors in other places. Whether we like it or not, this shows that we are interdependent. We can no longer exist in complete isolation.[71]

He elaborates further by saying that: 'All ... demarcations are artificially made.'[72] He posits that individuals 'fabricate' distinctions based on colour, geographical location, and so forth. But what really binds these individuals together is their need to find happiness and eschew suffering. He says: 'Human beings by nature want happiness and do not want suffering.'[73] It is here that the Dalai Lama brings in the concept of universal responsibility. He describes the concept of universal responsibility as the '...key to human survival and progress. It is also the best foundation for world peace and promotion of human rights and a political culture of non-violence and dialogue in resolving human conflicts.'[74] He contends that violent conflicts, destruction of nature, poverty, and hunger are all problems created by human beings, which can be resolved through effort, understanding and development of a sense of 'brotherhood' and 'sisterhood'. In his acceptance speech for the Nobel Peace Prize in 1989, he corroborated this by stating 'we need to cultivate a universal responsibility for one another and the planet we share.'[75] He further stressed that even though the Buddhist religion has helped him in generating love and compassion, universal responsibility, which entails 'responding with love and compassion,' can be practiced with or without religion[76] and that religion is not a pre-requisite for generating love and compassion within human beings. Universal responsibility is thus the recognition that our actions should benefit everyone. Schweitzer defined 'ethics' as 'unlimited responsibility for every living thing.' It has been suggested that Schweitzer's conception accords with man's subjective intention, which always prefers good to evil, and wants to be generous, compassionate, and just. Therefore, he says conclusively that 'no one should lighten his own burden of responsibility'.[77] Suggesting that environmental responsibility is an ethic of shared responsibility, Eliot Deutch says at least with regard to our ecosphere, we need to have a collective sense of responsibility, which he terms as '...an ethics of co-responsibility with regard to the effects of our collective activities (especially in view of the ecological crisis).'[78]

Defining the concept of universal responsibility, the Dalai Lama says: 'True compassion is universal in scope. It is accompanied by a sense of universal responsibility. To act altruistically, concerned only for the welfare of others, with no selfish or ulterior motive, is to affirm a sense of universal responsibility.'[79] The term universal responsibility literally means universal (chi in Tibetan) consciousness (sems in Tibetan) or chisems.[80] Commenting on universal responsibility in a speech at the Parliamentary Earth Summit held under the auspices of United Nations Conference on Environment and Development in Rio de Janeiro, Brazil on June 7, 1992, the Dalai Lama said it is the real key to human survival.[81] 'Universal responsibility ... is the best foundation for world peace, the equitable use of natural resources and, through concern for future generations, the proper care of the environment.'[82]

The present world, or as he calls it the 'modern' world, is in great need of universal responsibility according to the Dalai Lama. He insists on this because he feels significant events occurring in one part of the world eventually affect the entire planet. With such a perception comes the realization that each major local problem has to be treated as linked to global concerns. Even though the Dalai Lama knows that there are barriers like the national, racial, or the ideological that separate human beings, he cautions that one can no longer invoke them without oneself undergoing destructive repercussions.

This is due to the Buddhist principle of interdependence—a phenomenon as well as a principle—that is not absent in the 'modern' world.

The Dalai Lama insists that interdependence is a fundamental law of nature. He suggests that not only the myriad forms of life, but the subtlest level of material phenomena is also governed by the principle of interdependence. 'All phenomena, from the planet we inhabit to the oceans, clouds, forests, and flowers that surround us, arise in dependence upon subtle patterns of energy. Without their proper interaction, they dissolve and decay.'[83] This can be corroborated by another example:

Every thing that finds its way into streams finds its way sooner or later into rivers. Everything found in river water ultimately reaches the ocean, which are the lungs of our planet, its unique heat regulator, an enormous factory for producing food for men, as well as an all-embracing transport artery. Part of the refuse disintegrates in sea water, part settles to form deposits on the ocean bed while part proves resistant to the impact of sea water and spreads over great areas. The ocean can no longer serve mankind as a dumping ground—this becomes increasingly plain as the years go by.[84]

In a sense this embodies the essence of environmental concerns as reflected in Buddhism as well as in the Dalai Lama's thought. Thus, we see that by his understanding of how globalization has shrunk the world and the implications it has for man's attitude of responsibility, he draws a simple conclusion. Because of this interconnectedness that 'universal responsibility' recognizes, each individual is not only ethically responsible for the 'happiness' of each and every individual, but is also instrumental in recognizing and responding to one's universal responsibility.

He links the concept of universal responsibility to the environment by saying:

if humankind continues to approach its problems considering only temporary expediency, future generations will have to face tremendous difficulties. The global population is increasing, and our resources are being rapidly depleted. Look at the trees, for example. No one knows exactly what adverse effects massive deforestation will have on the climate, the soil, and global ecology as a whole. We are facing problems because people are concentrating only on their short-term, selfish interests, not thinking of the entire human family. They are not thinking of the earth and the long-term effects on universal life as a whole.[85]

Giving a utilitarian turn to his arguments advocating environmental care and awareness, the Dalai Lama has time and again emphasized that the environment is of consequence not only for this generation but is important for future generations as well.[86] Drawing inspiration from the Buddhist teachings that there is a very close interdependence between the natural environment and the sentient beings living in it, the Dalai Lama couches his argument in the language of those advocating a sustainable world. His utilitarian ethics comes forth in the following statement, which also sums up his thought on environmental ethics.

According to Buddhist teachings there is a very close interdependence between the natural environment and the sentient beings living in it. Human beings, as social animals, need companions in order to survive. Since I believe that human beings are basically gentle by nature, I feel that we should not only maintain non-violent relations with our fellow human beings, but that we should extend the same kind of attitude towards the environment.[87]

And further: '... resolving the environmental crisis is not just a question of ethics but a question of our own survival'[88] [and]

...taking care of our planet is like taking care of our houses. Since we human beings come from Nature, there is no point in our going against Nature, which is why I say the environment is not a matter of religion or ethics or morality. These are luxuries, since we can survive without them. But we will not survive if we continue to go against Nature.[89]

The Dalai Lama says:

For the sake of our future generations, we need to take care of our earth and of our environment. Environmental damage is often gradual and not easily apparent and by the time we become aware of it, it is generally too late. Since most of the major rivers flowing into many parts of Southeast Asia originate from the Tibetan plateau, it will not be out of place to mention here the crucial importance of taking care of the environment in that area.[90]

He insists that the vision in the Guidelines for future Tibet's Polity and the Basic Features of his Constitution are not conceived for the benefit of Tibet only but for the whole world, as the environmental degradation of the Tibetan Plateau will most certainly have global consequences.[91] However, his vision for the world at large has a clear concern for Tibet.

References to future generations are very interesting because it is by conceptualizing this aspect the Dalai Lama sums up the logic behind environmental protection and makes the universal reach of his thought on environment very obvious. In fact, he makes a special effort to make his thought seem utilitarian. The very fact that he refers to basic human qualities like kindness, compassion, sincerity, and honesty as 'secular ethics' highlights the utilitarian underpinnings of his thought.

Although the Dalai Lama has not gone into details about 'environmental rights' as a concept, he does allude to this idea. For him Tibet is a cause as well as the example of what environmental rights are, and what they have meant to the Tibetans. His writings speak about the violation of environmental rights in Tibet. In the context of the Tibetan attitude of protecting the environment, he makes a reference to the seventeenth century, when the Tibetans began enacting decrees to protect the environment.[92] However, he insists that the environment was protected chiefly because of the beliefs instilled in Tibetans when they were children. War violates nature. Bringing forth the Tibetan concern for the environment, he draws attention to the fact that virtually no army existed in Tibet for at least three hundred years. He states that Tibet had stopped waging wars in the eighth century. It is fairly clear when one reads the Dalai Lama that his conceptualization of environmental protection brings forth his Tibet agenda. Thus, the following statement, the fourth component in the Dalai Lama's peace plan comments on Tibet being used for the production of nuclear weapons and for the dumping of nuclear waste: '[T]he manufacture and use of nuclear power and other technologies which produce *hazardous waste* [italics added] would be prohibited.'[93]

The Dalai Lama explains this part of his peace plan as the

restoration and protection of Tibet's natural environment and the abandonment of China's use of Tibet for the production of nuclear weapons and dumping of nuclear waste...serious efforts must be made to restore the natural environment in Tibet. Tibet should not be used for the production of nuclear weapons and the dumping of nuclear waste.[94]

He sums up this nuclear threat in a philosophical tone by saying that the dangers for doing this are obvious: 'Not only living generations, but future generations are threatened by China's lack of concern for Tibet's unique and delicate environment.'[95]

Buddhist environmentalists have been linking human rights with environmental rights within the cosmological model. In their worldview hierarchical dominance of one human over another is rejected. Similarly, dominance of humans over nature is also rejected.[96] Thus the Dalai Lama finds a clear link between human rights and environmental rights: '... a clean environment is a human right like any other.'[97] He says further, 'All living beings have a right to breathe clean air, drink fresh water and find food ...'[98]

According to the Dalai Lama, war, pollution, poverty, and suffering are the results of ignorance and selfish action because of our inability to see the essential common relation of all beings. By this he implies the mutual dependence of all human beings and draws attention to the 'common basic feeling' that everyone shares.

Seeking the 'secular' need to protect the environment, the Dalai Lama shows that even though it may be a 'religious duty' to look after the environment, it is not as if having a non-religious or a secular attitude is not conducive to environmental awareness or concern. In his opinion, the environmental problem stems from insatiable desire, lack of contentment and the greed of human beings. Thus he says,

It is in the religious teachings that we find various instructions that enable us to keep a check on our desires and greed, and to positively transform our behavior and conduct. Therefore, I think religious traditions have not only a potential but also a great responsibility to make contributions in that direction.[99]

This is a point that has been stressed by other scholars who clearly state that 'No understanding of the environment is adequate without a grasp of the religious life that constitutes the human societies that saturate the natural environment and that, for better or worse, alter all the world's natural systems.'[100] The Dalai Lama's discerning vision clearly sees that any argument advocating environmental protection by religious motivation may not sound plausible in today's world—especially when people would seek clear scientific reasoning as against religious ones. Therefore, even though he gives the religious explanation behind environmental protection, his explanation is neither polemical nor dogmatic. In his explanation of Buddhist practice, one gets used to the idea of non-violence and of bringing an end to suffering. Hence destroying anything indiscriminately becomes impossible.[101] Although Buddhists do not believe that trees or flowers have minds, yet they have respect for them. This for the Dalai Lama is a clear instance of the Buddhist sense of universal responsibility for both mankind and nature. Pondering this, he establishes very logically that a Buddhist's belief in reincarnation is responsible for his sense of universal responsibility and thus of a concern for the future. 'Our belief in reincarnation is one example of our concern for the future.'[102] According to a scholar the role of religions in the environmental crisis is 'to get us past a preoccupation with our rights and move us to a sense of our responsibilities. That is the only way short of a global catastrophe.'[103]

The philosophy of the Dalai Lama, referred to as 'engaged', gives some guidelines on how to actually show one's concern through praxis. These guidelines are motivated chiefly by three factors: practical, religious, and psychological. From the practical point of view, the Dalai Lama considers the cultivation of fruit trees beneficial. These trees have an added advantage as they provide nourishment to humans while providing benefit to other sentient beings as well. In a reference to the *Mandala* offering, the Dalai Lama states that prayers are made for the ground to be covered with incense and to be strewn with flowers. Therefore, in the religious realm, flowers assist in accumulating merit and purifying obscuration. They are an indispensable offering in performing religious activities like visualization of meditational deities. On the psychological plane, people have been known to benefit, if they are under stress, by strolling in a garden. Some scholars have suggested that from the beginning of Buddhism, the forest has represented the ideal place of meditation for monks. The Dalai Lama points out how a deep commitment to environmental protection can be practically realized by not only protecting trees but also by planting new ones. In a speech made at a special tree planting ceremony in Mundgod on 6 December 1990, the Dalai Lama remarked that currently a movement towards a deeper commitment to environmental protection through planting trees and taking care of the existing ones is rapidly increasing all over the world. Here he also exhorted Tibetans to take a keen interest in environmental protection and in planting new trees. According to him, in this way Tibetans will be able to make small but significant contributions to the cause. Again the Dalai Lama gives utilitarian reasons for doing so. Trees create an atmosphere of natural beauty and security. Apart from being responsible for the nurture of these trees one can derive various benefits from them (like eating fruits and enjoying their shade).[104]

On 9 December 1990, in Sarnath, the Dalai Lama distributed seeds of fruit-bearing trees to encourage environmental protection through tree planting. Yet, the Dalai Lama is also trying to grapple with bigger issues like population and demilitarization—both very important in the environmental context.

The Dalai Lama interprets Buddhism for today's world by his total engagement with the concerns of the present time. His clear statements go to show that the Buddhist theory is not a dogma that is hermetically sealed. In fact since it stubbornly refuses to be categorized in the final analysis, it has been suggested that there is something ungraspable about it.[105] In his engagement and total concern for problems being faced by humanity, he clearly shows that his engagement with Buddhism is not strictly theoretical.

Thus, it has been suggested that the pragmatic attitude, which presupposes a permanent challenge to our habitual ways of thinking and acting, is the backbone of Buddhism. Even while it affirms that every event comes from a cause and brings on consequences, and attempts to establish interconnectedness, Buddhism has the capacity to do away with the theoretical speculation that may hamper real life.[106] In response to the question of whether he is strictly attached to the letter of his scriptures, the Dalai Lama replies, 'On the contrary. You would have (sic) to be crazy to maintain them with all your might in a world swept away by the movement of time. For example, if science shows that Scriptures are mistaken, the Scriptures have to be changed.'[107] The following views which have definite links with his environmental concerns will help to understand this aspect.

The Dalai Lama has spoken on a number of issues. It is apparent although his thought is strongly rooted in Buddhism, he is deeply sensitive to the contemporary context. His views on population instantiate this. Even though he acknowledges that in Buddhism each human life is precious, he realizes the implication this can have for the present state of the world's population. However, he is critical of cloning which he insists can overburden the earth. He says, '...if we suppress our death, by the same token we will have to suppress birth, because the earth will become too rapidly overburdened.' Thus, the view that Buddhism sees all lives as precious does not mean it considers population explosion as a virtue. He considers birth control good because without it from the global viewpoint, life would begin to threaten all life. Talking of abortion he says:

...abortion is a violent act, which we reject. But if we look at things from a certain distance, if we make an effort...to achieve a global viewpoint, then we see quite simply that there are too many of us on this planet. And tomorrow that overload is going to get worse...it's really a matter of survival...if we want to defend...precious lives now pressing on the planet, if we want to give them a little more prosperity, justice and happiness, we have to forbid ourselves to go on multiplying.[108]

With regard to birth control he gives an answer in the affirmative saying that it has to be 'publicized and promoted.'[109] Even though from the individual point of view he holds that birth control is pernicious because it prevents human life from existing, he asserts that from the global viewpoint human life can itself start to threaten all life. The Dalai Lama recognizes that looking at current issues from the religious point of view is not entirely helpful. Interpreting religion in a new light he says:

'...old religious prohibitions sometimes harm us.'[110]

The Dalai Lama's logical statement is that if population expands as rapidly as it is doing, eventually this planet may not be able to provide sufficient requirements for all human beings. In a deft turn of argument, he draws the conclusion that even though Buddhism is not in favour of annihilating life in any way, yet even from the Buddhist point of view, birth control can be justified. In his own words: '...from a Buddhist viewpoint, it is absolutely worthwhile to think about and seriously implement birth control.'[111] Thus, it can be seen that his thought on environment is linked to and also has a bearing on his social thought. By his unique insights, both into existing theory and emerging praxis, he balances artfully what he deems best for humankind at large. Sensitive to the current global problem, the Dalai Lama deviates from the Buddhist tradition. The Dalai Lama feels that humanity needs to be pragmatic and adopt birth control measures in order to ensure the quality of life in the southern countries today to protect the quality of life for future generations.[112] 'Buddhist' objections to contraception are limited—given that contraception 'prevents' a human life rather than 'destroys' it.[113]

In conclusion, it can be said that even though the picture of the Buddha seated under the tree of enlightenment has not traditionally been interpreted as a paradigm for ecological thinking, today's Buddhist environmental activists point out that decisive events in the Buddha's life occurred in natural settings: the Buddha was born and attained nirvana under trees.[114] It has been suggested that the textual record testifies to the importance of forests, not only as an environment preferred for spiritual practices such as meditation, but also as a place where the laity sought instruction. The Dalai Lama illustrates the importance of nature in Buddhism in the following excerpt from his poem:

Under a tree was the great Sage Buddha born
Under a tree, he overcame passion

And attained enlightenment
Under two trees did he pass in Nirvana

Verily, the Buddha held the trees in great esteem.[115]

Therefore, Swearer contends, 'Historically, in Asia and increasingly in the West, Buddhists have situated centers of practice and teaching in forests and among mountains at some remove from the hustle and bustle of urban life.'[116] For the Dalai Lama man's own constitutive nature is the key to understanding the relationality of the total 'reality', extending it as far as one would like it to go. The damage done to the environment will have consequences for our present well-being as well as for future generations. The Dalai Lama's thought is an appeal to humanity to slow down the deteriorating conditions in the environment, and if possible, to work judiciously toward the ideal of a healthy balance between man and his environment. Though the Dalai Lama recognizes science and technology as important, he still maintains that man is the master of both, and therefore, responsible for their use.

The Dalai Lama does not deal specifically with the environmental discourse. But, his persuasive thought gives cues for a philosophy which can harmoniously blend man and nature. Although he understands that change in terms of progress is a must, he suggests that it should be so articulated that it does not lead to the debasement of universally accepted human values. At many points, in consonance with Gandhi's thought, the Dalai Lama's thought can be understood in the Gandhian diktat, which states that the earth has enough to satisfy the 'need' of mankind, but never enough to satisfy its greed.

Notes

1. See Martine Batchelor and Kerry Brown (eds), *Buddhism and Ecology*, London: Cassell, 1992.

Duncan Ryuken Williams, *Buddhism and Ecology: The Interconnection of Dharma and Deeds*, Cambridge, Massachussetts: Harvard University Center for the Study of World Religions, 1997.

Bill Devall and George Sessions, *Deep Ecology: Living as if Nature Mattered*, Layton, UT: Gibbs Smith, 1985.

Allan Hunt Badiner (ed.), *Dharma Gaia: A Harvest of Essays in Buddhism and Ecology*, Berkeley, California: Parallax Press, 1990.

O.P. Dwivedi, *Environmental Ethics: Our Dharma to the Environment*, New Delhi: Sanchar Publishing House, 1994, p. 57.

Chatsumarn Kabilsingh, 'How Buddhism Can Help Protect Nature', in Nancy Nash (ed.), *Tree of Life: Buddhism and Protection of Nature*, Manchester: Alliance of Religions and Conservation, (1987) second edition 1999, p. 23.

2. H. Saddhatissa, (trans.), *The Sutta-Nipâta*, London: Curzon Press, 1985, p. 16

3. Ibid.

4. H. H. The Dalai Lama, 'Foreword', in M.L. Dewan, *Toward a Sustainable Society: Perceptions*, New Delhi: Clarion Books, 1995, p. 11.

5. Bhikkhu Rewata Dhamma, 'The Human and Environmental Crisis: A Buddhist Perspective', in Sulak Sivaraksa (hon. ed.), Pipob Udomittipong and Chris Walker (eds), *Socially Engaged Buddhism for the New Millennium: Essays in Honour of the Ven. Phra Dhammapitaka (Bhikkhu P.A. Payutto) on his 60th Birthday Anniversary*, Bangkok: Sathikoses-Nagapradipa Foundation and Foundation for Children, 12 May 2542 (1999), p. 491.

6. See Chandradhar Sharma, *A Critical Survey of Indian Philosophy*, Delhi: Motilal Banarsidass Publishers, (1960) 1991, pp. 72–3:

'The doctrine of Pratityasamutpada or Dependent Origination is considered the foundation of all the teachings of the Buddha. It is contained in the Second Noble Truth, which gives the cause of suffering, and in the Third Noble Truth, which shows the cessation of suffering. Suffering is *Samsara*; cessation of suffering is *Nirvana*. Both are only aspects of the same Reality. Pratityasamutpada, viewed from the point of view of relativity is *Samsara*; while viewed from the point of view of reality, it is Nirvana. It is relativity and dependent causation as well as the Absolute, for it is the Absolute itself, which appears as relative and acts as the binding threat giving them unity and meaning. Pratityasamutpada tells us that in the empirical world dominated by the intellect everything is relative, conditional, dependent, subject to birth and death and therefore impermanent. The causal formula is: "this being that arises", i.e., "Depending on the cause, the effect arises." Thus every object or thought is necessarily relative. And because it is relative, it is neither absolutely real (for it is subject to death) nor absolutely unreal (for it appears to arise). All phenomenal things hang between reality and nothingness, avoiding both the extremes. They are like the appearances of the Vedantic Avidya or Maya. It is in this sense that Buddha calls the doctrine the Middle Path, "Madhyama Pratipat", which avoids both eternalism and nihilism. Buddha identifies it with the Bodhi, the Enlightenment which dawned upon him under the shade of the "bo" tree in Gaya and which transformed the mortal Siddhartha into the immortal Buddha. He also identifies it with the Dharma, the Law: "He who sees the Pratityasamutpada sees the Dharma, and he who sees the Dharma sees the Pratityasamutpada." Failure to grasp it is the cause of misery. Its knowledge leads to the cessation of misery...Troubled by the sight of disease, old age and death, Buddha left his home to find a solution of the misery of earthly life. Pratityasamutpada is the solution which he found. Why do we suffer misery and pain? Why do we suffer old age and death? Because we are born. Why should there be this will to become? Because we cling to the objects of the world. Why do we have this clinging? Because we crave to enjoy the objects of this world. Why do we have this craving, this thirst for enjoyment? Because of sense-experience. Why do we have this sense-experience? Because of sense-object-contact. Why do we have this contact? Because of the six sense-organs (the sixth sense being the mind). Why do we have the six sense-organs? Because of the psycho-physical organism. Why do we have this organism? Because of the initial consciousness of the embryo. Why do we have this consciousness? Because of our predisposition or impressions of Karma. Why do we have these impressions? Because of Ignorance. Hence he postulated that ignorance is the root-cause of all suffering.'

7. Dhamma, n. 5, p. 491.

8. Ibid., p. 493.

9. Ibid., p. 496.

10. Ibid., pp. 491–2.

11. Donald K. Swearer, 'Buddhism and Ecology: Challenge and Promise', *Earth Ethics*, (Washington DC), vol. 10, no.1, Fall 1998, p. 22.

12. Nancy Nash, 'The Buddhist Perception of Nature Project', in Klas Sandell (ed.), *Buddhist Perspectives on the Eco-Crisis*, Buddhist Publication Society, 1987, as cited in Swearer, n. 11, p. 22. Considered very important to this movement and addressing international issues 'head-on', ranging from the disposal of nuclear waste to human rights violations, is the Dalai Lama and amongst key figures, Thich Nhat Hanh. Others in this movement are Sulak Sivaraksa, Ahangame T. Ariyaratne, Joanna Macy and Kenneth Kraft.

13. Albert Schweitzer, 'My Life and Thought', in J.J. Clarke, *Nature in Question: An Anthology of Ideas and Arguments*, London: Earthscan Publications, 1993, p. 182.

14. Swearer, n. 11, p. 19.

15. Sharma, n. 6, pp. 71–2.

16. Swearer, n. 11, p. 19.

17. J.J. Clarke, n. 13, pp. 182–3.

18. J. Baird Callicott and Roger T. Ames (eds), *Nature in Asian Traditions of Thought: Essays in Environmental Philosophy*, Delhi: Sri Satguru Publications, (1989) 1991, p. 243.

19. His Holiness The Dalai Lama, *The Heart of Compassion: A Dalai Lama Reader*, Delhi: Full Circle, 1997, p. 134.

20. Ibid., p. 135.

21. Daisetz Teitaro Suzuki, (trans. from Sanskrit), *The Lankavatara Sutra: A Mahayana Text*, London: Routledge and Kegan Paul, (1932) 1978, p. 212.

22. Dwivedi, n. 1, p. 60.

23. Swearer, n. 11, p. 20.

24. Lily De Silva, 'The Hills Wherein My Soul Delights', in Batchelor and Brown, n. 1, p. 20.

25. Swearer, n. 11, p. 20.

26. Ibid.

27. Ibid.

28. Ibid., pp. 20–1.

29. The Dalai Lama, *The Power of Compassion: A Collection of Lectures by His Holiness the XIV Dalai Lama*, trans. Geshe Thupten Jinpa, New Delhi: HarperCollins Publishers India Fvt. Ltd. (1995) 1998, p. 58.

30. The Dalai Lama and Jean-Claude Carrière, *The Power of Buddhism*, Dublin: Newleaf, 1988, p. 15.

31. His Holiness the Dalai Lama, n. 19, p. 70.

32. His Holiness the Dalai Lama, *Speeches Statements Articles Interviews: 1987 to June 1995*, Dharamsala: Department of Information and International Relations, Central Tibetan Administration, Gangchen Kyishong, 1995, p. 211.

33. Ibid., p. 179.

34. His Holiness the XIV Dalai Lama, 'Universal Responsibility and Our Global Environment', *On the Environment: Collected Statements*, Department of Information and International Relations, Central Tibetan Administration of His Holiness the XIV Dalai Lama, 1995, p. 37.

35. His Holiness the XIV Dalai Lama, 'Ecology and the Human Heart', in n. 34, p. 12.

36. His Holiness the XIV Dalai Lama, 'Caring for the Earth', in n. 34, p. 33.

37. Ibid.

38. Lawrence Sullivan, 'Toward a Geology of Religions', *News*, (Harvard University Centre for the Study of World Religions: Cambridge), vol. 6, no. 1, Fall 1988, p. 13.

39. Ibid.

40. His Holiness the XIV Dalai Lama, 'Universal Responsibility and the Environment', in n. 34, p. 16.

41. Ibid., p. 17.

42. 'Wildlife Conservation Decree Issued by Tagdra Rinpoche The Regent of Tibet in 1944', *Tibet: Environment and Development Issues*, 1992, Dharamsala: Department of Information and International Relations, Central Tibetan Administration, 1992, p. 94.

43. Batchelor and Brown, n. 1, p. 99.

44. Peter Harvey, *An Introduction to Buddhist Ethics*, Cambridge: Cambridge University Press, 2000, pp. 150–1.

45. Thich Nhat Hanh, 'The Individual, Society, and Nature', in Fred Eppsteimer (ed.), *The Path of Compassion: Writings on Socially Engaged Buddhism*, Berkeley, California: Parallax Press, (1985) revised edition 1988, p. 41.

46. (a) Ward F. Kingdon, *The Mystery Rivers of Tibet*, Philadelphia: Lippincott, 1923.

(b) Ward F. Kingdon, *The Riddle of Tsangpo Gorges*, London: Arnold, 1926.

47. Hugh Richardson, *Tibet and Its History*, Boston: Shambhala, 1984.

48. Roger Hicks and Ngakpa Chogyam, *Great Ocean: An Authorized Biography of the Buddhist Monk Tenzin Gyatso His Holiness The Fourteenth Dalai Lama*, London: Penguin Books, (1984) 1990, p. 140.

49. His Holiness the Dalai Lama, 'The Sheltering Tree of Interdependence: A Buddhist Monk's Reflections on Ecological Responsibility', in *Environment and Development: Annual Newsletter 1993–1999,* Environment and Development Desk, Department of Information and International Relations, Central Tibetan Administration, Gangchen Kyishong, Dharamsala, 1994, p. 2.

50. Tenzin Gyatso His Holiness the Dalai Lama, *Ancient Wisdom, Modern World: Ethics for the New Millennium*, London: Abacus, (1999) 2000, p. 7

51. Ibid., p. 6.

52. Ibid., p. 9.

53. His Holiness the Dalai Lama of Tibet, *My Land and My People,* New Delhi: Srishti Publishers and Distributors, (1962) 1997, p. 235.

54. His Holiness the XIV Dalai Lama, 'Press Conference Statement', in n. 34, p. 47.

55. His Holiness the XIV Dalai Lama of Tibet, 'An Ethical Approach to Environmental Protection', in Nancy Nash (ed.), *Tree of Life, Buddhism and Protection of Nature: With a Declaration on Environmental Ethics from His Holiness the Dalai Lama*, Manchester, UK: Buddhist Perception of Nature, (1987) second edition, 1999, p. 15.

56. Doboom Tulku Lama, *The Buddhist Path to Enlightenment: Tibetan Buddhist Philosophy and Practice*, California: Point Loma Publications, 1996, p. 146.

57. The Dalai Lama, *The Four Noble Truths*, New Delhi: HarperCollins Publishers India, (1997) 1998, p. 149.

58. Vandana Shiva, 'Recovering the Real Meaning of Sustainability', in David E. Cooper and Joy A. Palmer (eds.), *The Environment in Question: Ethics and Global Issues*, London: Routledge, 1992, p. 190.

59. See Appendix III.

60. 'Five Point Peace Plan for Tibet By His Holiness The Dalai Lama', in n. 42, p. 96.

61. His Holiness the XIV Dalai Lama, 'Universal Responsibility and the Environment', n. 34, p. 18.

62. Ibid.

63. Melvyn Goldstein and Cynthia Bell, *Nomads of Western Tibet*, Berkeley and Los Angeles: University of California Press, 1990.

64. n. 34, p. 65.

65. Ibid., p. 12.

66. Ibid., p. 13.

67. Ibid., p. 17.

68. H.H. The Dalai Lama, 'Foreword,' in M.L. Dewan, *Toward A Sustainable Society: Perceptions*, New Delhi: Clarion Books, 1995, p. 11.

69. Dalai Lama and Jean-Claude Carrière, *The Power of Buddhism*, Dublin: Newleaf, 1988, p. 29.

70. The Fourteenth Dalai Lama His Holiness Tenzin Gyatso, *Kindness, Clarity and Insight*, edited by Jeffrey Hopkins and Elizabeth Napper, trans. Jeffrey Hopkins, New York: Snow Lion Publications, 1984, p. 9.

71. Ibid., p. 61.

72. Ibid., p. 158.

73. Ibid.

74. His Holiness the Dalai Lama, 'I Believe ...', *Tibetan Bulletin*, (Dharamsala: Department of Information and International Relations), vol. 3, no. 1, January–February 1999, p. 29.

75. *Nobel Peace Prize Award Ceremony 1989: Speeches*, Dharamsala: Office of Information and International Relations, n.d., p. 13.

76. Ibid., pp. 13–14.

77. I. Laptev, *The World of Man and the World of Nature*, Moscow: Progress Publishers, (1978) 1979, pp. 195–6.

78. Eliot Deutsch (ed.), *Culture and Modernity: East–West Philosophic Perspectives*, Delhi: Motilal Banarsidass, (1991) 1994, pp. 264, 274.

79. 'Importance of Compassion in Human Life', *The Spirit of Tibet: Universal Heritage, Selected Speeches of HH the XIV Dalai Lama*, edited by A.A. Shiromany, New Delhi: Tibetan Parliamentary and Policy Research and Allied Publishers Ltd., 1995, p. 253.

80. Tenzin Gyatso His Holiness the Dalai Lama, 'Universal Responsibility', in n. 50, p. 168.

81. 'Speech At Parliamentary Earth Summit', in n. 79, p. 299.

82. Ibid.

83. His Holiness the XIV Dalai Lama, n. 34, pp. 36–7.

84. Laptev, n. 77, p. 20.

85. 'Human Approach to World Peace', in n. 79, p. 261.

86. 'World Peace and the Environment', *The Political Philosophy of His Holiness the XIV Dalai Lama: Selected Speeches and Writings*, edited by A.A. Shiromany, New Delhi: Tibetan Parliamentary and Policy Research Centre and Friedrich–Naumann–Stiftung, 1998, p. 130.

87. H.H. The Dalai Lama, in Dewan, n. 68, p. 11.

88. n. 86, p. 130.

89. The Dalai Lama, *Freedom in Exile: An Autobiography of the Dalai Lama of Tibet*, London: Abacus, (1990) 1998, p. 296.

90. *Demilitarization of the Tibetan Plateau: An Environmental Necessity*, Dharamsala: Environment and Development Desk, Department of Information and International Relations, Central Tibetan Administration, 2000, pp. 16–17.

91. Ibid., p 17.

92. His Holiness the XIV Dalai Lama, 'A Clean Environment is a Human Right', in n. 34, pp. 22–5.

93. 'A Zone of Peace, Excerpts from the Nobel Peace Prize Lecture of H.H. the Dalai Lama', in Martine Batchelor, *Buddhism and Ecology*, London and New York: Cassell Publishers Limited, 1992, p. 113.

94. *Tibet: Environment and Development Issues 1992*, Dharamsala: Department of Information and International Relations, Central Tibetan Administration, 1992, pp. 96–8. Apart from this report, the following also deal with the same issue: (a) UNI, 'China Plans to Bring Radioactive Waste,' 28 September 1998. (b) Michael Weiskopf, 'China Reportedly Agrees to Store Western Nuclear Wastes', *The Washington Post*, 18 February 1984.

95. *Tibet: Environment and Development Issues 1992*, ibid., p. 98.

96. Swearer, n. 11, p. 20.

97. The Dalai Lama, *Freedom in Exile: An Autobiography of the Dalai Lama of Tibet*, London: Abacus, (1990) 1998, p. 296.

98. 'True Meaning of Peace', in n. 86, p. 35.

99. The Dalai Lama, *The Power of Compassion: A Collection of Lectures by His Holiness the XIV Dalai Lama,* trans. by Geshe Thupten Jinpa, New Delhi: HarperCollins Publishers India Pvt. Ltd., (1995) 1998, pp. 116–17.

100. 'UN Meeting on Ecology and the Role of Religion', in *News*, n. 38, p. 1.

101. This gets verified in Harrer's book where he has clearly brought out the Tibetans' attitude of considering all life as sacred. See Heinrich Harrer, *Return to Tibet*, London: Weidenfeld and Nicolson, 1984.

102. His Holiness the XIV Dalai Lama, n. 34, p. 16.

103. n. 100, p. 3.

104. 'Speech On Importance of Tree Planting', in n. 79, pp. 288–9.

105. The Dalai Lama and Carrière, n. 30, p. 51.

106. Ibid., p. 49.

107. Ibid., pp. 37–8.

108. Ibid., pp. 33–4.

109. Ibid., p. 33.

110. Ibid., p. 40.

111. His Holiness the XIV Dalai Lama, n. 34, p. 46. Also see His Holiness The Dalai Lama with Fabien Ouaki, 'Living and Dying', *Imagine All the People: A Conversation with the Dalai Lama on Money, Politics, and Life As It Could Be,* Boston: Wisdom Publications, 1999, pp. 83–109.

112. His Holiness The Dalai Lama with Ouaki, ibid., pp. 83–109.

113. Harvey, n. 44, p. 326.

114. Swearer, n. 11, p. 21.

115. His Holiness the XIV Dalai Lama, 'The Sheltering Tree of Interdependence: A Buddhist Monk's Reflections on Ecological Responsibility', n. 34, p. 60.

116. Swearer, n. 11, p. 21.

'We are at the dawn of an age in which extreme political concepts and dogmas may cease to dominate human affairs. We must use this historic opportunity to replace them by universal human and spiritual values and ensure that these values become the fibre of the global family which is emerging.' ['Human Rights and Universal Responsibilities', in *The Dalai Lama*', *A Policy of Kindness: An Anthology of Writings By and About the Dalai Lama,* edited and compiled by Piburn Sidney, Delhi: Motilal Banarsidass Publishers Pvt. Ltd., (1990) 1997, p. 104].

'Let us not talk of karma, but simply of one's responsibility towards the whole world.' [His Holiness The Dalai Lama with Fabien Ouaki, *A Conversation with The Dalai Lama on Money, Politics, and Life As It Could Be,* Boston: Wisdom Publications, 1999, p. 52].

'Religion, according to (Gandhi), should pervade all our activities, it cannot and ought not to be pursued in seclusion from one's fellow-beings and in separation from life's other activities. The equivalent term for "religion" is *Dharma* in Sanskrit, which means moral obligation and connotes individual's integrity as well as social solidarity. Gandhi understood religion completely from that point of view.' [Geeta Methta, 'Gandhi's Integral Humanism', *Gandhi Marg,* (New Delhi), vol. 22, no. 2, July–September 1999, p. 222].

'I would not only not try to convert, but would not even secretly pray that anyone should embrace my faith. Cases of real, honest conversion are quite possible. If some people, for their inward satisfaction and growth change their religion, let them do so.' [*Young India*, June 27 1927, in Anand T. Hingorani and Ganga A. Hingorani, *The Encyclopaedia of Gandhian Thought*, New Delhi: All India Congress Committee (I), 1985, p. 62].

4

The Dalai Lama on
Religion and Humanism

Proponents of the problematic of 'progress' largely agree that the progress which humanity has made since its earliest days is so clear and so striking that any attempt to question it could be no more than an exercise in rhetoric. The argument therefore, is not to deny the fact of human progress, but to suggest that we might be more cautious in our conception of it.[1] Arguments that there are really no superior cultures and that the west has become infatuated by notions of technological progress and technical superiority, and is oblivious to other aspects of existence is an elaboration of this continuing dialogue of what is 'progress' or 'retrogression'.[2] It has been affirmed by others that while religion, mythology, history and philosophy as areas of study have apparently lost their credibility, science has triumphed in lodging the idea of natural 'progress' in the depths of human consciousness.[3]

In what can be considered a continuation of this critique, the Dalai Lama contends that progress can only be measured by evaluating the 'happiness' it engenders in mankind.[4] In this sense, for the Dalai Lama 'progress' clearly does not mean what *prima facie* is discerned as material progress and what he describes as 'numerical improvement'. He says:

There is no doubt about the increase in our material progress and technology, but somehow that is not sufficient as we have not yet succeeded in bringing about peace and happiness or in overcoming suffering. We can only conclude that there must be something seriously wrong with our progress and development.[5]

In his words: 'In many cases, progress has meant hardly anything more than greater numbers of opulent houses in more cities, with more cars driving between them.'[6] In his discussion of progress and development, he takes up the example of modern industrial society. Describing it as a huge self-propelled machine, he suggests that such a society reduces human beings to insignificant components of this machine, with no choice but to move when the machine does. In his words: 'Clearly a major reason for "modern" society's devotion to material progress is the very success of science and technology'.[7] He acknowledges the many positive results and outcomes from science, but suggests that comforts and necessities, which are by-products of science, do not necessarily guarantee the 'happiness'[8] they promise. He concludes therefore, that though outwardly successful, the populations of such materially developed countries suffer from anxiety, discontent, frustration, uncertainty and depression.[9] In his search for a utopian perfection, the Dalai Lama postulates the need for a society in which religion ought not to be considered archaic, and eventually brings out the significant role that religion and politics play in contemporary times. What emerges in the writings of the Dalai Lama is the strong view that in spite of their differences in terms of beliefs, rituals, practices, and philosophic tenets, all religious traditions and all great religious leaders seek in their unique ways to improve the human condition, to enable and uplift human life, to affirm respect for human dignity, and to see the interrelatedness of all life and of all constituents of the universe. In an example of religious motivation informing political motivation and political action, the Dalai Lama pleads for human welfare and for genuine efforts to save and serve society.[10] To cite him:

We must remember that the different religions, ideologies, and political systems of the world are meant for human beings to achieve happiness. We must not lose sight of this fundamental goal and at no time should we place means above ends; the supremacy of humanity over matter and ideology must always be maintained.[11]

He questions the 'popular' assumption that religion and ethics have no place in politics and that religious persons lead reclusive lives. He considers such a view as one-sided since it lacks a proper perspective on the individual's relation to society and of the role of religion in an individual's daily life.[12]

It has been suggested that the Dalai Lama's views on religion have immediate political connectivity, and his pronouncements on political situations and dilemmas are founded on the central teachings of his religion. Thus 'the worlds of religion and politics are brought together not through some successful effort at either intellectual or ethical synthesis, but because, at the core of life, from which station His Holiness speaks, they are in fact at one together.'[13] The Dalai Lama, like Gandhi, does not separate religion and politics, and attempts to establish that unless this truth dawns upon us, it would be impossible to live responsibly on this earth, or to establish happiness and peace in the world and to bring about qualitative improvement in human society. He expresses disagreement with the 'school of thought' that 'warns the moralist to refrain from politics, as politics is devoid of ethics and moral principles.' Considering that it is the instruments of our political culture that have been tampered with, and have distorted fundamental concepts to further selfish goals, politics as a concept is not 'dirty'. The Dalai Lama holds that should deep moral convictions form the guidelines for the political practitioner, then society would reap many benefits. He advocates the 'functional importance of religion' for promoting human values in politics. In arguing thus, he questions the assumptions that hermetically seal off the domain of politics from what is according to him, erroneously considered the hermitage of spirituality.[14]

In a striking argument the Dalai Lama brings forth his critique of 'progress' and 'modernity'. Citing the increasing urbanization of 'modern' society where a high concentration of people live in close proximity to one another he proffers the argument that 'modern' living is so organized that it demands the least possible 'direct dependence' on others. Although he chooses to see the positive points in the 'independence' that has resulted with the advancement of science and technology; he reckons that this has led to a 'sense' of individualism. The cognizance of interconnection between persons has been neglected. This fosters a way of thinking that regards the 'other' as dispensable. He says: 'We have, in my view, created a society in which people find it harder and harder to show one another basic affection.'[15] He observes further that progress may give material benefit for which a price needs to be paid: 'In some parts of Southeast Asia, it is observable that, as prosperity has increased, traditional belief systems have begun to lose their influence over people'.[16]

He comments on what this has done:

In...the...way that physical disease reflects its environment, so it is with psychological and emotional suffering: it arises within the context of particular circumstances. Thus...we find stress-related disease. All this implies that there are strong reasons for supposing a link between our disproportionate emphasis on external progress and the unhappiness, the anxiety, and the lack of contentment of modern society.[17]

In what can be interpreted as a warning, the Dalai Lama shows that worldviews generated from such phenomena can lead to two situations. First, because of self-reliance that science can generate, there is the increasing possibility of overlooking our dependence on others. Second, the strengthening of the belief that science has 'disproven' religion can lead to a situation where there will be no final evidence for any 'spiritual' authority. So 'morality' can easily become a matter of individual preference.[18] In this context he connects the concept of universal responsibility to religion.

While universal responsibility, as a concept, seeks a deep relationship with various interrelated subjects in the Dalai Lama's thought, he is profoundly convinced that, on the level of praxis, universal responsibility is fundamental to human survival. Universal responsibility in the context of religion shows that religions are primarily meant for self-improvement and that a truly religious person—belonging to any religious tradition—is first and foremost 'a human being with a good heart'. Such a person generates altruistic feelings through his good thoughts. Linking the desire for peace with religion, the Dalai Lama tries to establish that since the desire for peace is universal, therefore, if interreligious contacts are established and promoted with noble intentions, a peaceful atmosphere can be created, and conflicts, fears, suspicions, and prejudices can be reduced to a great extent.

It should be understood that the Dalai Lama is criticizing science primarily because he sees that despite extraordinary scientific achievements, science has not had a corresponding success in 'telling' us how we 'ought' to act morally. Even though science and technology reflect the human desire to attain a better, more comfortable existence, the Dalai Lama suggests:

We need also to recognize what happens when we rely too much on the external achievements of science. For example, as the influence of religion declines, there is mounting confusion with respect to the problem of how best we are to conduct ourselves in life. Now, many people, believing that science has 'disproven' religion, make the further assumption that because there appears to be no final evidence for any spiritual authority, morality itself must be a matter of individual preference.[19]

Therefore, the Dalai Lama says, keeping in view the danger of replacing religion as the final source of knowledge in popular estimation, science begins to resemble a new religion. What needs to be clearly understood is that the Dalai Lama does not envision supplanting religion with science, or vice-versa. In his view what is to be avoided is the 'intolerance of alternate views.'[20] The Dalai Lama contends that just as materialism does not signify success, similarly, spiritualism is not necessary for the development of man. He says:

Wealthy people, driven by the desire to accumulate greater wealth, realize soon enough that money alone does not give peace and mental satisfaction. With money also there is a problem...without money also....Use your wealth to be a happy person.

That is the answer to a balance between spiritualism and materialism. Do something good for society, develop deeper human insight. Cultivate sensitivity and engage in social action which will benefit society and eliminate fear.[21]

Though he holds the opinion that 'urbanization' generates 'disharmony', he is careful to insist that his intention is not to idealize 'old ways of life'. He is critical enough to realize the apparent 'high level of cooperation we find in underdeveloped rural communities may be based more on necessity than on goodwill.'[22] In a typical argument, which reveals his intent to bridge the gap between 'ancient' and the 'modern', he emphasizes 'the challenge we face is therefore to find some means of enjoying the same degree of harmony and tranquility as those more traditional communities while benefiting fully from the material development of the world as we find it at the dawn of a new millennium'.[23] Just as he argues against idealizing old ways of life, similarly he argues against intolerance of material progress which however, he concedes, has benefits.[24] Similarly, he does not think of progress or material growth and religion as being mutually exclusive.

Even if the Dalai Lama holds the idea that material progress alone is not sufficient to achieve an ideal society, he argues that mental development should be in harmony with material development. With this consideration he juxtaposes 'original Marxism' and Mahayana Buddhism in a comparative framework.

He contends that while Marxism and Buddhism have many differences, this should not detract from their common ground. The first shared belief is their emphasis on the common good of society. Hence, if everything depends on one's own karma in Buddhism, which is linked to individual motivation, similarly, in Marxist or communist theory, everything depends on one's own 'labour'. In his own words:

In Buddhism, it is explained that everything depends on one's own karma. This means that one's life situation in the present depends upon one's actions and their motivations in the past and that one's future is thus capable of being moulded through engaging in salutary actions with a pure motivation. Similarly, in Communist or Marxist Theory, everything is said to depend on one's own labour.[25]

Secondly, both in Marxism as well as in Buddhism, all practices are seen as a means for serving others. Whereas Marxist economic theory is related with ethical principles—in the sense that its prime concern is with the use of resources and wealth, not their mere accumulation—in Buddhism the practice of considering the needs of other beings is stressed to such an extent that sacrificing individual welfare for the benefit of the majority of sentient beings is advocated.[26]

He visualizes Marxist theory as not absolutely anti-religious, saying:

Since the thrust of Marxist thought is not absolutely anti-religious, there is no point in religious person's viewing Marxism as anti-religious, creating tension and distrust...Marxists, out of ignorance and lack of personal experience, see religion as totally counterproductive, which is wrong. A real Marxist must discard narrow and dogmatic attitudes, and be open to the values of spiritual teachings.[27]

He postulates that the original theme of communism was anti-exploitation and anti-corruption, which does not necessarily entail that it was anti-religion. He suggests that just as some religious institutions have become corrupt and should be opposed, similarly—although Marxism arguably has good points—the implementation of some of its practices are corrupt and therefore, have to be opposed. With this consideration he suggests, '...distinction must be made between systems and their practitioners'.[28] Particularly in reference to religion and Marxist debate, the Dalai Lama's writings reveal that while the earlier Dalai Lama was unsure of Marxism, the later Dalai Lama's thought evolves in strategic maturity. His earlier position is apparent in the following lines: '...the threat to us was not only more powerful, it was also different in its very nature...we were threatened not only with military domination, but also with the domination of an alien materialistic creed which, so far as any of us understood it in Tibet, seemed totally abhorrent'.[29]

Arguing from the historical perspective, he says:

History has shown that no single political, economic or social ideology has been sufficient. So it seems worthwhile for the two great systems of this large expanse of the world to take point from each other. Certainly, Buddhist Theory is not sufficient by itself for socio-economic policy in this or the next century; it can take many points from Marxist, Socialist and Democratic systems. Similarly, those systems can benefit from many points in Buddhist Theory, especially in terms of the development of socially beneficial attitudes. Such a partnership would help millions of people.[30]

It is with this stance that the Dalai Lama has managed to connect religion and the secular/political.

The Dalai Lama often stresses the notion that compassion is basic to all Buddhist practice, and insists that direct engagement with other people and their problems is necessary in the development of genuine compassion.[31] Too many Buddhists, he believes, withdraw from the world and cultivate their own minds, and although this is an important first step for many, he also urges Buddhists to become involved in the world. He says:

In the first stage, sometimes we need isolation while pursuing our own inner development; however, after you have some confidence, some strength, you must remain with contact, and serve society in any field—health, education, politics, or whatever. There are people who call themselves religious-minded, trying to show this by dressing in a peculiar manner, maintaining a peculiar way of life, and isolating themselves from the rest of society. This is wrong. A scripture of mind purification (mind-training) says, 'Transform your inner viewpoint, but leave your external appearance as it is'. This is important because the very purpose of practicing the great vehicle is service to others, you should not isolate yourselves from society. In order to serve, in order to help, you must remain in society.[32]

The Dalai Lama insists that most Buddhists should strive to achieve a balance between contemplation and social activism since both are essential components of a healthy spiritual life. He says that for most people no amount of contemplative activity can take the place of engagement in the world. On the other hand, he cautions that activism alone tends to become sterile and can lead to negative emotions such as frustration, anger, and hatred. However, in his view renunciation does not mean physically separating oneself from worldly activities, but cultivating an attitude of 'cognitive detachment' while working for others. He suggests that this is the proper attitude of a Bodhisattva.[33] Therefore, it is suggested that the Bodhisattva, while working within the world for the benefit of others, does so without getting dragged down by its negative elements.[34]

It has been suggested that the Dalai Lama's vision of Buddhist practice has had a profound impact on many of his followers, who see their social activism on behalf of the cause of Tibet as being intimately linked with their Buddhist practice, a sentiment that has been echoed by several individuals. Although a number of Buddhists are involved in various movements concerned with Tibet, some indicate that their activism interferes with their Buddhist practice. This sentiment is seen as an exception rather than a rule. In most cases, Buddhist activists have developed 'cognitive strategies' for integrating social activity and religious practice. The following statement expresses ideas held in common by many Buddhists working for the Free Tibet movement:

There is no question that activism is religious practice, and it's a way of putting into deed, attitudes like compassion for others that otherwise are just verbal. It gives...plenty of opportunities for acting together with other people and through acting, seeking to counteract what some other people have done.'[35]

Pleasure and pain come from the former actions (karmas) of an individual. The Dalai Lama explains karma: 'If you act well, things will be good, and if you act badly, things will be bad.' Karma, he explains, means 'action'. Karmas or actions are of three types: physical, verbal, and mental. From the viewpoint of their effects, actions are either virtuous, non-virtuous, or neutral. Temporally, there are two types of actions—actions of intention that occur while thinking of doing something and the intended actions that are expressions of those mental motivations in physical or verbal action. Whether these actions become good or bad depends on the motivation of the actor. 'If I speak from a good motivation out of sincerity, respect, and love for others, my actions are good, virtuous. If I act from a motivation of pride, hatred, cynicism, and so forth, then my verbal and physical actions become non-virtuous'.[36] Without leaving it at the metaphysical plane, the Dalai Lama draws the law of karma to our daily lives by contending,

...the important point is that such presentations of Buddhist Theories about actions can make a positive contribution to human society. It is my hope that whether religious or not, we will study each other's system to gather helpful ideas and techniques for the betterment of humankind.[37]

However, the point that needs clarification is that while the Dalai Lama emphasizes the importance of religion, his consideration is not for institutionalized religion. In fact what he has tried to bring forth in his writings is the spiritual aspect, which is present in all religions. Thus, it becomes important to understand the distinction he draws between religion and spirituality in this sense.

The Dalai Lama draws a clear distinction between religion as an institution and spirituality as a mental attitude. He believes even though the teachings of the Buddha are relevant and useful for humanity, enabling people to lead constructive and satisfying lives as other religions do, it is not mandatory for anyone to be religious in the conventional sense, although it is important to be spiritual.

For the Dalai Lama, Buddhism is a rational, deep, and sophisticated approach to life, one that does not emphasize something external, rather, one that emphasizes personal responsibility towards inner development. He quotes the Buddha's teaching: 'You are your own master; things depend upon you. I am a teacher and like a doctor, I can give you effective medicine, but you have to take it yourself and look after yourself'.[38]

He says initially, *Shakyamuni* Buddha was Siddhartha, an ordinary being troubled by delusion and engaged in harmful thoughts and wrong actions.

In other words, he was an ordinary man. However, with the help of certain teachings and teachers, he gradually purified himself and in the end became enlightened. From this the Dalai Lama draws the conclusion that 'through this same causal process, we too can become fully enlightened'.[39]

In attempting to bridge the gap between material progress and spiritual development, he concludes that although both are important, we need not choose one over the other, but should attempt to balance the two. In fact he asserts that with the ever-growing impact of science on our lives, religion and spirituality will 'remind us of our humanity'. Seeing no contradiction between the two, he says that both science as well as the teachings of the Buddha tell us of the fundamental unity of all things.[40] Drawing an analogy from the Buddha's writings, he says:

Buddha always emphasized a balance of wisdom and compassion; a good brain and a good heart should work together. Placing importance just on the intellect and ignoring the heart can create more problems and more suffering in the world. On the other hand, if we emphasize only the heart and ignore the brain, then there is not much difference between humans and animals. These two must be developed in balance, and when they are, the result is material progress accompanied by good spiritual development. Heart and mind working in harmony will yield a truly peaceful and friendly human family.[41]

This stance has an interesting interpretation. Clearly, the Dalai Lama recognizes two domains, namely, the rational and the emotional. He terms these domains as belonging to the 'mind' and belonging to the 'heart' respectively. According to him, a balance between the two is required. He extols goodness, which he rates as being higher than having a religious or a ritualistic attitude.[42] He observes that in the 'developed' world the influence of religion on people's lives is marginal. Therefore, he concludes, '...we humans can live quite well without recourse to religious faith.'[43] Despite the fact that he is a religious leader, the Dalai Lama is of the opinion that 'religion' is not mandatory for human survival. To him 'basic human qualities' ought to take precedence:

...there are more than 5 billion of us on the planet. Three billion have no sort of religion. Of the 2 billion who call themselves religious, I would say that only a billion of the follower of this or that religion are a sincere believer. One billion in five that means a minority...everything starts with us, with each one of us. The indispensable qualities are peace of mind and compassion...we can reject every form of religion, but we can't reject and cast off compassion and peace of mind.[44]

One distinct feature in the thought of the Dalai Lama is his flexible attitude to religion. His thoughts on religion are ruled by his consideration of the tolerance of dissent. His thought lacks the polemic rigidity that dogmatism would otherwise entail. In this sense he is also not strictly attached to the letter of Buddhist scriptures. He responds to queries about whether he is moving away from the 'words' of the scriptures, which amounts to sacrilege, thus: 'On the contrary, you would have to be crazy to maintain them with all your might in a world swept away by the movement of time. (For example, if science shows that the scriptures are mistaken, the scriptures have to be changed)'.[45] The scriptures, venerable and sacred as they are, are relative and impermanent, like all things. Commenting on this, Carrière says:

This is certainly a point in Buddhism that at first surprises and then attracts us. In the monotheistic religions that constitute one tradition we are used to scriptures revealed, now by God, now by one of his angels or prophets. In any event, they come from somewhere else. The man who proclaimed them or wrote them down was nothing but the spokesman of a supposed beyond. It was, it still is in many cases, out of the question, unimaginable, to modify even so slightly a saying held to be strictly divine. There is no such thing in Buddhism. It must be repeated that Buddha drew his four fundamental truths and all the teachings that followed from deep within him. He never stopped saying that this teaching had to be meticulously verified at every moment by experience, and by personal experience at that. Even though in certain currents of Buddhism and in Hinduism (which saw in Siddhartha the ninth avatar of Vishnu, after Krishna), Buddha has sometimes been enlisted in the ranks of the gods, he remains today a human being.[46]

In this spirit the Dalai Lama believes permanent recourse to religion can paralyse us. It is his conviction that above all the ideal position is to remain open and sensitive. Thus, if one has the means, one has to show others what must be done. It is in this spirit that he considers the old religious prohibitions to be harmful sometimes. However, he expresses his inability to actually handle them and asks, 'But how to bend them? With what weapons?'[47]

In acknowledgement of the special responsibility he has towards Tibetans—as a Dalai Lama and a monk—he recognizes the specific need to foster inter-religious harmony. By extending the same logic, he concludes that as a human being he has a much larger responsibility towards the entire human family. While 'the earlier Dalai Lama' was less flexible and believed that Buddhism was the best way, 'the later Dalai Lama' finds a larger concern in serving all humanity, without appealing to religious faith.[48] Though the earlier Dalai Lama had tried to advocate proselytization, the later Dalai Lama concedes that this was due to ignorance.[49] Drawing a distinction between the 'religious' and the 'spiritual,' the Dalai Lama shows that it is neither dogmatism nor religious fanaticism that he advocates. On the contrary, his emphasis is on looking for universal ethical principles in all religions. Because all religions emphasize similar values, he sees no use in proselytization. Even though he contends that his philosophy of developing a 'good heart' is based on core Buddhist principles, he also believes this is in accordance with the best principles of all religions.[50] He says: 'I believe all religions pursue the same goals, that of cultivating human goodness and bringing happiness to all human beings. Though the means might appear different, the ends are the same.'[51] He concludes that all religions have a similar motivation—that of love and compassion.[52]

Deeply reflective of his tolerant views on religion is the Dalai Lama's categorical stand against proselytization. In what has been an area of much debate, the Dalai Lama has taken a middle stand based on respect for all religions. He insists that respecting other systems enriches one's own system or one's practice of religion.[53] Comparing the varying tastes that people exhibit with regard to various things, he suggests that just as 'various people have various tastes ... different religions are suitable for different people.'[54] In the context of Buddhism in Tibet, he says:

We believe in oracles, omens, interpretations of dreams, reincarnation. But these beliefs, which for us are certainties, are not something we try to impose on others in any way. I repeat: we do not want to convert people. Buddhism's main attachment is to the facts. It is an experience, a personal experience even.[55]

His anti-proselytization stand is evident in the following observation made about him:

The Dalai Lama has been able to reach beyond his Buddhist devotees to find a universal relevance. He has followers from among the Catholic, Jewish, Muslim, agnostic, and even atheist communities. Those who revere him do not necessarily adopt Buddhist practices, but virtually all derive *spiritual* [italics added] and *mental* [italics added] enrichment from his insights on daily living, inner peace, compassion, peace and justice, and the environment.[56]

He acknowledges that he does not give importance to propagating the Dharma, that is, Buddhism. This he says is in consonance with Buddhist tradition, which does not seek to persuade people to change their religion since this is considered a lack of respect for others. However, if someone were to approach him seeking teachings, he feels it would be his responsibility to grant such a request. Yet he maintains that it is better for people to follow their own tradition.[57] He also attributes practical reasons against proselytization. For instance, he says, the Jewish community is small and if some of its best scholars are attracted to Buddhism it may cause a practical problem.

Previously, the various religious communities were more isolated. As long as Buddhists, Muslims, and Christians remained in their countries it did not matter if they had one religion or a specific concept of God. He knows the situation is very different today. He says: 'now, if I try to propagate Buddhism while other religious leaders try to spread Catholicism or Islam, sooner or later there will be a clash.' The Dalai Lama's humanistic interpretation of religion is reflected in his words: 'religion is important for humanity, but it should evolve with humanity'.[58] With this consideration he announces that the first priority is to establish and develop the principle of pluralism in all religious traditions. The next step, he states categorically, is to accept that the idea of propagating religion is outdated.

The Dalai Lama is careful not to be accused of proselytization. He says:

I recognize the wide variety of mental dispositions among human beings. This is totally acceptable to me. The Buddha himself clearly acknowledged that some of his followers believed in the bodhisattva's path and others did not...this is why there are four schools of Buddhists thought with many contradictions between them. The Buddha created all these schools to accommodate the different mental dispositions of his followers. If in Buddhism alone so many dispositions exist, then there must be many more in the human family. Buddhism alone cannot fulfill all these different needs.[59]

Therefore, the Dalai Lama makes it clear that he would not like people to convert to Buddhism since it could result in a clash of cultural and religious traditions. This 'liberal compromise', which the Dalai Lama emphasizes, makes Buddhism attractive to Westerners, who can hold on to the comfort of their original faiths while adopting those elements of Buddhism they find attractive. This liberal attitude towards conversion has brought Buddhism to mainstream western society:

There are many programmes starting up with American corporations that employ various Buddhist meditation techniques to help relieve stress among their employees ... Thich Nhat Hanh has started a programme called 'Engaged Buddhism' that uses Buddhism in social work, like meditation programmes for prisons and Buddhist hospices for people dying of AIDS and cancer. There is even a Jewish revival movement in America that is drawing from Buddhism in order to emphasize spirituality within Judaism.[60]

The Dalai Lama acknowledges that this is the way he would like to see Buddhism work in the West. He advises:

I...think it is very important to remember that you are a Westerner. Your social and cultural background and your environment are different from mine. If you want to practice an Eastern philosophy, such as Tibetan Buddhism, you should take the essence and try to adopt it to your cultural background and the conditions here. As you engage in spiritual practice, for example, Buddhism over the course of time, you can gradually integrate it with your own culture and the values here, just as in the past occurred with Indian Buddhism, Tibetan Buddhism, and so on. There must gradually evolve a Western Buddhism or an American Buddhism'.[61]

At the same time, with his deep regard for all spiritual traditions he does not see the need for a 'single' world religion, which, as some claim, would establish a unified single world religion.

Although he is an advocate of universal human rights, the Dalai Lama realizes that the 'universal' criteria would be dangerous if applied to religion. Thus while he advocates universal human rights, he argues against the universalizing vision of religion. It has been noted that he aims at non-proselytization. It follows logically that for him all religions are important and there is no requirement for a single—'one' world religion. He says: 'Forming a world religion is not desirable.'[62] He cogently argues against an enterprise that suggests the 'unification of all religions' under a global umbrella. He says: 'I believe that we need different religious traditions because a single tradition cannot satisfy the needs and mental dispositions of the great variety of human beings.'[63] Consequently, even though he argues for equality at the level of rights, he extends the same logic to the sphere of religion, where having rights entails a non-coerced situation, in which religion is a matter of personal choice. If the same logic were to be extended, then proselytization would automatically become coercion, and thus, a violation of human rights. Says the Dalai Lama:

I believe the protection of religious freedoms and the diversity of our many different faiths is a matter of our fundamental Human Rights. Beyond a matter of personal or national preference, it is obligated by international law and convention. We have no alternative but to live in religious harmony. For the same reasons, if the proponents of different religious systems are unable to show each other respect, they must a least observe mutual tolerance.[64]

Arguments show that even though Tibetans were *ignorant* of other religions, they were *tolerant* of them and never sought to run them down. In fact, since they had no problems with these other religions, they did not find the need to address those needs. The Dalai Lama says:

We Tibetans had, of course, heard of other religions. But what little we knew about them came from Tibetan translations of secondary Buddhist sources. Naturally, these focused on those aspects of other religions, which are more open to debate from a Buddhist perspective. This was not because their authors wished deliberately to caricature their opponents. Rather, it reflected the fact that they had no need to address all those aspects with which they had no argument.[65]

With time the Dalai Lama has come to recognize the value of 'major faith traditions' and his writings are revelatory of this. To him, Buddhism has remained the most precious 'path'. He believes it corresponds best with his personality. However, he regards the 'universal ethical principles' to be paramount in achieving the happiness that everyone aspires to. But he makes it clear that he is in no way trying to propagate Buddhism by stealth.[66]

Reiterating what was said earlier, the Dalai Lama states that 'religion' by itself is something we can actually do without. What he qualifies as spirituality—a concern with qualities of the human spirit, such as love and compassion, patience, tolerance, forgiveness, contentment, a sense of responsibility, a sense of harmony—is considered indispensable. He says:

While ritual and prayer, along with the questions of *nirvana* and salvation, are directly connected with religious faith, these inner qualities need not be, however. There is thus no reason why the individual should not develop them, even to a high degree, without recourse to any religious or metaphysical belief system.[67]

The unifying characteristic of the qualities described above as 'spiritual' may, be at some level, concern for the well being of others. In Tibetan '*shen-pen kyi-sem*', means 'the thought to be of help to others.'[68] Similarly, the spiritual qualities noted by the Dalai Lama are implicit in one's concern for others. Thus he says:

Spiritual practice...involves, on the one hand, acting out of concern for others' well being. On the other, it entails transforming ourselves so that we become more readily disposed to do so....My call for a spiritual revolution is thus not a call for a religious revolution. Nor is it a reference to a way of life that is somehow otherworldly, still less to something magical or mysterious. Rather, it is a call for a radical reorientation away from our habitual preoccupation with self. It is a call to turn toward the wider community of beings with whom we are connected, and for conduct, which recognizes others' interests alongside our own.[69]

At this point the engaged ethic in the Dalai Lama's consideration of religion emerges. The Dalai Lama's religious and spiritual concerns are two categories, and it is the 'spiritual quest'—be it on the individual or social plane—that enhances human life and reduces suffering. It is at the social level that he would suggest the idea of spiritualizing political life.

The Dalai Lama's contribution to religion primarily consists in conceiving a humanistic religion that centres on man and his life in this world. According to him, religion should pervade all human activity since it is not separate from life's other activities and cannot be pursued in seclusion from one's fellow beings. It is in consonance with the integral totality of his thought and based on the logic that human life cannot and should not be segregated into separate compartments, that the Dalai Lama conceptualizes religion and politics in his Weltanschauung. A well-known concept since ancient times in Tibet, 'chos-srid-zung-brel' literally means 'the harmonious blend of religion and politics'.[70] According to the Dalai Lama:

... spirituality is far more important for a politician than for someone who remains secluded in the mountains seeking spiritual awakening. A hermit, even if he is not involved in spirituality, will not be able to harm the public, but the same cannot be said for a politician. A politician is an important figure in society and has a great need for spirituality. If such a person's mind becomes crooked, then he or she can be truly harmful to many people. Therefore, it is essential that leaders of nations cultivate peace of mind, an altruistic attitude and a true sense of universal responsibility.[71]

In the Dalai Lama's vision, all religions exist to serve and help man and therefore, in his opinion, any divorce from politics is to forsake a powerful instrument for social welfare. He suggests that religion and politics are a useful combination for the welfare of man when tempered by correct ethical concepts and a minimum of self-interest. Thus, he argues against the opinion of 'spiritual people' who are voicing their concern about the intermingling of politics with religion since they fear the violation of ethics by the corrupt politics. According to them politics contaminates the 'purity' of religion, an argument that the Dalai Lama clearly does not share.[72]

It is here again that the engaged ethic in the Dalai Lama's thought comes to the fore vis-à-vis man's relation to society and the role of politics in social life. He makes it clear that 'a man of religion' should not isolate himself from society:

In the correlation between ethics and politics should deep moral convictions form the guidelines for the practical practitioners, man and his society will reap far-reaching benefits. It is an absurd assumption that religion and morality have no place in politics and that a man of religion and a believer in morality should seclude himself as a hermit. These ideas lack proper perspective vis-à-vis man's relation to his society and the role of politics in our lives. Strong moral ethics are as concomitantly crucial to a man of politics as they are to a man of religion, for dangerous consequences are foreseen when our politicians and those who rule forget their moral principles and convictions....We need human qualities such as moral scruples, compassion and humility....The functional importance of religion and social institutions towards promoting these qualities thus assumes a serious responsibility and all efforts should be concentrated sincerely in fulfilling these needs.[73]

The Dalai Lama maintains that every major religion of the world— Buddhism, Christianity, Confucianism, Hinduism, Islam, Jainism, Judaism, Sikhism, Taoism, Zoroastrianism—have similar ideals of love and the same goal of benefiting humanity through spiritual practice as well as the same effect of transforming their followers into better human beings. All religions teach moral precepts for perfecting the functions of mind, body, and speech. All teach us not to lie or steal, or to take other's lives and so on. He thus contends that the common goal of all moral precepts laid down by the great teachers of humanity is 'unselfishness'. He says that each religion teaches a path leading to a spiritual state that is 'peaceful', 'disciplined', 'ethical', and 'wise', and each religion agrees upon the necessity of controlling the indisciplined mind that harbours selfishness and other roots of trouble.[74]

According to the Dalai Lama the most important thing is to look for the purpose of religion and not at the details of theology or metaphysics. It is his belief that all major religions of the world can contribute to world peace and work together for the benefit of humanity if they put aside subtle metaphysical differences, which to him are really the 'internal business of each religion.'[75] Even though he takes cognizance of the metaphysical foundations of different religions, he bridges the chasm between metaphysics and reality through his conviction that all religions essentially hold a message that is similar. He says:

Differences of dogma may be ascribed to differences of time and circumstance as well as cultural influences; indeed, there is no end to scholastic argument when we consider the purely metaphysical side of religion. On the contrary, he considers it much more beneficial to implement in one's daily life, the shared precepts for goodness taught by all religions, rather than to argue about differences in their approach.[76]

At the same time doctrinal differences that exist among various faiths also do not entail that a 'universal belief' or a universally accepted religion is needed. In fact he insists that humanity needs all the world's religions to suit the ways of life, diverse spiritual needs, and inherited national traditions of individual human beings.[77] His insistence that all the religions are needed for establishing peace in the world is expressed in the following statement:

> We practitioners of different faiths can work together for world peace when we view different religions as essentially instruments to develop a good heart—love and respect for others, a true sense of community. The most important thing is to look at the purpose of religion and not at the details of theology or metaphysics, which can lead to mere intellectualism. I believe that all the major religions of the world can contribute to world peace and work together for the benefit of humanity if we put aside subtle metaphysical differences ....[78]

While on the one hand religion promotes human happiness, on the other it is also a source of discord, conflict, and blood-shed. The Dalai Lama indicates that a choice must be made to maintain and nurture religious traditions while trying to minimize conflicts. Therefore, he advocates interfaith dialogue in order to improve understanding between different religious traditions. He says: '... dialogue ... builds a healthy spirit of harmony on the basis of mutual understanding. With full knowledge of our differences and similarities, we have developed mutual respect, mutual understanding', referring to the Buddhist-Christian dialogue that he had with Thomas Merton, a Christian practitioner.[79] The Dalai Lama has clearly stated that what is ultimately important is to imbibe secular, spiritual ethics, and that there is actually no need to focus on religion. He insists that there should be some way of increasing deeper human values, compassion, sharing, responsibility, and concern. 'It is not necessary to have religious faith,' he says.[80] In viewing religion as one of the major causes of conflict throughout human history, he even abandons religion—as a concept, if all it effects is conflict. But on the other hand, he discerns that religion can play the positive role of engendering moral and ethical values. Thus he says, 'Religion can go a long way in promoting world peace and happiness.'[81]

The Dalai Lama thinks it is important that religious leaders and practitioners should occasionally meet and be acquainted on a personal level; he considers it important in the political sphere for leaders to get to know each other because their personal relationships have a great bearing on the decisions they take. He holds the same view with regard to religious practitioners, believing that the establishment of close relations based on a personal acquaintance can be of profound significance.[82] Citing his own example, he says:

I meet with other religious leaders as often as possible. We walk together; we visit one religious site or another, whatever tradition it may belong to. And there we meditate together; we share a moment of silence. I get a great sense of well-being from that. I continue to believe that in the name of religion, we are making progress by comparison with the beginning of the century.[83]

Taking a clear stand against instances where religious faith is misused and made a basis for conflict and violence, he promulgates 'active steps' to create harmony and mutual respect amongst different religious traditions. In the preface to 'Creeds of our Times',[84] he charts the path to religious harmony. According to the Dalai Lama religious harmony can be initiated at various levels:

1. He suggests that meetings should be arranged between scholars and academicians where the differences and similarities of different traditions can be discussed.

One type of dialogue involves scholars meeting in a more academic way to clarify the differences and similarities between their traditions. This type of dialogue provides a valuable way to help people understand and appreciate each other's religions and build bridges between different religious communities.[85]

2. Meetings between serious practitioners of various spiritual traditions can be arranged in which they can exchange their inner experiences. In his view: 'This is a very powerful and extremely helpful way to develop respect for spiritual paths other than your own. In my own experience, it was meeting profound practitioners of other religious traditions that really opened my eyes to the value of other spiritual traditions.'[86]

3. He suggests that groups of people from various traditions should visit each other's holy places together and spend some time praying together or meditating together. He shares his own experience of having been moved by visits to various places of worship. Describing one such visit, the Dalai Lama says:

In a similar spirit, some of my Christian brothers and sisters recently came to spend a few days in Bodh Gaya....In addition to the dialogue we held together, each morning under the Bodhi Tree, we all, Buddhists and Christians, sat and meditated. From experiences like these, I have come to the conclusion that when we overcome our doubts and suspicions and approach each other with respect, there is much that we can learn from one another.[87]

4. He insists that it is through dialogue that religious leaders can discuss various crucial matters: '... a meeting like the "Day of Prayer for Peace" in

Assisi in 1986...religious leaders came together and exchanged a few nice words.'[88]

According to the Dalai Lama events depend heavily on one's motivation. He contends that what holds true for politics also holds true for religion. He realizes that sometimes politics is looked down upon and criticized as being 'dirty.' However, conceived objectively, politics in itself is not wrong or dirty. It is an instrument to serve human society. With good motivation—sincerity and honesty—politics becomes an instrument in the service of society. But when motivated by selfishness, hatred, anger or jealousy it becomes dirty. This is true, he suggests, not only for politics but also for religion. Speaking about religion with selfish motives or with hatred is not useful because the motivation that guides it is not good. By taking this stand the Dalai Lama attempts to show that motivation is the most important factor for any action and that, in the ultimate analysis, what defines an act is the motivation behind it.[89]

Despite the progressive secularization brought about by global modernization and despite systematic attempts to destroy spiritual values, a vast majority of people continue to believe in one religion or another. Faith in religion, evident even under non-religious political systems, clearly demonstrates the potency of religion. The spiritual energy and power can be purposefully used to bring about the conditions necessary for world peace. The Dalai Lama says: 'Religious leaders and humanitarians all over the world have a special role to play in this respect.'[90] He suggests two ways of going about this. One, by promoting better inter-faith understanding so as to create a workable degree of units among all religions. He suggests that this can be done in part by respecting each other's beliefs, and by emphasizing a common concern for human well-being. Two, by bringing about a viable consensus on basic spiritual values that touch every human heart and enhance general human happiness. He suggests: 'We must emphasize the common denomination of all religions—humanitarian ideals.' He believes these two steps will together lead to the creation of the necessary spiritual conditions for world peace.[91]

The Dalai Lama's contribution to religion consists in conceiving a humanistic religion that centres almost wholly on the human being and his/her evolution. According to him religion, or the humanitarian ideals in spirituality, should pervade all our activities and should not be pursued in seclusion from one's fellow-beings and in separation from life's other activities.

As a humanist the Dalai Lama's attitude of tolerance for all religions is derived from his conviction of the fundamental unity of religious beliefs of mankind, and hence the possibility of universal religious peace. It is on the concept of 'chos-srid-zung-brel', which means 'the harmonious blend of religion and politics' that the Dalai Lama bases his religio-political thought.[92] It has been suggested: 'With the passing of years, intentionally or not, the Dalai Lama has become a seasoned politician.'[93] This statement solicits attention—in the light of the Engaged Buddhist ethic the Dalai Lama employs—first, to show that religion cannot be pursued in seclusion and in separation from the activities of life, and second, by conjoining religion and politics.

In his attempt to extricate himself and the system he represents from the past, the Dalai Lama has been searching for more democratic and transparent methods of religious succession, without entirely abandoning the doctrine of reincarnation. In fact, the Dalai Lama has said that his reincarnation could be born in any human form: 'Next Dalai Lama could be an Indian or European or African—even a woman. Body doesn't matter.'[94] He says further: 'My name, my popularity are useful in other fields, like promotion of human values and of harmony among world religions. It is wise that my energy should be devoted to these things rather than remain Dalai Lama'.[95] As one of the most persistent advocates of reform, the Dalai Lama has tried to change the political system he himself embodies by promulgating a charter for Tibetans in exile. By his own admission, the Chinese did the Tibetans a favour by forcing them to purify their religion, which according the Dalai Lama had—in some cases—become obsessed with form and splendour at the expense of content.[96]

Another radical change is that even within the monastic tradition, the Dalai Lama gives precedence to a candidate 'knowingly entering' the monastic order:

Generally it is the parents who wish to see their child join the monastery. Novice vows can be taken at the age of seven, but full *bhikshu* ordination can only be taken after the age of twenty. I think we should adopt the system of the Christian nuns and monks, where the candidate is allowed to mature before entering the monastic order. We should extend the 'probation' period. That way our young people could enter the order knowingly and according to their own decision.[97]

He adds:

I believe that despite the rapid advances made by civilization in this century, the most immediate cause of our present dilemma is our undue emphasis on material development alone. We have become so engrossed in its pursuit that, without even knowing it, we have neglected to foster the most basic human needs of love, kindness, cooperation, and caring. If we do not know someone or find another reason for not feeling connected with a particular individual or group, we simply ignore them. But the development of human society is based entirely on people helping each other. Once we have lost the essential humanity that is our foundation, what is the point of pursuing only material development?[98]

Though the Dalai Lama institution is closely linked to religion and is fostered by it, the Dalai Lama himself makes a break from it by clearly asserting that any sectarian view of religion would lead to the situation where politics or religion cannot be viewed as two related domains.

Thus, the Dalai Lama's rejection of the view that politics is inherently 'dirty' is typically non-Gandhian. For Gandhi politics may not be inherently sinful but is definitely 'inherently impure', and can never be an ideal in any sense, although it can be purified.[99] The Dalai may not state it outright but for him, as for Gandhi, the aim is to 'spiritualize' politics. Thus, for both, religion cannot remain isolated from activity. The Dalai Lama clearly discerns he could not be leading a religious life without seeing the interrelatedness of the various activities of human life. Perhaps for this reason notions of religion and politics blend and harmonize in the Dalai Lama's thought, being evolved and articulated in practical terms for the needs of the contemporary world.

Notes

1. Claude Levi-Strauss, *Race and History*, Paris: Unesco, 1952, pp. 20–1.

2. Richard Kearney, *Modern Movements in European Philosophy*, Manchester: Manchester University Press, 1987, pp. 258–9.

3. Philip Alott, *Eunomia* (New Order for a New World), Oxford: Oxford University Press, 1990, p. 105.

4. Tenzin Gyatso His Holiness the Dalai Lama, *Ancient Wisdom, Modern World: Ethics for the New Millennium*, London: Abacus, (1999) 2000, p. 5.

5. His Holiness Tenzin Gyatso the Fourteenth Dalai Lama, *A Human Approach to World Peace*, London: Wisdom Publications, 1984, p. 3.

6. Tenzin Gyatso His Holiness the Dalai Lama, n. 4, p. 7.

7. Ibid., p. 10.

8. The Dalai Lama reiterates that the ultimate aim of humanity is genuine happiness and satisfaction. Taking this as a 'basic starting point', he suggests that there is the need to understand everything as connected in mankind's quest for

happiness, whether it be in the field of matter or in the spiritual field. See H.H. XIV Dalai Lama, 'Meeting-Points in Science and Spirituality—A Buddhist View', *Tibetan Review,* (New Delhi), vol. XVIII, no. 10, October 1983, p. 12.

9. Tenzin Gyatso, His Holiness the 14th Dalai Lama, 'What Can Religion Contribute to Mankind', Chöyang, (Dharamsala, Council for Religious and Cultural Affairs), vol. 1, no. 2, 1987, p. 3.

10. Ramesh Chandra Tewari, 'Introducton,' In Ramesh Chandra Tewari and Krishna Nath (eds), *Universal Responsibility: A Collection of Essays to Honour Tenzin Gyatso the XIVth Dalai Lama,* New Delhi: Foundation for Universal Responsibility of His Holiness the Dalai Lama and ANB Publishers Pvt. Ltd., 1996, p. xxii.

11. His Holiness Tenzin Gyatso the Fourteenth Dalai Lama, *A Human Approach to World Peace,* London: Wisdom Publications, 1984, p. 5.

12. Ibid., pp. 20–1.

13. Walter H. Capps, 'Religious and Political Perspectives', in n. 10, 1996, p. 166–7.

14. His Holiness XIV Dalai Lama, 'Place of Ethics and Morality in Politics', *Tibetan Review,* (New Delhi), vol. XIV, no. 7, July 1979, pp. 15–16.

15. Tenzin Gyatso His Holiness the Dalai Lama, n. 4, p. 9.

16. Ibid.

17. Ibid., p. 10.

18. Ibid., p. 11.

19. Ibid.

20. Ibid., p. 12.

21. Swati Mitra (ed.), *Walking With The Buddha: Buddhist Pilgrimages in India,* New Delhi: Eicher Goodearth Limited, 1999, p. 158.

22. Tenzin Gyatso His Holiness the Dalai Lama, n. 4, p. 14.

23. Ibid.

24. Ibid., p. 15.

25. 'Spiritual Contribution to Social Progress', 'Spiritual Contribution to Social Progress,' *The Spirit of Tibet, Vision for Human Liberation: Selection Speeches and Writings of His Holiness the XIV Dalai Lama,* edited by A.A. Shiromany, New Delhi: Tibetan Parliamentary and Policy Research Centre in Association with Vikas Publishing House, 1996, p. 64.

26. Ibid.

His Holiness the XIV Dalai Lama, 'Spiritual Contributions to Social Progress,' *Tibetan Review,* vol. XVI, no. 2, November 1981, p. 19.

27. Ibid.

28. Ibid.

In fact the Dalai Lama sees Marxism and Buddhism so closely aligned that he actually envisages a society where the two can live together in harmony. In an interview, the Dalai Lama responds to the question 'Have you a dream of a society where Marxism and Buddhism may live together?' The Dalai Lama answers: 'Yes it is possible in Marxist dominated Asian parts. In these countries, there are traces of Buddhism. So I think that in these countries, it will be very fruitful to have a dialogue between Marxism and Buddhism and particularly Mahayana Buddhism. It is because Marxism is running towards failure. Marxism is wasting energy on destructive side instead of the constructive side and this destruction has broken all limits. It is destroying trust between man and wife, child and parents and so on. It is the failure of Marxism. Now it is clear that real communism is not the child of force but it is created by making people give up selfishness. The edifice of real communism can stand only on altruism for masses' benefit. Gun cannot do this. China is a glaring example of this. All their efforts of force and fear have failed to bring real communism in China and a slight liberalization used there give rise to corruption. It is therefore essential that altruism like teachings of Mahayana Buddhism must be preached through love and reason and not by force. It shall achieve ideal socialism in China.' Ather Farouqui, 'Practising Non-Violence', *Thirdworld*, (Karachi), July 1990, p. 44.

29. His Holiness, the Dalai Lama of Tibet, *My Land and My People*, New Delhi: Srishti Publishers & Distributors, (1962) 1997, p. 81.

30. n. 25, p. 65.

31. The Dalai Lama, 'Conflicts Based on Religious Differences Are Sad, Futile', *Tibetan Review*, vol. XXX, no. 2, February 1995, p. 18.

32. (a) Tenzin Gyatso, 'A Talk to Western Buddhists,' *The Dalai Lama: A Policy of Kindness: An Anthology of Writings By and About The Dalai Lama*, edited by Sidney Piburn, Delhi: Motilal Banarsidass Publishers Pvt. Ltd., (1990) 1997, p. 82.

(b) The above is also cited by Christopher S. Queen (ed.) in *Engaged Buddhism in the West*, Boston: Wisdom Publications, 2000, p. 231.

33. The Bodhisattva is a Buddhist practitioner who is committed to achieving Buddhahood in order to benefit others. This is the ideal of Mahayana Buddhism. Queen, n. 32, pp. 231, 243.

34. Ibid., p. 231.

35. Ibid., p. 233.

36. The Fourteenth Dalai Lama His Holiness Tenzin Gyatso, *Kindness, Clarity and Insight*, edited by Jeffrey Hopkins and Elizabeth Napper, trans. Jeffrey Hopkins, New York: Snow Lion Publications, 1984, p. 26.

37. Ibid., p. 28.

38. Ibid., pp. 29–30.

39. Ibid., p. 30.

40. 'The Nobel Peace Prize Acceptance Speech: Oslo, Norway, December 10, 1989', in Sidney Piburn (ed.), *The Nobel Peace Prize and the Dalai Lama*, New York: Snow Lion Publications, 1990, pp. 26–7.

41. The Fourteenth Dalai Lama His Holiness Tenzin Gyatso, n. 36, pp. 30–1.

42. Tenzin Gyatso His Holiness the Dalai Lama, n. 4, pp. 19–20.

43. Ibid., p. 20.

44. His Holiness The Dalai Lama and Jean Claude Carrière, *The Power of Buddhism*, Dublin: Newleaf, 1988, p. 86. (However, he does not elucidate anywhere as to how he derives or reaches the particular figures mentioned).

Furthering this argument the Dalai Lama again expresses a similar thought in the following words: 'Religion is a question of individual freedom. Basically, I cannot say that humanity needs religion because observation proves that we can survive perfectly well without it. In fact, a great majority of the 5.7 billion humans on this planet are non-believers. Still, I do not think that religion has an important role in human societies. But I normally make a distinction between religion and spirituality. Spirituality has two levels: internal and external. The external level is simply to remain a kind, warm-hearted human being who does not harm others, who is law abiding, and does not lie or kill, as we mentioned earlier. We can do that without belonging to any religion. Inner spirituality helps develop and strengthen our intrinsic qualities and in this sense I think that religion has an important role to play, since it gives hope to some individuals. In this way, the major religious traditions have great potential. It is wrong to assume that all human requirements can be fulfilled by external means, without using our inner qualities. As human beings, a positive call is essential for survival. Religions can help with this.' His Holiness the Dalai Lama and Fabien Ouaki, *Imagine all the People: A Conversation with the Dalai Lama on Money, Politics and Life As It Could Be*, Boston: Wisdom Publications, 1999, pp. 55–6.

45. His Holiness The Dalai Lama and Carrière, ibid., pp. 37–8.

46. Ibid., p. 39.

47. Ibid., p. 40.

48. The Fourteenth Dalai Lama His Holiness Tenzin Gyatso, n. 36, p. 29.

49. Also see the writer's interview with His Holiness the XIV Dalai Lama in Appendix I.

50. The Fourteenth Dalai Lama His Holiness Tenzin Gyatso, n. 36, pp. 9–17 and pp. 45–50.

51. *Nobel Peace Prize Award Ceremony 1989: Speeches*, Office of Information and International Relations, Dharamsala, n.d., p. 14.

52. The Fourteenth Dalai Lama His Holiness Tenzin Gyatso, n. 36, p. 21.

53. Ibid., p. 49.

54. Ibid., p. 29.

The Dalai Lama says: '...there are differences between various religions but the common purpose is the same. If we emphasize this aspect of religion then there is no difference. If you look from a wider perspective and ask the question: what is the purpose of religion? Then you will find that all religions lead to the same common goal. There are differences and there are similarities between religions. If we lay more emphasis on similarities, then we realize that all men are the same. But if we lay too much emphasis on the differences then we quarrel.' A.J. Singh, 'Interview with the Dalai Lama: "God is your Business, Karma is my Business"', *The Tibet Journal*, (Dharamsala, the Library of Tibetan Works and Archives), vol. II, no.3, Autumn 1977, p. 12.

55. His Holiness The Dalai Lama and Carrière, n. 44, p. 18.

56. Mathew E. Bunson (ed.), *The Dalai Lama's Book of Wisdom*, London: Rider, 1997, p. x.

57. Explaining this, he says: 'In different places at different times, according to local conditions and circumstances, different masters arise and teach different philosophies: in just this way over time were born, for example, the Buddhist, the Christian and the Muslim worlds. For this reason, I feel it is basically safer and better to follow one's own traditional religion because I have noticed that some Westerners who have hurried to adopt the Buddhadharma as a personal religion have only become more confused.' His Holiness the Dalai Lama, 'Address to the Buddhist Society', *The Middle Way*, (London), vol. 71, no. 3, November 1996, p. 147.

The Dalai Lama says, 'All religions are different with different origins, philosophies and practice, but all provide paths by which mankind can come to truth.' Olaf Caroe, 'Tibet and the Dalai Lama', *The Tibet Journal*, (Dharamsala: Library of Tibetan Works and Archives), vol.II, no. 4, Winter 1977, p. 11.

58. His Holiness the Dalai Lama and Fabien Ouaki, *Imagine All The People: A Conversation with the Dalai Lama on Money, Politics, and Life As It Could Be*, Boston: Wisdom Publications, 1999, pp. 58–9.

59. Ibid., p. 57.

60. William Rhode, 'In Search of Nirvana: What Accounts for the Renewed Interest in Buddhism?' *Sunday*, (Calcutta), 7–13 May 1995, p. 53.

61. His Holiness The Dalai Lama, *Worlds in Harmony: Dialogues on Compassionate Action*, Delhi: Full Circle, 1998, p. 91.

62. The Fourteenth Dalai Lama His Holiness Tenzin Gyatso, n. 36, p. 49.

63. *Creeds of Our Time*, Delhi: Full Circle Publishing and the Foundation for Universal Responsibility of His Holiness the Dalai Lama, 2000, p. IX.

64. 'Universal Responsibility and Religion,' *The Spirit of Tibet: Universal Heritage, Selected Speeches and Writings of His Holiness the XIV Dalai Lama*, edited by A.A. Shiromany, New Delhi: Tibetan Parliamentary and Policy Research Centre and Allied Publishers Ltd., p. 204.

65. Tenzin Gyatso His Holiness the Dalai Lama, n. 4, p. 21.

66. Ibid., p. 22.

67. Ibid., p. 23.

68. Ibid.

69. Ibid., p. 24.

70. Namkhai Norbu, *The Necklace of gZi: A Cultural History of Tibet*, Dharamsala: Narthang Publications, (1981) 1989, p. 28.

71. His Holiness the Dalai Lama with Ouaki, n. 58, p. 18.

72. 'Place of Ethics and Morality in Politics', in n. 25, p. 60.

73. Ibid., p. 60.

74. 'World Religions for World Peace', in n. 64, p. 265.

75. Ibid., p. 267.

76. Ibid., p. 265.

77. Ibid., p. 266.

78. Ibid., p. 267.

79. His Holiness the Dalai Lama, *Spiritual Advice for Buddhists and Christians*, New Delhi: New Editions Publishing House (1998) 1999, p. 27.

80. Mitra, n. 21, p. 158.

81. Ibid., p. 157.

82. n. 64, p. 203.

83. His Holiness The Dalai Lama and Carrière, n. 44, pp. 10–11.

84. n. 63, pp. vii–x.

85. His Holiness the Dalai Lama, n. 79, p. 20.

86. n. 63, p. viii.

87. Ibid., pp. viii–ix and His Holiness The Dalai Lama, n. 79, pp. 20–1.

88. His Holiness The Dalai Lama, ibid., p. 21.

89. 'Compassion in Global Politics', in n. 25, pp. 207–8.

90. 'World Religions for World Peace', in n. 64, p. 267.

Sunita Aron, 'Can Dalai Lama Do What Others Couldn't?', *Hindustan Times*, (Delhi), January 18, 2004.

Hemendra Singh Bartwal, 'Dalai New Honest Broker on Ayodhya', *The Hindu*, (Delhi), January 9, 2004. 'In a significant development on the Ayodhya issue, Tibetan spiritual head Dalai Lama has now appeared on the scene to help resolve the imbroglio'.

91. 'Compassion in Global Politics', in n. 64, p. 267.

92. Norbu, n. 70, p. 28.

93. Pierre-Antoine Donnet, *Tibet: Survival in Question*, trans. Tica Broch, Delhi: Oxford University Press, 1994, p. 176.

94. 'Dalai Lama Desires Apolitical Role,' *Tibetan Review,* vol. XXXIV, no. 9, September 1999, p. 11.

95. Ibid., p. 10.

96. Roger Hicks and Ngakpa Chogyam, *Great Ocean: An Authorized Biography of the Buddhist Monk Tenzin Gyatso His Holiness the Fourteenth Dalai Lama*, London: Penguin Books, (1984) 1990, pp. 136–7.

For a detailed exposition of how and what factors contributed to the formation and persistence of the 'romance' of Tibet see Donald S. Lopez Jr., *Prisoners of Shangrila*, Chicago: University of Chicago Press, 1998.

'We may be disillusioned to learn that Tibet is not the place we have dreamed of. Yet to allow Tibet to circulate in a system of fantastic opposites (even when Tibetans are the "good" Orientals) is to deny Tibetans their agency in the creation of contested quotidian reality....The question considered is not how knowledge is tainted but how knowledge takes form....[Lopez's book] is an exploration of some of the mirror-lined cultural labyrinths that have been created by Tibetans, Tibetophiles, and Tibetologists....' (pp. 11–12)

97. His Holiness the Dalai Lama and Ouaki, n. 58, p. 86.

98. Ibid., pp. 144–5.

99. Raghavan Iyer, *The Moral and Political Thought of Mahatma Gandhi*, London: Concord Grove Press, 1983, p. 61.

Conclusion

Taking into account the large body of the Dalai Lama's writings and his global impact, it is apparent that no assessment of Buddhism in the contemporary world can be considered adequate without acknowledging his recommendations concerning the problems faced by the world community. While they seem compelling, can a mixture of deontic injunctions, precepts, euphemisms, exhortations and appeals qualify as philosophical thought?

It may be said in response that in addressing his Engaged Buddhist ethics, the Dalai Lama's thought has varied consequences for non-violent conflict resolution, peace, human rights, religious understanding and protection of the environment—thus qualifying as applied ethics/philosophy. His position as the Dalai Lama does not reduce his thought to an expediency; his formulations, expressive of a deep concern for Tibet, also succeed in establishing a universal ethic founded on the concepts of non-violence, interdependence and compassion. Therefore in assessing his thought, his concern should not be seen as limited to, or limited by, his Tibetan identity. On the contrary the Dalai Lama's thought discusses ways of thinking, acting, and applying the Buddhist ideals of wisdom and compassion to the social, political, and environmental issues in the world. His Engaged Buddhist ethic does not approve of anything that might lead men away from activity in the outside world to mere inward contemplation that suggests the self-sufficiency of a monk.

His assumptions sound more like convictions about the positive aspect of human nature. His emphases on the role of human choice—which can either brutalize itself by seeking recourse in violence, or allow the manifestation of compassion and non-violence in human life by being aware of the interdependent nature of reality—can be best described as an optimistic view of human nature. The Dalai Lama recognizes certain innate or natural tendencies and qualities in humans. He concedes that human nature can be subject to ignorance and wretchedness,[1] although he is mostly firm about the view that human nature is basically non-violent and good,[2] and that a 'sense of peace' already exists in it.[3] In this respect the Dalai Lama's thought is a unique blend of the ideal, which considers all human beings as ends and not means, and of the Buddhist tradition which considers, isolated and egoistic existence as antithetical to cosmic and human interdependence. Violence is inherent in overlooking 'interdependence', a concept that emerges as a seminal point in the context of writings on Engaged Buddhism.

'Engaged Buddhism' is open to diverse interpretations and meanings.[4] There are suggestions that 'all Buddhism is engaged'[5] and that 'every moment of life is engagement; every moment of life is Buddhist.'[6] As efforts to define Engaged Buddhism continue, the indeterminate and contested aspects of the subject can function fruitfully as stimuli rather than impediments to the understanding of what this movement is about. Scholars have still to pin down the definition of the term; meanwhile, the movement continues to grow. Therefore, it would be pertinent to ask what Engaged Buddhism is not.

Aum Shinrikyo, the 'new-new religion' in Japan, whose members released the lethal sarin gas on Tokyo subways, uses Buddhist terminology and has definite ideas about changing the world for the better. The group's founder, Shoko Asahara, has a photograph with the Dalai Lama being greeted warmly. Yet this does not qualify *Aum Shinrikyo* as a form of Engaged Buddhism.[7]

There is a general consensus even among the Engaged Buddhists that any living religion or vital social movement changes constantly. In the event of the failure of the movement for Tibetan autonomy and if the succession of the Dalai Lama is disrupted, it would not be inaccurate to say that however serviceable, designations such as 'Engaged Buddhist' or 'Buddhist' are only constructions, limited and ultimately insubstantial.[8] However, it is also true that as an 'act of dividing and shaping reality', it is pertinent and significant for Engaged Buddhist studies to consider the Dalai Lama's worldview on Engaged Buddhism. Again, one does not make much headway by suggesting that considerations of the Dalai Lama are of significance only if he succeeds in getting autonomy for Tibet—as is symbolically suggested by Kenneth Kraft[9] because that would undermine the significance of the Dalai Lama's thought which is permeated with his concern for human values.

The range of concerns that motivate Buddhists engaging in public service and political activism encompass nearly every area of social experience—conflict and suffering, war and violence, race, human rights, environmental destruction, gender relations, sexual orientation, ethnicity, health care, prisons, schools, and the workplace. The great unity among the many Engaged Buddhists is that the existence of suffering evokes in them a feeling of 'universal responsibility,' as the Dalai Lama calls it. By seeking to give redressal to the Tibet problem and by going beyond it, the Dalai Lama's arguments have been transformed into ethical paradigms which have an explicit universal meaning and value. An explanation for this emerges from within various studies that insist that it is necessary to consider the efforts of personal and social actions on others especially in the realms of speech and symbolic manipulation in the contemporary information age, and in the policies, programmes, and products of large and small institutions. '"The others" affected by these actions must be understood not only as unit selves, but as significant collectivities: families, neighbours, and workplace teams; social, ethnic, and economic group; national and international populations; and, not least, biological species and ecosystems.'[10] This conception has been spelt out in the following way again:

Social suffering...brings into a single space an assemblage of human problems that have their origins and consequences in the devastating injuries that social force can inflict on human experience. Social suffering results from what political, economic, and institutional power does to people and, reciprocally, from how these forms of power themselves influence responses to social problems. Included under the category of social suffering are conditions that are usually divided among separate fields, conditions that simultaneously involve health, welfare, legal, moral, and religious issues. They destabilize established categories. For example, the trauma, pain, and disorders to which atrocity gives rise are health conditions; yet they are also political and cultural matters. Similarly, poverty is the major risk factor for ill health and death; yet this is only another way of saying that health is a social indicator and indeed a social process.[11]

The Dalai Lama has sought unique ways of seeking representation in a world order where peace and non-violence have more varied implications than can be easily imagined. He stresses on the human need to seek new routes to a harmonious world, be it through religion or by standing up for human dignity, environmental protection or cleaner politics. As a follower of Gandhi, his articulations seek to show the interdependence of all life and thereby the role of compassion as the pure emotive force, which resonates with universal responsibility. However, a perfect shift between the Dalai Lama and Gandhi's perspectives emerges when seen in a comparative framework in which Babasaheb Ambedkar (Indian dalit leader of the 1930s and 1940s) emerges as the third protagonist on the issue of karma.

While Gandhi advocated compassion and improved social services for India's 'untouchables', Ambedkar demanded the abolition of the caste system itself. Gandhi held caste to be a deeper issue, indeed 'like a cosmic law not to be abrogated by human struggle of legislative fiat.' He believed that each person is limited or empowered by the cumulative effects of his or her own karma, and therefore cannot be rescued by outside forces. Suggestions have been made that Gandhi, separated his political philosophy in this respect from his morality,[12] imagined a society transformed by legislation and the action of courts, without paying heed to the idea that religious identities, practices, beliefs, and morality were negotiable or subject to reform.[13] But to Ambedkar

if the collective, institutionalized expression of greed, hatred, and delusion was India's legacy of colonialism, bureaucratic corruption, and the religious-based caste system, then all of these structures, fashioned by human hearts and minds, could be repaired, remodeled, or removed. The key was the notion of collective action—both in the genesis of human suffering, and in relief.[14]

In this respect the Dalai Lama's formulation differs from Gandhi's, especially when seen in the context of karma and human rights. While Gandhi considered an individual's human condition as being designated by Karmic law, the Dalai Lama goes a step beyond by making the individual larger than karma.

As a concept, karma is seminal to Buddhism. In Buddhism various manifestations of suffering, natural as well as unnatural, are taken to be the consequence of karma.[15] Yet in the Dalai Lama's view an individual cannot shirk the responsibility of finding himself/herself in a particular situation. Says the Dalai Lama, 'To say that every misfortune is the result of karma is tantamount to saying that we are totally powerless in life.'[16] Going to the root of the word karma in Sanskrit, the Dalai Lama sees it as denoting an active force, the inference being that the outcome of future events can be influenced by our actions. He suggests that to suppose karma to be some sort of independent energy that predestines the course of our whole life is incorrect. He asks the question, 'Who creates karma?' and answers his own question in the following words:

We ourselves. What we think, say, do, desire and omit creates *karma*...In everything we do, there is cause and effect, cause and effect. In our daily lives the food we eat, the work we undertake, our relaxation are all a function of action: our action. This is *Karma*. We cannot, therefore, throw up our hands whenever we find ourselves confronted by unavoidable suffering. If this were correct, there would be no cause for hope.[17]

This stance shows the extremely difficult task that the Dalai Lama has taken up, that of treading the middle path between the preservation of tradition and the necessity of progress.[18] He has fused the metaphysics of Buddhism with social activism. His considerations of the human condition are based on egalitarian motives. Although anthropological studies reveal the class hierarchies within Tibet and within the Tibetan Diaspora, the Dalai Lama himself holds all human beings to be equally precious to the world. This is clearly seen in his concept of 'universal responsibility', which emerges fully in his views on human rights and environmental protection. He discerns that the entire reality is linked in a fragile cohesiveness; any dissonance in one of these links is bound to have a ripple effect on the whole. However, it would be more accurate to say that in his views on human rights his egalitarian impulse blooms completely. He says, 'The universal principles of equality of all human beings must take precedence',[19] and adds, 'from a broader viewpoint...we are all brothers and sisters',[20] he explicitly rejects distinctions based on colour or geographical location as fabrications. In an interview with the writer the Dalai Lama clearly stated his view on the caste system (see Appendix I). He considers caste to be a dehumanizing influence. Clearly, the reason for the Dalai Lama's immense popularity in the West, it may be suggested, is primarily because he does not parry difficult questions. The least judgmental of sacred figures, he does not recoil from what could be taken as 'profane' issues. He discusses with ease topics like introducing sex education in schools, its positive results as well as its repercussions,[21] which establishes a deep contact between him and his audiences. Without debunking the original issue of relating non-violence to various strands in the fabric of his thought, he clearly places the worth of human beings as paramount. His thought does not permit any subjugation of human agency. He establishes with ease a link between traditional Buddhist thought and contemporary concerns.

Although the Dalai Lama and Gandhi have been seen to have been at variance with one another,[22] the Dalai Lama's agenda of non-violence is free of dogma, and never refrains from facing issues that need redressal. Observations on meat eating Tibetans have drawn some flak as they are seen as being at loggerheads with his non-violent agenda. Veering towards the middle path, the Dalai Lama has not been able to give any certain answers on meat eating and non-violence other than those in the case of Tibet, for which geographical and other reasons have been cited. Are the two at variance in their spirit and essence, or is it non-violent to eat meat? Clearly, it is the butcher who is seen getting bad treatment. In the Tibetan community, meat eating is not taboo, but killing is. Thus, the butcher still remains ostracized, as he was in the past. The ethical outcome of this discussion is still open-ended. One of the most important religious texts in Buddhism is a poetic collection of aphorisms known as the *Dhammapada*, roughly meaning 'Path of Virtue,' which speaks of killing in the following way: 'Everyone fears punishment; everyone fears death, just as you do. Therefore do not kill or cause to kill; everyone loves life, as you do. Therefore do not kill or cause to kill.' A related passage says: 'Him I call a Brahmin who has put aside weapons and renounced violence toward all creatures. He neither kills nor helps others to kill.'[23]

It has been observed that the XIII Dalai Lama had avoided any direct involvement in cases of capital punishment because of his religious rule. Struggling to modernize Tibet, he also reformed Tibet's feudal legal system. Among the changes was the abolition of the death penalty by about 1920.[24] The XIV Dalai Lama has continued to evolve a more direct approach. He refers to capital punishment as a form of violence. It is significant that he has an abolitionist stance on capital punishment, a stance which finds strong support in Buddhist thought and history. The Buddha is said not only to have taught non-violence and peace, he even went to a battlefield and intervened personally to prevent a war between the Sakyas and the Koliyas over the waters of the Rohini river. It is also said that his words once prevented King Ajatsatru from attacking the Kingdom of the Vajjis. The Buddha's views on conflict resolution become clear in his teaching of the 'Ten Duties of the King' (*dasa-raja-dhamma*) as given in the Jataka text. In the eighth of the 'Ten Duties of the King' he says: 'Non-violence (ahimsa), which means not only that he should harm nobody, but also that he should try to promote peace by avoiding and preventing war and everything that involves violence and destruction of life'.[25]

Like Gandhi, the Dalai Lama finds reasons to say that violence can at times be useful. He cites an example: 'The anger that causes us to go to the assistance of someone who is being attacked in the street could be characterized as positive.'[26] Commenting on the seeming paradox regarding non-violence and violence in Gandhi's thought, the Dalai Lama says:

Positive aggressive actions arise out of sincere motivation, self-confidence and tireless effort. Sometimes that appears to be aggressive, but it is positive and there is no intention to disregard other's rights. I think some of Gandhi's actions were quite aggressive, but there was a strong positive motivation towards a correct goal.[27]

So much for the similarity. The difference between the two is made clear in the following passage:

The former is not descended from a line of wise men, institutionalized and anchored in history. Indeed, Mahatma Gandhi was a man of his time and had an intellectual flexibility that allowed him to adapt to the new social and political environment of the era. The Dalai Lama, on the other hand, is a prisoner of monastic tradition; he does not have the power to change anything whatsoever and it is difficult for him to adapt to a new social and political environment without hurting the feelings of certain monks and lamas.[28]

Indeed, the Dalai Lama and Gandhi are two different figures at two different times in history. Yet if Gandhi is allowed his intellectual flexibility, it would not be wrong to say that the Dalai Lama has deliberately not frozen his ideas within tradition. His thought seems contemporary and very relevant. He absolves himself of dogmatism by openly suggesting that there is nothing wrong in abandoning scriptures when they do not serve any practical purpose. He strives for a tolerant religious attitude and a flexible stance vis-à-vis 'religious' issues that can have a questioning attitude towards the merely textual/ritualistic stance of the scriptures. The Dalai Lama's worldview has a marked utilitarian flavour in terms of his advocacy of human rights, environmental protection, non-violent conflict resolution, and the quest for religious harmony. In all these areas he seeks the amelioration of human life. He says, 'you should be "wisely" selfish'.

The institution of the Dalai Lama is the 'guarantor of social order' for Tibetans. Without it an institutional void, political and social chaos can occur.[29] However, the Dalai Lama clearly states that if the institution serves no purpose for Tibetans, it should be abandoned. In his words:

The existence of the Dalai Lama institution is the choice of the Tibetans. It was made clear in the sixties by me. But this institution is useful in the present situation for Tibetans and their culture. Dalai Lama's institution will cease to exist in future, if it is no longer useful. So I sometimes say that I am the last Dalai Lama.[30]

In this context observations have been made that the Dalai Lama's position as the leader of an exiled community has forced him to come to terms with a world that is very different from the traditional Buddhist society in which he was born. He has become the most prominent advocate of the Tibet cause and is its main 'theoretician'. Although much of his focus is on Tibet, he believes he is responsible for the welfare of all sentient beings. This is apparent in his declarations: 'My motivation is directed towards all sentient beings. There is no question, though, that on the second level, I am directed towards helping Tibetans.'[31] As a corollary, he acknowledges 'ancient traditions' to be relevant today and he emphasizes the combination of modern knowledge and ancient wisdom. While he talks about preserving 'traditions' that are capable of propagating human values and calls upon people to preserve spiritual and social values, he also talks about disbanding the caste system and practices like *sati* and the dowry system.[32] He belongs to a tradition in which—as the Dalai Lama—he is important enough to serve as the 'daily regenerator' of the Tibetan founding myth.[33] But he does not hesitate to say that in his opinion China did Tibet a favour by extricating it from past evils.

In the same spirit his remarks on 'caste' or 'sati' bring out his focus on human values and as a logical corollary, on human dignity in the dynamic paradigms of other cultures or as well as Tibet. He observes:

If we maintain obsolete values and beliefs, a fragmented consciousness and self-centered spirit, we will continue to hold on to outdated goals and behaviours. Such an attitude by a large number of people would block the entire transition to an independent yet peaceful and cooperative global society.[34]

He has emphasized this view repeatedly to reinforce his concept of non-violence. In his vision, non-violence as a concept does not have restrictive application. Inspired by the correct non-violent motivation, it can be applied in daily lives, whatever an individual's position or vocation. It is relevant to medical procedures, education systems, legal procedures and so forth.[35]

The Dalai Lama links the issue of human dignity as gleaned from the essence and spirit of Buddhist philosophy, and places it firmly in the context of current debates on human rights. The Dalai Lama's thought moves away from the existential approach when he says: 'It is a major error, a "root-error," to isolate human life, to attribute to it an essence, an in-itself.'[36] However, this stance should not be mistaken for a rejection of the dignity of the individual, either in terms of denial of human rights or in terms of individual growth. In the debates on rights and responsibilities the Dalai Lama recognizes rights of the human being as being inherent in the Buddhist notions of human 'dignity' and 'compassion', and conceptualizes them by postulating the reciprocity of 'rights' and 'responsibilities'. Although lacking formal character, his thesis—springing from his Buddhist concerns—offers a normative understanding of the issue.

Such a stance is aptly summed up in the following words: 'Human rights are rights, which belong to human beings, *qua* human beings, as beings who can exercise freedom through reason. Such rights, therefore, are unique to human beings and apply universally to all human beings.'[37] A violation of these, as emphasized by the Dalai Lama, points to a lack of recognition of the 'essential unity' of all phenomena. It is suggested that the notion of human rights is primarily a moral notion and that 'the human rights discourse can become practically relevant for us...can enter the density of our everyday practical concerns only by shedding its pristine universality and uniqueness—at least to a large extent.'[38] Since the notion of human rights is directly linked to questions like 'how does it (human rights) enter into our idea of the good life?' One way of understanding the 'good life' is 'through one's active intelligent engagement in moral practice'. In this context it can be said that in the Gandhian notion of satyagraha knowledge and practice are inalienably interwoven: 'Knowledge and articulacy about *Satya*, which for Gandhi, is the same as the good, is to be achieved only through active and contemplative moral engagement in actual human situations'. Again, 'if it is agreed, therefore, that the idea of human rights is a moral idea, then the human rights discourse must be rescued from its abstract, disengaged universality and placed firmly in the context of localized moral discourses and the practices from which these discourses derive their sustenance.'[39] In an attempt to move away from hollow rhetoric about human rights, he suggests that a serious and mature human rights advocate must already know and act in ways which show, for instance, what it is like to be a good parent, a good friend, a good spouse, a good member of a community, a good citizen, and so on.

In this context, the Dalai Lama proposes that the dichotomy of 'we' and 'they' creates chasms between individuals. In the ultimate analysis, there are no actual differences between individuals, since all individuals are linked to one another.[40] He turns the argument around, and instead of rights, he focuses attention on the notion of responsibility. Extending the argument of responsibility, he mobilizes it into a concept and gives it the name of 'universal responsibility'. By emphasizing the aspect of universal interconnectedness through the concept of universal responsibility, he attempts to articulate a moral vision in which rights become important, but only vis-à-vis responsibility.

There is no attempt to debunk social responsibility in his arguments. The social aspect is as important as the individual, the universal, and the global. Where his thesis is discernibly utilitarian, there he sublimates and qualifies it with his considerations of respect for others and concern for their rights. He stands for the view that there is no single set of Western, Islamic, or Asian cultural values, and clearly rejects Huntington's thesis.[41] The Dalai Lama also realizes that at times economy becomes larger than human rights. He says: 'I believe economics and human rights are interlinked...when China did not heed to world appeals on human rights....The US should have put economic pressure on China'. This view also reveals his understanding and knowledge of the modus operandi of political economy in contemporary times. Grounded in compassion, the Dalai Lama's discourse on human rights is not ecliptic; his approach to this issue addresses many domains— the moral versus the individual, the private versus the social, and the social versus the universal. His thought does not contain seeds of dissent or discord because, like the concept of non-violence, he has based the assumption of human rights exactly where it belongs—in the human being. This notion is clearly described in the following words: 'So although the world may become large or small ultimately it is the relation between two individuals only. As soon as the second man is visualized the concept of the world also arises. The second man, therefore, includes in him all the rest of individuals in the world.'[42] The Dalai Lama concludes: 'we need to develop concern for the problems of others, whether they be individuals or entire people.'[43] The Buddhist interpretation of compassion is based on the recognition that others, like oneself, want happiness and wish to eschew suffering. On that basis one develops some kind of concern about the welfare of others, irrespective of one's attitude to oneself. This is what the Dalai Lama refers to as 'compassion'.[44] He extends his belief in the non-violent nature of humans to their ability to have non-violent relations among themselves. This aspect finds a logical coherence in his seeking advocacy of a non-violent attitude towards the environment.

Since nothing can exist independently, any harm done to humans, animals, or the environment is tantamount to a violation of the phenomenon of interrelatedness. The Dalai Lama's thesis on environmental protection is a logical corollary to his non-violent thesis. It is also an extension of his arguments on the legitimacy of human rights. He says: 'we should not only maintain non-violent relations with our fellow human beings, but...we should extend a similar attitude towards the environment' [as well].[45]

Traditional moral philosophy showed little concern for the relationship between human beings and nature. When philosophers examined the moral status of animals and natural objects, it was usually for the purpose of ruling them out of ethical bounds, in the manner of Descartes' famous statement—'*cogito ergo sum*' ('I think therefore I am')—from which it is derived that what does not think' 'is not'. Of course Descartes was referring to consciousness at a different level—but not without implications for issues pertaining to nature. Well into the middle of the twentieth century, environmental ethics was simply inconceivable as a subject for philosophy.[46]

Environmental ethics was something only environmentalists talked about. If you had asked a philosopher what he knew about the subject, you would most likely have been greeted by stunned silence....Environmental ethics was entirely alien to the normal kinds of things that philosophers talked about.[47]

However the intensity of environmental concerns in the 1970s, coupled with an unprecedented eagerness on the part of philosophers who sought to apply philosophy to contemporary issues, created a new field—environmental philosophy.[48] It would be overstating the case to imply that no philosopher was interested in the ethics of human-nature relationships prior to the age of environmentalism.[49] But philosophical attempts to widen the moral circle were far-sporadic and relatively unnoticed, compared to the sudden burgeoning of environmental philosophy in the 1970s. The Dalai Lama's thought strikes a chord with thinkers who argued 'that there is no individual welfare (or liberty) apart from the ecological matrix in which the individual life must exist.'[50]

E.F. Schumacher re-appraised Western economic attitudes in the book *Small is Beautiful*, and suggested that 'Buddhist Economics' is not a nostalgic dream and that 'modernization', as currently practiced without regard to religious and spiritual values, is not actually producing agreeable results. Buddhist economics, on the other hand, is based on 'Right Livelihood' which is one of the requirements of the Buddha's Noble Eightfold Path. In Schumacher's opinion, the Buddhist point of view takes the function of work to be at least threefold: to give man a chance to utilize and develop his faculties; to enable him to overcome his egocenterdness by joining other people in a common task; and to bring forth the goods and services needed for a 'becoming' existence. One important aspect—the use of natural resources—illustrates the difference between modern economics and Buddhist economics in a striking way, and is connected with the Dalai Lama's thought on environment. Schumacher suggests that the 'modern' man does not seem to mind how much he wastes or destroys:

He does not seem to realize at all that human life is a dependent part of an ecosystem of many different forms of life. As the world is ruled from towns where men are cut off from any form of life other than human, the feeling of belonging to an ecosystem is not revived. This results in a harsh and improvident treatment of things upon which we ultimately depend, such as water and trees.[51]

Significantly, the teaching of the Buddha enjoins a reverent and non-violent attitude not only to all sentient beings but also to the natural world, for instance, trees. Injunctions found in the Buddhist texts instruct that every follower of the Buddha ought to plant a tree every few years and look after it until it is safely established. Schumacher says: 'the Buddhist economist can demonstrate without difficulty that the universal observation of this rule would result in a high rate of genuine economic development...'[52] Also, modern economics does not distinguish between renewable and non-renewable materials. Its very method is to equalize and quantify everything by means of money price. Thus, the only significant difference drawn by modern economists is of 'the relative cost per equivalent unit,' as Schumacher says. From a Buddhist point of view, non-renewable goods must be used only if they are indispensable, and then too, with the greatest care and the 'most meticulous concern for conservation.' It is here that the Dalai Lama's concept of non-violence becomes more coherent when seen through Schumacher's approach. To cite Schumacher again:

To use them [non-renewable goods] heedlessly or extravagantly is an act of violence, and while complete non-violence may not be attainable on this earth, there is nonetheless an ineluctable duty on man to aim at the ideal of non-violence in all he does....As the world's resources of non-renewable fuels—coal, oil and natural gas—are exceedingly unevenly distributed over the globe and undoubtedly limited in quantity, it is clear that their exploitation at an ever-increasing rate is an act of violence against nature, which must almost inevitably lead to violence between men.[53]

This is an argument that the Dalai Lama has also considered. In his visualization, the 'Zone of Non-Violence', namely Tibet, is also the zone where, apart from its implication for de-militarization and peace, the environment is respected and taken care of. The Dalai Lama, even though he does not consider it wrong for 'humans to use nature to make useful things', takes a categorical stand against exploiting nature unnecessarily and excessively.[54] The Dalai Lama has taken it upon himself to define the definite practical role of the media and of education as tools to disseminate information on the significance of environmental protection. He believes both have a special responsibility:

If there is one area in which both education and the media have a special responsibility, it is, I believe, our natural environment. This responsibility has less to do with questions of right or wrong than with the question of survival. The natural world is our home. It is not necessarily sacred or holy. It is simply where we live. It is therefore in our interest to look after it.[55]

It can be said that the Dalai Lama's thought on the environment is an appeal to humanity to slow down the deteriorating conditions. McLeod Ganj in Dharamsala is not exactly a haven, representative of the Dalai Lama's worldview. However, his thought *is* a radical departure from the conventional, and from it implications can be drawn for his thought on religion.

The Dalai Lama emphasizes the egalitarian spirit of 'religion'. Therefore he abandons notions of proselytization. He also draws out the significant role of development, progress, and scientific evolution in the context of religion. He emphasizes that although mankind has made enormous material progress, the human spirit still yearns for the inner development which he terms as spiritual development, and which is felt by most individuals irrespective of religious faith. However, his view on what he conceives as the gift of the technologically advanced Western world to its populace is stereotypical. This gift, he visualizes, as the lack of faith in the spiritual quest. So although he argues for equality among human beings and is considered an upholder of human rights, his considerations on religion somehow seem to stereotype two sets of people—the non Western and the Western:

...when he speaks about the West the Dalai Lama is sometimes content, for convenience's sake, to stick with an image that has no nuances. We regularly do the same when we speak of the Arab countries, of Africa, or Japan: we keep only striking features that simplify everything. Yet Buddhism keeps teaching us that every simplification, if indeed it claims to describe a whole society, is false and hence dangerous.[56]

Discernibly a constant feature in his writings, such indistinct expressions and idioms make the Dalai Lama's thought simplistic and cliché-ridden; yet these alone cannot be taken as being truly representative of his 'thought'. Therefore, if in attempting to assess its essence, only aberrations in his thought are taken into cognizance, and if only *these* should be highlighted, the Dalai Lama's central message would be lost.

In a statement made during his tour of the USA in September–October 1979, the Dalai Lama said: 'Material progress should be seen primarily as a source of physical comfort, but should not be confused with mental peace.'[57] Clearly, he is not derisive of science and what he refers to as the 'Western' material culture brought about by scientific progress. He says, 'No religion basically believes that material progress alone is sufficient for humankind. All religions believe in forces beyond material progress. All agree that it is very important and worthwhile to make a strong effort to serve human society.'[58]

The Dalai Lama's discussion on religion is an insightful examination of the role of religion in conflict, and of methods of conflict resolution. His improvizations of ways in which social, political, and religious conflicts can be resolved at various levels comprehensively move away from mere rhetoric to an actual mapping out of a discourse that offers real solutions to conflict-ridden situations, to finding ways and means to eschew conflicts. He authenticates and justifies the 'spiritual' underpinnings of all religions, while emphatically condemning all fanaticism. The emperor Ashoka, while refraining from warfare and the slaughter of animals, also planted trees, dug wells and established health care,[59] conforming to the Buddhist ideal of a positive programme of action. In the contemporary times this finds an apt representation in the Dalai Lama's vision of Engaged Buddhism.

If there are traces of the 'utopian', particularly in the Dalai Lama's considerations of 'realpolitik', emerging from the 'idealpolitik' of non-violence, it would be well to remember that utopias represent and embody the eternal quest for all that is authentic and perfect in the world. Acknowledged as a way to accomplish renunciation and purity, Buddhism, as seen by the Dalai Lama, cannot be described as a mere shrinking away from the world but as active engagement with it.

Notes

1. His Holiness the Dalai Lama, 'Understanding Human Nature Cultivate the Compassion Within', *Speeches, Statements, Articles, Interviews: 1987 to June 1995*, Dharamsala: The Department of Information and International Relations, Central Tibetan Administration, Gangchen Kyishong, 1995, pp. 179–82.

2. His Holiness The Dalai Lama, *The Heart of Compassion: A Dalai Lama Reader*, Delhi: Full Circle, 1997, p. 70.

3. The Dalai Lama and Jean-Claude Carrière, *The Power of Buddhism*, Dublin: Newleaf, (1994) 1996, p. 15.

4. Kenneth Kraft, 'New Voices in Engaged Buddhist Studies', in Christopher Queen (ed.), *Engaged Buddhism in the West*, Boston: Wisdom Publications, 2000, p. 486.

5. Queen, 'Introduction: A New Buddhism', in n. 4, p. 24.

6. Paula Green, 'Walking for Peace: Nipponzan Myohoji', in Queen, n. 4, p. 154.

7. Kraft, n. 4, pp. 486–7.

8. Ibid.

9. Ibid., p. 486.

10. Queen, n. 4, p. 3.

11. Arthur Kleinman, Veena Das, and Margaret Lock (eds), *Social Suffering*, Berkeley: University of California Press, 1996, p. IX.

12. Queen, n. 4, p. 16.

13. Eleanor-Zelliot, 'Gandhi and Ambedkar: A Study in Leadership', in *From Untouchable to Dalit: Essays on the Ambedkar Movement*, New Delhi: Manohar, 1992, pp. 150–78.

Asha Krishnan, *Ambedkar and Gandhi: Emancipators of Untouchables in India*, Mumbai: Himalaya Publishing House, 1997, as cited in Queen, n. 4, p. 16.

14. Queen, n. 4, pp. 16–17.

15. There is a category of natural suffering which includes phenomena like war, poverty, and crime, into which the Dalai Lama has incorporated contemporary issues like illiteracy and certain diseases also. The second category is of natural suffering like old age, sickness, and death. His Holiness the Dalai Lama, *Ancient Wisdom, Modern World: Ethics for the New Millennium*, London: Abacus, 2000, pp. 138, 141.

16. Ibid., p. 141.

17. Ibid., pp. 141–2.

18. Fredrick R. Hyde-Chambers, 'Buddhism in Action: The Dalai Lama and the People of Tibet', *The Middle Way*, (London), May 1996, vol. 71, no. 1, p. 9.

19. *The Political Philosophy of His Holiness The XIV Dalai Lama: Selected Speeches and Writings*, edited by A.A. Shiromany, New Delhi: Tibetan Parliamentary and Policy Research Centre, 1998, p. 130.

20. The Fourteenth Dalai Lama His Holiness Tenzin Gyatso, *Kindness, Clarity, and Insight*, New York: Snow Lion Publications, 1984, p. 158.

21. His Holiness The Dalai Lama with Fabien Ouaki, *Imagine All the People: A Conversation With The Dalai Lama on Money, Politics and Life As it Could Be*, Boston: Wisdom Publications, 1999, p. 93.

22. Jamyang Norbu, 'Non-Violence or Non-Action: Some Gandhian Truths about the Tibetan Peace Movement', *Tibetan Review*, (Delhi), vol. XXXII, no. 9, September 1997, pp. 18–21.

23. Damien Horigan, 'Buddhist Perspectives on Death Penalty', *Turning Wheel,* (Berkeley, California), Winter 1999, p. 17.

24. Ibid., p. 19.

25. Jataka I, 260, 399; II 400, 274, 320, V, 119, 378 as cited in Fred Eppsteimer (ed.), *The Path of Compassion: Writings on Socially Engaged Buddhism*, Berkeley, California: Parallax Press, (1985), rev. ed. 1988, p. 108.

26. His Holiness the Dalai Lama, n. 15, p. 100.

27. *Dialogues on Universal Responsibility and Education*, Dharamsala: Library of Tibetan Works and Archives, 1995, p. 118.

28. Huitzi, 'The Institution of the Dalai Lama in Question,' *Lungta,* (Switzerland), no. 7, August 1993, p. 31.

29. Ibid., p. 30.

30. Ather Farouqui, 'Practicing Non-Violence', *Thirdworld,* (Karachi), July 1990, p. 45.

31. *The Dalai Lama, A Policy of Kindness: An Anthology of Writings By and About the Dalai Lama*, edited and compiled by Sidney Piburn, Delhi: Motilal Banarsidass Publishers, (1990), 1997, p. 40

32. The Dalai Lama, 'Eschew Violence', *Tibet Foundation Newsletter,* (London), no. 31, February 2001, p. 3.

33. Huitzi, n. 28, p. 24.

34. 'Statement of His Holiness the Dalai Lama on the 38th Anniversary of Tibetan National Uprising Day—March 10, 1997,' *Adarsha: Tibetan Nyingma Buddhist Review*, (Lisboa, Portugal), no. 3/4, Janeiro/Juhno, 1997, p. 6.

35. 'World Peace and the Environment', in n. 19, pp. 128–9.

36. His Holiness the Dalai Lama and Carrière, n. 3, p. 35.

37. Mrinal Miri, 'A Note on the Idea of Human Rights', *Journal of Indian Council of Philosophical Research*, (New Delhi), vol. XVII, no. 2, January–April, 2000, p. 160.

38. Ibid., p. 161.

39. Ibid., pp. 161–2.

40. See Interview with His Holiness the Dalai Lama in Appendix I.

41. Samuel P. Huntington, *The Clash of Civilizations and the Remaking of the World Order,* New Delhi: Penguin Books, (1996) 1997.

42. S.S. Barlingay, 'Responsibility, University and Religion,' in Ramesh Chandra Tewari and Krishna Nath (eds), *Universal Responsibility: A Felicitation Volume in Honour of His Holiness the Fourteenth Dalai Lama, Tenzin Gyatso, on His Sixtieth Birthday*, New Delhi: Foundation for Universal Responsibility of His Holiness The Dalai Lama and ANB Publishers, 1996, p. 123.

43. 'Speech on Human Rights and Responsibilities', in n. 19, p. 38.

44. The Dalai Lama, *The Power of Compassion: A Collection of Lectures by His Holiness the XIV Dalai Lama*, trans. Geshe Thupten Jinpa, New Delhi: HarperCollins Publishers, (1995) 1988, pp. 62–3.

45. H.H. The Dalai Lama, 'Foreword', in M.L. Dewan, *Towards a Sustainable Society: Perceptions*, New Delhi: Clarion Books, 1995, p. 11.

46. Roderick Frazier Nash, *The Rights of Nature: A History of Environmental Ethics*, Madison, Wisconsin: The University of Wisconsin Press, 1989, p. 122.

47. Eugene C. Hargrove (ed.), *Religion and Environmental Crisis*, Athens: Ga, 1986, p. IX.

48. Nash, p. 122.

49. Ibid.

50. Ibid., p. 160.

51. E.F. Schumacher, *Small is Beautiful: A Study of Economics as if People Mattered*, London: Vintage, (1973) 1993, p. 44.

52. Ibid.

53. Ibid., pp. 44–55.

54. 'Environmental Responsibility', *The Spirit of Tibet: Universal Heritage, Selected Speeches and Writings of HH The Dalai Lama XIV*, edited by A.A. Shiromany, New Delhi: Tibetan Parliamentary and Policy Research Centre and Allied Publishers Limited, 1995, p. 286.

55. His Holiness the Dalai Lama, n. 15, p. 195.

56. 'Education and Contamination', n. 3, p. 55.

57. James Nashold, 'The Meeting of East and West: The Dalai Lama's First Trip to the United States', *The Tibet Journal*, (Library of Tibetan Works and Archives), no. 1 and 2, vol. V, Spring/Summer, 1980, p. 37.

58. *The Dalai Lama*, n. 31, p. 55.

59. Romila Thapar, *Ashoka and the Decline of the Mauryas*, Oxford: Oxford University Press, 1961, pp. 251, 265.

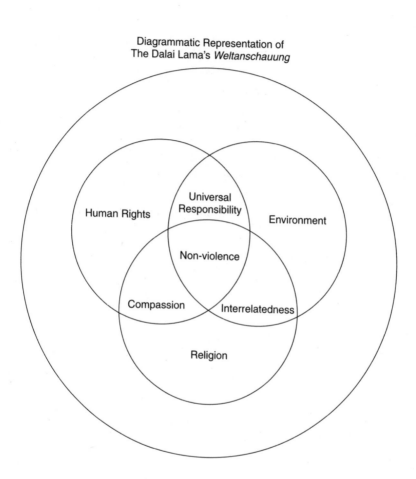

Diagrammatic Representation of
The Dalai Lama's *Weltanschauung*

Human Rights

Universal
Responsibility

Environment

Non-violence

Compassion

Interrelatedness

Religion

How does the story end?
... Guess.
I don't know. Just tell me.
Who cares about the end?
What?
All this fuss about endings.
All this fuss...

From *Phorpa*, a film by Khyentse Norbu

Appendix I

Interview with his Holiness the XIV Dalai Lama
Tenzin Gyatso, at his Private Office, McLeod Ganj,
Dharamsala, on 27 August 2001*

QUESTION 1   Interdependence, Non-violence and Compassion, according to my readings are the fundamental concepts in your thought. Are
there any other fundamental concepts in your thought, apart from these
three?

ANSWER 1   I think these three things, [are] fundamental ... beside that ... I
think they my fundamental thought, they my personal level. Then ... another
level which mainly deals with humanity or peace or environment. *So, on
the level of peace and environment, these three things are the most important.*
Beside that I don't know ... or certainly, personal level ... monk ... monkhood
... as a bhikshu ... including in my dream, I always remember I am monk,
I am bhikshu ... so there is a thought as a bhikshu ... it is fundamental.
Then perhaps some other practice. That's in my personal level. So on that
level may be you see few more thought ... thoughts on compassion ... non-
violence, interdependence. Then perhaps deity yoga also. Deity yoga ...
visualization of oneself as a deity, or one might go through practice. Then I

---

*   *Note*: This interview has been edited minimally to preserve the original essence
of His Holiness The XIV Dalai Lama's answers in English, with a very occasional
translation by Lhakdor (Present Director of the Library of Tibetan Works and
Archives, (LTWA), Dharamsala then Joint Secretary, Religious Assistant and
Translator, Office of His Holiness The Dalai Lama) and Tenzin Geshe Tethong
(Secretary to His Holiness The Dalai Lama). The text has been italicized to
highlight issues of importance.

think basic thing is monk. Buddhist follower. I think ... of course Buddhist. As a practitioner taking refuge, I think always, Buddha as my teacher. And also in a way ... model. And then some of the Indian context like Nagarjuna and these things. That's my personal level. Of course *when I deal with world peace or environment then I talk about compassion or interdependence.* Then of course the Buddhist concept very much involved there .... But itself, I do not ... carry these ... certain thought as a part of Buddhism. No. On these level as a human value. *Interdependence ... effects reality. Because everything is reality. You see everything interdependent. You see something happen here, its effect reaches elsewhere.* So this I feel, you see, very useful in our bhikshu's life. And especially when we think about the world, ... think about our own future with ... the concept of interdependence then ... now for example *when we talk about Tibet, Tibetan freedom, then ... you cannot ignore the world or humanity as a whole because Tibet is part of the world. Tibet ... part of humanity. So therefore when you realize everything ... you see ... everything interconnected, then they [are] one particular sort of problem now trying to find solution, that since that thing very much related ... connected with other, you have to take serious consideration about these factors. You can't find solution on [sic] one particular thing because this is not isolated.* Isolate things. If things are isolated then of course you can find solution just there. *That things are interconnected. So you have to find ... you have to ... [take the] whole picture.* That's the I think, concept of reality and realization of reality. ... that idea *... that concept also brings [out the] importance of our action rather than prayer. Prayer of course, ... but prayer alone will not change all situation. So you have to act.*

QUESTION 2(a)   As you would be aware, there is a very visible group of writers who call themselves 'Engaged Buddhists'. They are represented by Sulak Sivaraksa and Thich Nhat Hanh amongst others. Engaged Buddhism is a movement that shows that Buddhism has a practical relevance. In this way, Engaged Buddhism is a critique of writers and thinkers who have tried to show that Buddhism does not have any social or practical relevance. Your Holiness, you are being seen as an 'Engaged Buddhist' by several writers primarily because of your deep involvement in issues like human rights, environmental rights, non violent means to conflict resolutions, and ways and means to religious harmony.

(a) Do you think that Buddhism at any point could have been 'disengaged' or has it always been 'engaged'?

(b) What are the chief issues that you see yourself engaged in?

ANSWER 2(a)   ... [At the] Individual level if someone really wants to practice deep *samadhi* ... or *vipassana*. Then ... that person can practice ... *then it is worthwhile to remain completely isolated situation*. Many big practitioners, great masters in India as well as in Tibet in the past in certain period remain like ... wounded wild animal ... Hide. Hide themselves because they remain in remote area. ... meditate. Buddhism practice. *So that ... directly, yes they are disengaged ... with the welfare of others. But indirectly, they themselves improve or increase in their energy, their motivation, so that [in] later days, later part, they can serve more effectively.* That's Buddhist way. So in certain period it's disengaged.

Now my own case. Now many years ago I expressed my wish, three years retreat. But that did not materialize

So ... in certain stage ... yes ... you see they are disengaged. They concentrate on own meditation. ... one of my fundamental belief[s] is, *what is the purpose of religious practice? All religions you see, teach us sense of concept of brotherhood and sisterhood, so that means you should not forget them. You should respect them, you should have sense of concern for them.* So therefore, for example, all the theistic religions—those religions which believe in God or Creator, and I think those people who believe in creator ... their aim is not like everything .... Everything you see put on the God, on the creator, and do nothing oneself, not that way. Isn't it? So as *I mentioned earlier, Christian brothers, sisters and Muslims, they are also very much actively involved for improvement of society for education field or health field or some other fields.* So therefore sometimes, you see, Latin America, some Christian or Catholic, I think Catholic priests are very much active in the revolution or whatever cause, some movement. So some people, [are] little critical about ... their attitude ... or their involvement. *So there I feel their involvement is very right. So now for example [in] Buddhism, our very concept of no creator but that one individual himself or herself, I feel ... everything depends on one's own action.* Then, I think Buddha, I feel, spoke very critically about [the] caste system. So that is, I think, his involvement in the society. If he just took his bowl and taught his own few disciples ... then no need to take certain position[s] [on] caste, racial discrimination ... [is] ... and Jesus Christ also I think similar. Very similar. So all these great masters, you see not only [are they serious about] their own practice, but they take serious concern about the society and existing situation.

Then I think another thing [is] 'Brahmacharya' or celibacy [in] Buddhism, like possibly some ancient Indian tradition ... Hindu tradition .... So Buddha himself became a *brahmachari*, a celibate, so do his followers, the main adherents, the main followers of his teachings—the monks. So eventually certain area where monks remain, monks stay ... that you see usually become a monastery. So the Buddha clearly mentioned monastery should remain isolated from the society and monks' daily routine ... certain daily routine, as you said. Therefore like Thailand and also [to] some extent, I think, Tibet also ... eventually [remains] in [a] remote area in the monastery. So not much contact or interaction with the society. So with that, the involvement with society was also becoming much less.

This does not mean theoretically that monk or nun should not be engaged in the society. But on the practical level I think monks remained in the remote area in the monastery. So now in daily basis [to be in] morning time with the society and do some work then return in the evening ... that's impractical. Some distance. Isn't it? I think, that's one reason. Then perhaps some lazy monk, could [cited that as the] ... main reason [for] not wanting to do any work. But in the pretext that is also possible. (laughter).

QUESTION 2(b)   What are the chief issues you see yourself engaged in, since you have been called an Engaged Buddhist?

ANSWER 2(b)   I think the practical reason. If I am just an ordinary monk ... I always sort of attracted ... to some ... like in recent years ... now visible. Now there is a very good monk from Ladakh. (Lhakdor La translates, 'very high ranking monk from Ladakh'). So he often used to come here. Listen my teaching. Also perform some *poojas*. When he takes leave for Ladakh then often I feel (Lhakdor La translates, 'Then often His Holiness will feel how happy he is ... kind of envious') [goes on] You see, he goes back to Ladakh and at least for a few months retreat or relaxes ... holiday in his own area. So that means if I am just a simple monk, with no responsibility, perhaps I may engage in more retreat or study. But then you know being the 'Dalai Lama' there is more chance to serve, to usefully serve. There is one story from the first Dalai Lama's biography. He mentioned after he established one big monastery, 'Tashi Lhumpo'. That time he was very very active. Recording his daily routine he spent time teaching new young monks. One portion supervised construction. One time he sent some appeal to some of the richer families for donation for the construction of monastery. So [he] almost an architect! Inspite of old age, with stick, he always used to go around [became] supervising this construction. So then one time he expressed as a response to some of his followers who had become rather lazy

(Tenzin Geshe Tethong translates: 'complaining a little bit for lack of appreciation for what he was doing, in that kind of an attitude he expressed') that in the past he had spent one year in one area, in retreat as an individual monk. He did serious practice. At that time he really developed certain spiritual experiences. So then he mentioned, 'If I continue to practice *dharma* in remote area, then today my spiritual practice would be much higher. But I sacrifice that to serve you but if you are not doing well then my effort is useless, small effort is useless, wasted.' So that inspired me. *He chose active engagement in the society rather than going to remote area, although he sacrificed his own spiritual development. So now my case is exactly the same. If I have, you see more time, and I remain in some remote area, perhaps my spiritual practice, I think, I am quite sure would be, I think little bit more. But then that of course, [in the] long run could be beneficial to others but for [the moment, I see] no direct sort of benefit. So things are serious. So therefore you see, I can balance. This is very necessary, you have to carry some work in the society like that.*

I think you may have heard main three things. Number one, *I as a human being. As my own share ... contribution for promotion of human values ... for betterment of humanity and that is inclusive of world peace or happier society, peaceful society. For that, I believe human values are very essential, I believe they are the basis of a happier society, happier family.* Therefore on the level of human being, *I try to promote ... make contribution regarding promotion of human values. 'Environment' is taking care of one's own home. This world is our home. So because of mainly population, and also I think lifestyle, major resources are becoming limited.* And then I think exploitation of nature. So now because of population and because of their lifestyle ... extent of damage to nature has reached such a stage .... Now nature cannot cope. (Lhakdor La adds, 'if damage is small then nature can recover itself'). Now for example, when we have 'teachings' here. For a few days the area becomes very dirty. ... there is a bad smell. But after few weeks if rains come then everything is alright. Unless we take care, nature cannot (Lhakdor La translates, 'recover itself'). So these are the concerns. That is number one.

Number two, *being a Buddhist monk and more importantly I think name of one Buddhist leader, Dalai Lama. So there is opportunity and my responsibility, my share, for promotion of religious harmony. That's on the basis of ... level of Buddhist monk. These two things are, of course indirectly related with the Tibetan issue. But directly? No. No direct relations.*

Then third, my responsibility being a Tibetan. And then even more as the Dalai Lama of Tibet. So, and then the most important, is the Tibetan people outside as well as inside Tibet. Specially inside. They trusted me. They put on me lot of hope, so therefore, I have a very heavy moral responsibility to look after them, to serve them. *So now I am fully committed to struggle for Tibetan survival. Struggle for freedom. I will be precise. Certain degree of freedom. Not independence. That is my commitment.*

QUESTION 3   Seen from the contemporary angle could you please specify the relevance of Buddhism for four issues:

   (i) Human Rights
   (ii) Non-Violence
   (iii) Environmental Protection and
   (iv) Religious Harmony

How is Buddhism important for these? Or, what kind of contribution can Buddhism make for these issues?

ANSWER 3   I think Buddhism has great potential for all these. I think great potential. Number one, *Buddhism not only talks of human rights but right of all sentient beings. All living sentient beings. ... [have the] same rights.* The basic thing is that so long as sentient beings have desire to overcome suffering. That is the main thing. So, their shapes, are ... different matter. Whether they have the same intellect or not, that's secondary. *The important thing is the desire, the feeling of 'I' ... the desire on that basis, desire to overcome suffering. Wanting happiness. So ... all sentient beings, who have the feeling ... are the same. Therefore, in Buddhism you see all other sentient beings, specially in the Buddhist Mahayana tradition we always say ... we always pray for all sentient beings, all other sentient being. So then certainly, particularly human beings have such nice intelligence. Great potential and furthermore human beings also have negative potential. So therefore, it is very essential to take special care about human beings. So human right is very much relevant.*

Of course the basis of Buddhism, or the basic teaching of Buddha Dharma is 'Karuna,' or Compassion. 'Karuna' is the basis or the root of non-violence. Demarcation between non-violence and violence is motivation. Compassionate motivation, then action which come out of compassionate movitation, that's non violence. Any action which comes out of hatred or desire to cheat, are essentially violent actions. So therefore the concept of non-violence is I think the reflection of the Buddhist message of 'Karuna'. Compassion is motivation. Non-violence is an expression of compassion. So compassion is there, non-violence automatically comes.

Compassion not there, then superficially it may look non-violent but still not very sure ... whether true non-violence or not.

The Buddhists I think, unlike some ancient Indian tradition, which believes that plants also have life as sentient beings [do not do so]. Buddhism does not believe that these plants also have the consciousness or the soul. But you see the plants, and of course all these wild animals, are also sentient beings—they also have feelings. So one should help them, not harm them. ... although we do not consider these as sentient beings ... these also have the experience of pain and pleasure. *One's own lifestyle should be ... [a] contented one. You should use material in the minimal way. Of course, Buddha himself when he arranged his own seat, had to collect some trunks, some leaves, if necessary ... but very limited. Isn't it? So lifestyle contented ... simplicity.* I think this is one way to make contribution regarding the environment. *Then second, the environment, also there are lot of insects ... lot of animals ... their whole life depends on the forest.* So in Tibet, traditionally some farmers in certain area, for cultivation, we are very much against it. Main reason, once you start that in a small area, the limited insects will be killed. Will burn. [sic] *Then of course in Tibet ... government in the past had ... prohibitions on fishing, hunting ... of course they ... [slaughtered] some yaks, some sheep, goats—that's exceptional ...* (Laughter) But basically you see there is some prohibition and I think that is quite practical. *But hunting down mouse is exceptional because it harms farmers. Then wolf, hunting down wolf is also exceptional because it is very harmful for nomads and their cattle. So ... even at government level there is some prohibition. So therefore those are I think come out of Buddhist concept. Then today as I think, to me, the Buddhist concept of interdependence is that if environment is damaged, eventually it is irrecoverable. Then who'll suffer? The world itself! So maximum exploitation of forests and things which are short-sighted. Actually, I think the maximum exploitation of the natural resources means the destruction of one's own home. So these are I think, due to lack of realization in being interconnected.*

Buddhism is also like any other religion ... you see ... the belief, their own teaching is the best. For Buddhists ... we should not take refuge in other master. We should have belief in our own master. Our 'Buddha Dharma Sangha' is the supreme, ultimate. But the, I think big difference is, that Buddha himself taught some different philosophy and different concepts. Why? Because Buddha accepted that among his followers there are different mental dispositions, different mental capacities. So therefore, as a recognition and respect for these differences ... you see ... he taught different philosophies, different concept. So this brings us, this sort of attitude. Yes, among the humanity, there are so many different people, different mental capacities, therefore, just one Buddhist teaching naturally cannot satisfy a variety of people. Therefore we need a variety of philosophies, variety of religions. Now of course for Buddhists some sort of tradition like animal sacrifice, in Tibet in some very remote area, is there. (Lhakdor La translates, 'These kind of malpractices cannot be accepted saying that this is the tradition. We need to find some means to discourage such practices.') Basically, all teachings that bring peace of mind and give hope like Christian or Muslim or Judaism of course, all the ancient Indian tradition, just as in Jainism *'ahimsa'* is the supreme message. (Lhakdor La translates, 'Very strong message which is very good'.) *So they respect, all other traditions. Perhaps I think, it is a little easier for Buddhists to accept, to respect other traditions because within Buddhism itself, you see, there are so many different (Lhakdor La translates, 'Philosophies.') taught by one Buddha, one teacher. So that gives us some kind of thought.* (Lhakdor La translates, 'that naturally activates us and makes us think that why Buddha taught us so many different philosophies.') Then ... answer (Lhakdor La translates, 'that brings the answer that Buddha thought of giving such teaching because there are so many different types of disposition and capacities.') (Lhakdor La translates, 'so that will naturally help us appreciate the need to have different religious traditions, to be able serve people with different mental capacities.')

QUESTION 4   It has been suggested that your position as the leader of an exiled community has forced you to come to terms with a world that is very different from the traditional Buddhist society. (My reference being Christopher Queen's book *Engaged Buddhism in the West*, p. 230). My question Your Holiness is that, do you really agree with this? Do you think that this has made you compromise on your Buddhist perceptions? Can you still link your true Buddhist perceptions with the contemporary needs of the 'modern' world?

ANSWER 4   No need any change (sic). I think specially the so-called *Mahayana* tradition. *Mahayana* tradition, very much emphasized service to others. The *Theravada* tradition, mainly lay emphasis on salvation. Of course that way accordingly, in *Theravada* tradition also, the main practice is *'Karuna'* - *'Metta'*. *But then they are I think very actively engaged in the society.* I think they are serving or are engaged in service of society. Then society where it is usually little bit negligent about basic human values, that I think is because of ignorance. Because of short-sightedness. Then that develops a very extreme self-centered attitude. This helps to create immoral activities. Then killing other, bullying other, abuse, cheating, all these things happen ... scandals (sic).

So basically ... modern society is still a human society. So human values are still very much appreciated . Look at children—students in kindergarten. I think they [are] immediately appreciative if you give smile and show them care or compassion or sense of concern-all children appreciate. If you try to cheat them they don't like it, or if you try to beat them ... if you show bad face, of course, they don't like. So that is human being. Animal also. If you treat them with compassionate attitude [they are] more peaceful, respect their need ... their requirement, and they appreciate. (Lhakdor La translates, *'in the modern society there is a clear negligence of the fundamental human values. But this does not belittle the importance of fundamental values. So therefore these fundamental human values that go into traditional values are not only important and relevant but more, they are even more necessary at this time because of negligence of these fundamental human values.'*) I think main Buddhist message is dealing with emotion and not economy, not health, not of construction ... *so therefore, you see as far as human emotion is concerned ... the level of human emotion today in the 21st century when compared with Buddha's time, I think is basically the same. So there's no need for any change of concept or teaching. It came 2500 years ago and is still very relevant in today's world. Now modernity means change of external things. Modernization has nothing to do with human emotion. I think through education you can change, can transform, can make differences about emotion.* But the modern education is very much related with external things ... How to make economy work, how do we improve health, how to remove corruption, how do we develop civil society. These things not talking much about human emotions. That's why modern education now seems *something not complete ... not sufficient.* Today's world as compared even to hundred years ago, has changed ... is still changing.

QUESTION 5   Do you think your perceptions on various issues changed after 1959? For instance in your book *Ethics for the New Millennium* on pages 21–2, you say 'I told myself it would be marvelous if everyone converted.' This perhaps was your earlier position? Or, has your position changed? Could you elab orate please.

ANSWER 5   That's right! ... *There's some change.* I think in the second part of the twentieth century, one Tibetan scholar visited India. His name is

Gedun Chophel. Once he mentioned in one of his books ... non-Buddhist sort of ideas ... [and spoke of] all the weakest points with pleasure. It is easier to argue in order to refute ... . (Laughter) *So you have the feeling that Buddhism is the best and very superior, that kind of thing. And ... then I think because of lack of contact. When I was in Tibet one translation ... Tibetan translation of Bible was there. But otherwise you see there was ... no personal contact with Christian practitioners ... so you have no idea how much benefit is brought by non-Buddhist and other traditions. After I came to India and had the opportunity to meet people ... followers of different traditions such as some Christian monks and nuns and also some 'sadhus', some Jains and I was also introduced to some Muslims and some Jews and Parsis ... there are many good human beings ... really warm-hearted human beings, very devoted and contented. Then Mother Teresa. And of course I think one great example amongst the many Indian freedom fighters, like Vinoba Babaji [Reference to Vinoba Bhave]. You know I personally know these great souls. Great human beings.*

And Rajendra Babu the first Indian President. Very religious-minded. But Nehru seems not much religious minded. More westernized ... it seems! Then of course I never had the opportunity of seeing *Mahatma Gandhiji. But of course I saw his statue ... some pictures. I think he is the great spiritual master. You get the feeling that all other traditions also have same potential to produce wonderful good human beings.* So that realism [realization] makes differences of attitude to other tradition.

QUESTION 6   Although your 'non-violence' stand is visionary, some people think that it is not practical. What is your view? Do you think that your non-violent stand has helped to strengthen the Tibetan people in exile?

ANSWER 6   O yes! I think the great number of supporters of Tibetan issue in the outside world ... *are mainly due to our non-violent principle. Especially among the young people and then also nowadays you see, amongst Chinese also, specially amongst the intellectuals ... some writers, thinkers, some artists; who know something about Tibet; they automatically show their sympathy and their solidarity.* I think one of the main reasons that brings their sympathy and their solidarity is because we are fighting for our freedom through the non-violent way. Non-violence is not only just restraint from harming others but keeping a compassionate attitude towards them. *There is one Tibetan monk who spent 18 years in Chinese prison ... Chinese 'gulag'. .... In the early 80's he joined here ... since we know each other before 1959, so on one occasion he mentioned that during those years he faced some dangers ... I asked 'what* danger?' *His answer was 'the danger of losing compassion towards the Chinese.'* *So you see genuine Tibetan Buddhists, genuine practitioner consider keeping of compassionate attitude towards enemy as something very important. That's the reasoning of non-violence.* So I feel there is a lot of observation of positive results. Of course even we Tibetan involve some violence (sic). Then some headlines, more publicity in the world. Like Middle-East crisis and also Kashmir ... problems of India. Some area ... some one or two people killed then immediately you see reports in all the newspapers, some headlines sometimes. But does that really help for solution of the problem? I don't think. *More violence ... this side ... involve violence ... then counter violence. That creates more violence. More hurt ... that I think is very bad for development of mutual trust ... And mutual suspicion, mutual hate are easy things. Things which can be easily solved ... it creates then impossible barrier.* So that is what exactly happened.

QUESTION 7   What do you think are the most important means for resolving conflicts? Which are the most important ways to resolve conflicts?

ANSWER 7   (Lhakdor La translates, 'Unless you have clairvoyance. Unless you have pre-cognition it is difficult to say.' [His Holiness's laughter]). I mean, that each conflict has many aspects. Some cases religion, faith, some cases purely politics, some cases economy, some cases racial ... in each case there are so many different aspects ... although you see all violent conflicts, they have the same aspect. But within that there are difference of aspects. So difficult to say ... But perhaps *I think one thing which we can discover everywhere ... that's ... we should recognize the other also is a part of you. Not external. So according to the concept of interdependence ... the other also is a part of you.* Now for example India Pakistan. Pakistan also you see although the political (Lhakdor La translates, 'politically separate, different states.') two countries (sic). *But in economy or environment or education if you work together ... it would be mutually beneficial.* Isn't it? If you isolate Pakistan from India's side ... Pakistan side, India isolated ... and try every way and means to harm India. It actually suffer-Pakistan (sic). ... *So I think in every case, the old concept ... 'we' and 'they' is a very strong concept. According to that concept ... you know the reality. According to that concept, when we try to gain every sort of victory, every gain to oneself and try to harm the other—that is a mistake. That's I think an outdated concept. In ancient times may be, your economy, your environment had nothing to do with your neighbour. Under those circumstances, maybe it is justified that complete destruction of your neighbour is victory on yourself. But now in modern time that reality ... completely gone. [Laughter]*

Appendix II

The Nobel Peace Prize Acceptance Speech, Oslo, Norway, December 10, 1989*

Your Majesty, Members of the Nobel Committee, Brothers and Sisters:

I am very happy to be here with you today to receive the Nobel Prize for Peace. I feel honoured, humbled, and deeply moved that you should give this important prize to a simple monk from Tibet. I am no one special. But, I believe the prize is a recognition of the true value of altruism, love, compassion, and non-violence which I try to practice, in accordance with the teachings of the Buddha and the great sages of India and Tibet.

I accept the prize with profound gratitude on behalf of the oppressed everywhere and for all those who struggle for freedom and work for world peace. I accept it as a tribute to the man who founded the modern tradition of non-violent action for change—Mahatma Gandhi—whose life taught and inspired me. And, of course, I accept it on behalf of the six million Tibetan people, my brave countrymen and women inside Tibet, who have suffered and continue to suffer so much. They confront a calculated and systematic strategy aimed at the destruction of their national and cultural identities. The prize reaffirms our conviction that with truth, courage, and determination as our weapons, Tibet will be liberated.

No matter what part of the world we come from, we are all basically the same human beings. We all seek happiness and try to avoid suffering. We have the same basic human needs and concerns. All of us human beings

* *The Nobel Peace Prize and The Dalai Lama*, compiled and edited by Sidney Piburn, Ithaca: Snow Lion Publications, 1990, pp. 24–7.

want freedom and the right to determine our own destiny as individuals and as peoples. That is human nature. The great changes that are taking place everywhere in the world, from Eastern Europe to Africa, are a clear indication of this.

In China the popular movement for democracy was crushed by brutal force in June this year. But I do not believe the demonstrations were in vain, because the spirit of freedom was rekindled among the Chinese people and China cannot escape the impact of this spirit of freedom sweeping many parts of the world. The brave students and their supporters showed the Chinese leadership and the world the human face of that great nation.

Last week a number of Tibetans were once again sentenced to prison terms of up to nineteen years at a mass show trial, possibly intended to frighten the population before today's event. Their only 'crime' was the expression of the widespread desire of Tibetans for the restoration of their beloved country's independence.

The suffering of our people during the past forty years of occupation is well documented. Ours has been a long struggle. We know our cause is just. Because violence can only breed more violence and suffering, our struggle must remain non-violent and free of hatred. We are trying to end the suffering of our people, not to inflict suffering upon others.

It is with this in mind that I proposed negotiations between Tibet and China on numerous occasions. In 1987, I made specific proposals in a five-point plan for the restoration of peace and human rights in Tibet. This included the conversion of the entire Tibetan plateau into a Zone of Ahimsa, a sanctuary of peace and non-violence where human beings and nature can live in peace and harmony.

Last year, I elaborated on that plan in Strasbourg, at the European Parliament. I believe the ideas I expressed on those occasion are both realistic and reasonable, although they have been criticized by some of my people as being too conciliatory. Unfortunately, China's leaders have not responded positively to the suggestions we have made, which included important concessions. If this continues we will be compelled to reconsider our position.

Any relationship between Tibet and China will have to be based on the principle of equality, respect, trust, and mutual benefit. It will also have to be based on the principle which the wise rulers of Tibet and China laid down in a treaty as early as 823 AD, carved on the pillar which still stands today in front of the Jo-khang, Tibet's holiest shrine in Lhasa, that 'Tibetans will live happily in the great land of Tibet, and the Chinese will live happily in the great land of China.

As a Buddhist monk, my concern extends to all members of the human family and, indeed, to all sentient beings who suffer. I believe all suffering is caused by ignorance. People inflict pain on others in the selfish pursuit of their happiness or satisfaction. Yet true happiness comes from a sense of inner peace and contentment, which in turn must be achieved through the cultivation of altruism, of love and compassion, and elimination of ignorance, selfishness and greed.

The problems we face today, violent conflicts, destruction of nature, poverty, hunger, and so on, are human created problems which can be resolved through human effort, understanding, and the development of a sense of brotherhood and sisterhood. We need to cultivate a universal responsibility for one another and the planet we share. Although I have found my own Buddhist religion helpful in generating love and compassion, even for those we consider our enemies, I am convinced that everyone can develop a good heart and a sense of universal responsibility with or without religion.

With the ever-growing impact of science on our lives, religion and spirituality have a greater role to play reminding us of our humanity. There is no contradiction between the two. Each gives us valuable insights into the other. Both science and the teachings of the Buddha tells us of the fundamental unity of all things. This understanding is crucial if we are to take positive and decisive action on the pressing global concern with the environment.

I believe all religions pursue the same goal, that of cultivating human goodness and bringing happiness to all human beings. Though the means might appear different the ends are the same.

As we enter the final decade of this century I am optimistic that the ancient values that have sustained mankind are today reaffirming themselves to prepare us for a kinder, happier twenty-first century.

I pray for all of us, oppressor and friend, that together we succeed in building a better world through human understanding and love, and that in doing so we may reduce the pain and suffering of all sentient beings.

Thank you.

The Nobel Peace Prize Lecture*
Oslo, Norway

Brothers and Sisters:

It is an honor and pleasure to be among you today. I am really happy to see so many old friends who have come from different corners of the world, and to make new friends, whom I hope to meet again in the future. When I meet people in different parts of the world, I am always reminded that we are all basically alike: we are all human beings. Maybe we have different clothes, our skin is of a different color, or we speak different languages. This is on the surface. But basically, we are the same human beings. That is what binds us to each other. That is what makes it possible for us to understand each other and to develop friendship and closeness.

Thinking over what I might say today, I decided to share with you some of my thoughts concerning the common problems all of us face as members of the human family. Because we all share this small planet, we have to learn to live in harmony and grace with each other and with nature. That is not just a dream, but a necessity. We are dependent on each other in so many ways that we can no longer live in isolated communities and ignore what is happening outside those communities. We need to help each other when we have difficulties, and we must share the good fortune that we enjoy. I speak to you as just another human being, as a simple monk. If you find what I say useful, then I hope you will try to practice it.

I also wish to share with you today my feelings concerning the plight and aspirations of the people of Tibet. The Nobel Prize is a prize they well deserve for their courage and unfailing determination during the past forty years of foreign occupation. As a free spokesman for my captive countrymen and women, I feel it is my duty to speak out on their behalf. I speak not with a feeling of anger or hatred towards those who are responsible for the immense suffering of our people and the destruction of our land, homes, and culture. They too are human beings who struggle to find happiness and deserve our compassion. I speak to inform you of the said situation in my country today and of the aspirations of my people, because in our struggle for freedom, truth is the only weapon we possess.

* Piburn, pp. 35–45. See also 'The 14th Dalai Lama-Nobel Lecture, December 11, 1989', http://nobelprize.org/peace/laureates/1989/lama-lecture.html

The realization that we are all basically the same human beings, who seek happiness and try to avoid suffering, is very helpful in developing a sense of brotherhood and sisterhood—a warm feeling of love and compassion for others. This, in turn, is essential if we are to survive in this ever-shrinking world we live in. For if we each selfishly pursue only what we believe to be in our own interest, without caring about the needs of others, we not only may end up harming others but also ourselves. This fact has become very clear during the course of this century. We know that to wage a nuclear war today, for example, would be a form of suicide; or that to pollute the air or the oceans, in order to achieve some short-term benefit, would be to destroy the very basis for our survival. As individuals and nations are becoming increasingly interdependent we have no other choice than to develop what I call a sense of universal responsibility.

Today, we are truly a global family. What happens in one part of the world may affect us all. This, of course, is not only true of the negative things that happen, but is equally valid for the positive developments. We not only know what happens elsewhere, thanks to the extraordinary modern communications technology, we are also directly affected by events that occur far away. We feel a sense of sadness when children are starving in Eastern Africa. Similarly, we feel a sense of joy when a family is reunited after decades of separation by the Berlin Wall. Our crops and livestock are contaminated and our health and livelihood threatened when a nuclear accident happens miles away in another country. Our own security is enhanced when peace breaks out between warring parties in other continents.

But war or peace, the destruction or the protection of nature, the violation or promotion of human rights and democratic freedoms, poverty or material well-being, the lack of moral and spiritual values or their existence and development, and the breakdown or development of human understanding, are not isolated phenomena that can be analysed and tackled independently of one another. In fact, they are very much interrelated at all levels and need to be approached with that understanding.

Peace, in the sense of the absence of war, is of little value to someone who is dying of hunger or cold. It will not remove the pain of torture inflicted on a prisoner of conscience. It does not comfort those who have lost their loved ones in floods caused by senseless deforestation in a neighbouring country. Peace can only last where human rights are respected, where the people are fed, and where individuals and nations are free. True peace with ourselves and with the world around us can only be achieved through the development of mental peace. The other phenomena mentioned above are similarly interrelated. Thus, for example, we see that a clean environment, wealth, or democracy mean little in the face of war, especially nuclear war, and that material development is not sufficient to ensure human happiness.

Material progress is of course important for human advancement. In Tibet, we paid much too little attention to technological and economic development, and today we realize that this was a mistake. At the same time, material development without spiritual development can also cause serious problems. In some countries too much attention is paid to external things and very little importance is given to inner development. I believe both are important and must be developed side by side so as to achieve a good balance between them. Tibetans are always described by foreign visitors as being a happy, jovial people. This is part of our national character, formed by cultural and religious values that stress the importance of mental peace through the generation of love and kindness to all other living sentient beings, both human and animal. Inner peace is the key: if you have inner peace, the external problems do not affect your deep sense of peace, the external problem do not affect your deep sense of peace and tranquility. In that state of mind you can deal with situations with calmness and reason, while keeping your inner happiness. That is very important. Without this inner peace, no matter how comfortable your life is materially, you may still be worried, disturbed, or unhappy because of circumstances.

Clearly, it is of great importance, therefore, to understand the interrelationship among these and other phenomena, and to approach and attempt to solve problems in a balanced way that takes these different aspects into consideration. Of course it is not easy. But it is of little benefit to try to solve one problem if doing so creates an equally serious new one. So, really, we have no alternative: we must develop a sense of universal responsibility not only in the geographic sense, but also in respect to the different issues that confront our planet.

Responsibility does not only lie with the leaders of our countries or with those who have been appointed or elected to do a particular job. It lies with each of us individually. Peace, for example, starts within each one of us. When we have inner peace, we can be at peace with those around us. When our community is in a state of peace, it can share that peace with neighbouring communities, and so on. When we feel love and kindness towards others, it not only makes others feel loved and cared for, but it helps us also to develop inner happiness and peace. And there are ways in which we can consciously work to develop feelings of love and kindness. For some of us, the most effective way to do so is through religious practice. For others it may be non-religious practices. What is important is that we each make a sincere effort to take seriously, our responsibility for each other, and for the natural environment.

I am very encouraged by the developments which are taking place around us. After the young people of many countries, particularly in northern Europe, have repeatedly called for an end to the dangerous destruction of the environment which was being conducted in the name of economic development, the world's political leaders are now starting to take meaningful steps to address this problem. The report to the United Nations Secretary General by the World Commission on the Environment and Development (the Brundtland Report) was an important step in educating governments on the urgency of the issue. Serious efforts to bring peace to war-torn zones and to implement the right to self-determination of some people have resulted in the withdrawal of Soviet troops from Afghanistan and the establishment of independent Namibia. Through persistent non-violent popular efforts, dramatic changes bringing many countries closer to real democracy have occurred in many places, from Manila in the Philippines to Berlin in East Germany. With the Cold War era apparently drawing to a close, people everywhere live with renewed hope. Sadly, the courageous efforts of the Chinese people to bring similar changes to their country were brutally crushed last June. But their efforts too are a source of hope. Military might has not extinguished the desire for freedom and the determination of the Chinese people to achieve it. I particularly admire the fact that these young people, who have been taught that 'power grows from the barrel of the gun,' chose, instead, to use non-violence as their weapon.

What these positive changes indicate is that reason, courage, determination, and the inextinguishable desire for freedom can ultimately win. In the struggle between forces of war, violence, and oppression on the one hand, and peace, reason, and freedom on the other, the latter are gaining the upper hand. This realization fills us Tibetans with hope that some day we too will once again be free.

The awarding of the Nobel Prize to me, a simple monk from far away Tibet, here in Norway, also fills us Tibetans with hope. It means that, despite the fact we have not drawn attention to our plight by means of violence, we have not been forgotten. It also means that the values we cherish, in particular our respect for all forms of life and the belief in the power of truth, are today recognized and encouraged. It is also a tribute to my mentor, Mahatma Gandhi, whose example is an inspiration to so many of us. This year's award is an indication that this sense of universal responsibility is developing. I am deeply touched by the sincere concern shown by so many people in this part of the world for the suffering of the people of Tibet. That is a source of hope not only for us Tibetans, but for all oppressed peoples.

As you know, Tibet has, for forty years, been under foreign occupation. Today, more than a quarter of a million Chinese troops are stationed in Tibet. Some sources estimate the occupation army to be twice this strength. During this time, Tibetans have been deprived of their most basic human rights, including the right of life, movement, speech, worship, only to mention a few. More than one sixth of Tibet's population of six million died as a direct result of the Chinese invasion and occupation. Even before the Cultural Revolution started, many of Tibet's monasteries, temples, and historic building were destroyed. Almost everything that remained was destroyed during the Cultural Revolution. I do not wish to dwell on this point which is well documented. What is important to realize, however, is that despite the limited freedom granted after 1979 to rebuild parts of some monasteries and other such tokens of liberalization, the fundamental human rights of the Tibetan people are still today being systematically violated. In recent months this bad situation has become even worse.

If it were not for our community in exile, so generously sheltered and supported by the government and people of India and helped by organizations and individuals from many parts of the world, our nation would today be little more than a shattered remnant of a people. Our culture, religion, and national identity would have been effectively eliminated. As it is, we have built schools and monasteries in exile and have created democratic institutions to serve our people and preserve the seeds of our civilization. With this experience, we intend to implement full democracy in a future free Tibet. Thus, as we develop our community in exile on modern lines we also cherish and preserve our own identity and culture and bring hope to millions of our countrymen and—women in Tibet.

The issue of most urgent concern at this time is the massive influx of Chinese settlers into Tibet. Although in the first decades of occupation a considerable number of Chinese were transferred into the eastern parts of Tibet—in the Tibetan province. Amdo (Chinghai) and Kham (most of which has been annexed by the neighbouring Chinese have been encouraged by their government to migrate to all parts of Tibet, including central and western Tibet (which the PRC refers to as the so-called Tibet Autonomous Region). Tibetans are rapidly being reduced to an insignificant minority in their own country. This development, which threatens the very survival of the Tibetan nation, its culture, and spiritual heritage can still be stopped and reversed. But this must be done now, before it is too late.

The new cycle of protest and violent repression, which started in Tibet in September of 1987 and culminated in the implosion of martial law in the capital, Lhasa, in March of this year, was in large part a reaction to this tremendous Chinese influx. Information reaching us in exile indicates that the protest marches and other peaceful forms of protest are continuing in Lhasa and a number of other places in Tibet despite the severe punishment and inhumane treatment given to Tibetans killed by security forces during the protest in March and of those who died in detention afterwards is not known but is believed to be more than two hundred. Thousands have been detained or arrested and imprisoned, and torture is commonplace.

It was against the background of this worsening situation and in order to prevent further bloodshed, that I proposed what is generally referred to as the Five Point Peace Plan for the restoration of peace and human rights in Tibet. I elaborated on the plan in a speech in Strasbourg last year. I believe the plan provides a reasonable and realistic framework for negotiations with the People's Republic of China. So far, however, China's leaders have been unwilling to respond constructively. The brutal suppression of the Chinese democracy movement in June of this year, however, reinforced my view that any settlement of the Tibetan question will only be meaningful if it is supported by adequate international guarantees.

The Five Point Peace Plan addresses the principal and interrelated issues, which I referred to in the first part of this lecture. It calls for (1) Transformation of the whole of Tibet, including the eastern provinces of Kham and Amdo, into a zone of Ahimsa (non-violence); (2) Abandonment of China's population transfer policy; (3) Respect for the Tibetan people's fundamental human rights and democratic freedoms; (4) Restoration and protection of Tibet's natural environment; and (5) Commencement of earnest negotiations on the future status of Tibet and of relations between the Tibetan and Chinese peoples. In the Strasbourg address I proposed that Tibet become a fully self-governing democratic political entity.

I would like to take this opportunity to explain the Zone of Ahimsa or peace sanctuary concept, which is the central element of the Five Point Peace Plan. I am convinced that it is of great importance not only for Tibet, but for peace and stability in Asia.

It is my dream that the entire Tibetan plateau should become a free refuge where humanity and nature can live in peace and in harmonious balance. It would be a place where people from all over the world could come to seek the true meaning of peace within themselves, away from the tensions and pressure of much of the rest of the world. Tibet could indeed become a creative center for the promotion and development of peace.

The following are key elements of the proposed Zone of Ahimsa:

- the entire Tibetan plateau would be demilitarized;
- the manufacture, testing, and stockpiling of nuclear weapons and other armaments on the Tibetan plateau would be prohibited;
- the Tibetan plateau would be transformed into the world's largest natural park or biosphere. Strict laws would be enforced to protect wildlife and plant life; the exploitation of natural resources would be carefully regulated so as not to damage relevant ecosystems; and a policy of sustainable development would be adopted in populated areas;
- the manufacture and use of nuclear power and other technologies which produce hazardous waste would be prohibited;
- national resources and policy would be directed towards the active promotion of peace and environmental protection. Organizations dedicated to the furtherance of peace and to the protection of all forms of life would find a hospitable home in Tibet;
- the establishment of international and regional organizations for the promotion and protection of human rights would be encouraged in Tibet.

Tibet's height and size (the size of the European Community) as well as its unique history and profound spiritual heritage make it ideally suited to fulfill the role of a sanctuary of peace in the strategic heart of Asia. It would also be in keeping with Tibet's historical role as a peaceful Buddhist nation and buffer region separating the Asian continent's great and often rival powers.

In order to reduce existing tensions in Asia, the President of the Soviet Union, Mr Gorbachev, proposed the demilitarization of Soviet-Chinese borders, and their transformation into a 'frontier of peace and good-neighbourliness.' The Nepal government had earlier proposed that the Himalayan country of Nepal, bordering on Tibet, should become a zone of peace, although that proposal did not include demilitarization of the country.

For the stability and peace of Asia, it is essential to create peace zones to separate the continent's biggest powers and potential adversaries. President Gorbachev's proposal, which also included a complete Soviet troops withdrawal from Mongolia, would help to reduce tension and the potential for confrontation between the Soviet Union and China. A true peace zone must clearly also be created to separate the world's two most populous states, China and India.

The establishment of the Zone of Ahimsa would require the withdrawal of troops and military installations from Tibet, which would enable India and Nepal also to withdraw troops and military installations from the Himalayan regions bordering Tibet. This would have to be achieved by international agreements. It would be in the best interest of all states in Asia, particularly China and India, as it would enhance their security, while reducing the economic burden of maintaining high troop concentration in remote areas.

Tibet would not be the first strategic area to be demilitarized. Parts of the Sinai peninsula, the Egyptian territory separating Israel and Egypt, have been demilitarized for some time. Of course, Costa Rica is the best example of an entirely demilitarized country. Tibet would also not be the first area to be turned into a natural preserve or biosphere. Many parks have been created throughout the world. Some very strategic areas have been turned into natural 'peace parks'. Two examples are the La Amistad park on the Cost Rica-Panama border and the Si A Paz project on the Costa Rica-Nicaragua border.

When I visited Costa Rica earlier this year, I saw how a country can develop successfully without an army, to become a stable democracy committed to peace and the protection of the natural environment. This confirmed my belief that my vision of Tibet in the future is a realistic plan, not merely a dream.

Let me end with a personal note of thanks to all of you and our friends who are not here today. The concern and support which you have expressed for the plight of the Tibetans has touched us all greatly, and continues to give us courage to struggle for freedom and justice; not through the use of arms, but with the powerful weapons of truth and determination. I know that I speak on behalf of all the people of Tibet when I thank you and ask you not to forget Tibet at this critical time in our country's history. We too hope to contribute to the development of a more peaceful, more humane, and more beautiful world. A future free Tibet will seek to help those in need throughout the world, to protect nature, and to promote peace. I believe that our Tibetan ability to combine spiritual qualities with a realistic and practical attitude enables us to make a special contribution in however modest a way. This is my hope and prayer.

In conclusion, let me share with you a short prayer which gives me great inspiration and determination:

For as long as space endures,
And for as long as living beings remain,
Until then may I, too, abide
To dispel the misery of the world.

Thank you.

Appendix III

Five Point Peace Plan for Tibet Strasbourg Proposal, June 15, 1988, His Holiness the Dalai Lama*

Five Point Peace Plan

The world is increasingly interdependent, so that lasting peace—national, regional, and global—can only be achieved if we think in terms of broader interest rather than parochial needs. At this time, it is crucial that all of us, the strong and the weak, contribute in our own way. I speak to you today as the leader of the Tibetan people and as a Buddhist monk devoted to the principles of a religion based on love and compassion. Above all, I am here as a human being who is destined to share this planet with you and all others as brothers and sisters. As the world grows smaller, we need each other more than in the past. This is true in all parts of the world, including the continent I come from.

At present in Asia, as elsewhere, tensions are high. There are open conflicts in the Middle East, Southeast Asia, and in my own country, Tibet. To a large extent, these problems are symptoms of the underlying tensions that exist among the area's great powers. In order to resolve regional conflicts, an approach is required that takes into account the interests of all relevant countries and peoples, large and small. Unless comprehensive solutions are formulated, that take into account the aspirations of the people most directly concerned, piecemeal or merely expedient measures will only create new problems.

* Published by: Office of Information & International Relations, Central Tibetan Secretariat, Gangchen Kyishong, Dharamsala (H.P.), n.d.

The Tibetan people are eager to contribute to regional and world peace, and I believe they are in a unique position to do so. Traditionally, Tibetans are a peace loving and non-violent people. Since Buddhism was introduced to Tibet over one thousand years ago, Tibetans have practiced non-violence with respect to our country's international relations. Tibet's highly strategic position in the heart of Asia, separating the continent's great powers—India, China, and the USSR—has throughout history endowed it with an essential role in the maintenance of peace and stability. This is precisely why, in the past, Asia's empires went to great lengths to keep one another out of Tibet. Tibet's value as an independent buffer state was integral to the region's stability.

When the newly formed People's Republic of China invaded Tibet in 1949/50, it created a new source of conflict. This was highlighted when, following the Tibetan national uprising against the Chinese and my flight to India in 1959, tensions between China and India escalated into the border war in 1962. Today large numbers of troops are again massed on both sides of the Himalayan border and tension is once more dangerously high.

The real issue, of course, is not the Indo-Tibetan border demarcation. It is China's illegal occupation of Tibet, which has given it direct access to the Indian sub-continent. The Chinese authorities have attempted to confuse the issue by claiming that Tibet has always been a part of China. This is untrue. Tibet was a fully independent state when the People's Liberation Army invaded the country in 1949/50.

Since Tibetan emperors unified Tibet, over a thousand years ago, our country was able to maintain its independence until the middle of this century. At times Tibet extended its influence over neighbouring countries and peoples and, in other periods, came itself under the influence of powerful foreign rulers—the Mongol Khans, the Gorkhas of Nepal, the Manchu Emperors, and the British in India.

It is, of course, not uncommon for states to be subjected to foreign influence or interference. Although so-called satellite relationships are perhaps the clearest examples of this, most major powers exert influence over less powerful allies or neighbours. As the most authoritative legal studies have shown, in Tibet's case, the country's occasional subjection to foreign influence never entailed a loss of independence. And there can be no doubt that when Peking's communist armies entered Tibet, Tibet was in all respects an independent state.

China's aggression, condemned by virtually all nations of the free world, was a flagrant violation of international law. As China's military occupation of Tibet continues, the world should remember that though Tibetans have lost their freedom, under international law Tibet today is still an independent state under illegal occupation.

It is not my purpose to enter into a political/legal discussion here concerning Tibet's status. I just wish to emphasize the obvious and undisputed fact that we Tibetans are a distinct people with our own culture, language, religion, and history. But for China's occupation, Tibet would still, today, fulfill its natural role as a buffer state maintaining and promoting peace in Asia.

It is my sincere desire, as well as that of the Tibetan people, to restore to Tibet, her invaluable role, by converting the entire country comprising the three Provinces of U-Tsang, Kham, and Amdo—once more into a place of stability, peace, and harmony. In the best of Buddhist tradition, Tibet would extend its services and hospitality to all who further the cause of world peace and the well-being of mankind and the natural environment we share.

Despite the holocaust inflicted upon our people in the past decades of occupation, I have always strived to find a solution through direct and honest discussions with the Chinese. In 1982, following the change of leadership in China and the establishment of direct contacts with the government in Peking, I sent my representatives to Peking to open talks concerning the future of my country and people.

We entered the dialogue with a sincere and positive attitude and with a willingness to take into account the legitimate needs of the People's Republic of China. I hoped that this attitude would be reciprocated and that a solution could eventually be found which would satisfy and safeguard the aspirations and interest of both parties. Unfortunately, China has consistently responded to our efforts in a defensive manner, as though our detailing of Tibet's very real difficulties was criticism for its own sake.

To our even greater dismay, the Chinese government misused the opportunity for a genuine dialogue. Instead of addressing the real issues facing the six million Tibetan people, China has attempted to reduce the question of Tibet to a discussion of my own personal status.

It is against this background and in response to the tremendous support and encouragement I have been given by you and other persons I have met during this trip, that I wish today to clarify the principal issues and to propose, in a spirit of openness and conciliation, a first step towards a lasting solution. I hope this may contribute to a future of friendship and cooperation with all of our neighbours, including the Chinese people.

This peace plan contains five basic components:

1. Transformation of the whole of Tibet into a zone of peace;
2. Abandonment of China's population transfer policy which threatens the very existence of the Tibetans as a people;
3. Respect for the Tibetan people's fundamental human rights and democratic freedoms;
4. Restoration and protection of Tibet's natural environment and the abandonment of China's use of Tibet for the production of nuclear weapons and dumping of nuclear waste;
5. Commencement of earnest negotiations on the future status of Tibet and of relations between the Tibetan and Chinese peoples.

Let me explain these five components.

1

I propose that the whole of Tibet, including the eastern provinces of Kham and Amdo, be transformed into a zone of 'Ahimsa', a Hindi term used to mean a state of peace and non-violence. [italics added]

The establishment of such a peace zone would be in keeping with Tibet's historical role as a peaceful and neutral Buddhist nation and buffer state separating the continent's great powers. It would also be in keeping with Nepal's proposal to proclaim Nepal a peace zone and with China's declared support for such a proclamation. The peace zone proposed by Nepal would have a much greater impact if it were to include Tibet and neighbouring areas.

The establishment of a peace zone in Tibet would require withdrawal of Chinese troops and military installations from the country, troops and military installations from the Himalayan regions bordering Tibet. This would be achieved under an international agreement which would satisfy China's legitimate security needs and build trust among the Tibetan, Indian, Chinese, and other peoples of region. This is in everyone's best interest, particularly that of China and India, as it would enhance their security, while reducing the economic burden of maintaining high troops concentrations on the disputed Himalayan border.

Historically, relations between China and India were never strained. It was only when Chinese armies marched into Tibet, creating for the first time a common border, that tensions arose between these two powers, ultimately leading to the 1962 war. Since then numerous dangerous incidents have continued to occur. A restoration of good relations between the world's two most populous countries would be greatly facilitated if they were separated—as they were throughout history—by a large and friendly buffer region.

To improve relations between the Tibetan people and the Chinese, the first requirement is the creation of trust. After the holocaust of the last decades in which over one million Tibetans—one sixth of the population— lost their lives and at least as many lingered in prison camps because of their religious beliefs and love of freedom, only a withdrawal of Chinese troops could start a genuine process of reconciliation. The vast occupation force in Tibet is a daily reminder to the Tibetans of the oppression and suffering they have all experienced. A troop withdrawal would be an essential signal that in future a meaningful relationship might be established with the Chinese, based on friendship and trust.

2

The population transfer of Chinese into Tibet, which the government in Peking pursues in order to force a 'final solution' to the Tibetan problem by reducing the Tibetan population to an insignificant and disenfranchised minority in Tibet itself, must be stopped. [italics added]

The massive transfer of Chinese civilians into Tibet in violation of the Fourth Geneva Convention (1949), threatens the very existence of the Tibetans as a distinct people. In the eastern parts of our country, the Chinese now greatly outnumber Tibetans. In the Amdo province, for example, where I was born, there are, according to Chinese statistics, 2.5 million Chinese and only 750,000 Tibetans. Even in the so-called Tibet Autonomous Region (that is, central and western Tibet), Chinese government sources now confirm that Chinese outnumber Tibetans.

The Chinese population transfer policy is not new. It has been systematically applied to other areas before. Earlier in this century, the

Manchus were a distinct race with their own culture and traditions. Today only two to three million Manchurians are left in Manchuria, where 75 million Chinese have settled. In Eastern Turkestan, which the Chinese now call Sinkiang, the Chinese population has grown from 200,000 in 1949 to 7 million, more than half of the total population of 13 million. In the wake of the Chinese colonization of Inner Mongolia, Chinese number 8.5 million, Mongols 2.5 million.

Today in the whole of Tibet 7.5 million Chinese settlers have already been sent, outnumbering the Tibetan population of 6 million. In central and western Tibet, now referred to by the Chinese as the 'Tibet Autonomous Region,' Chinese source admit the 1.9 million Tibetans already constitute a minority of the region's population. These numbers do not take the estimated 300,000–500,000 troops in Tibet into account—250,000 of them in the so-called Tibet Autonomous Region.

For the Tibetans to survive as a people, it is imperative that the population transfer is stopped and Chinese settlers return to China. Otherwise, Tibetans will soon be no more than a tourist attraction and a relic of a noble past.

3

Fundamental human rights and democratic freedoms must be respected in Tibet. The Tibetan people must once again be free to develop culturally, intellectually, economically, and spiritually, and to exercise basic democratic freedoms. [italics added]

Human rights violations in Tibet are among the most serious in the world. Discrimination is practiced in Tibet under a policy of 'apartheid' which the Chinese call 'segregation and assimilation'. Tibetans are, at best, second class citizens in their own country. Deprived of all basic democratic rights and freedoms, they exist under a colonial administration in which all real power is wielded by Chinese officials of the Communist Party and the army.

Although the Chinese government allows Tibetans to rebuild some Buddhist monasteries and to worship in them, it still forbids serious study and teaching of religion. Only a small number of people, approved by the Communist Party, are permitted to join the monasteries.

While Tibetans in exile exercise their democratic rights under a constitution promulgated by me in 1963, thousands of our countrymen suffer in
prisons and labour camps in Tibet for their religious or political convictions.

4

Serious efforts must be made to restore the natural environment in Tibet. Tibet
should not be used for the production of nuclear weapons and the dumping of
nuclear waste. [italics added]

Tibetans have a great respect for all forms of life. This inherent feeling is
enhanced by the Buddhist faith, which prohibits the harming of all sentient
beings, whether human or animal. Prior to the Chinese invasion, Tibet was
an unspoiled wilderness sanctuary in a unique natural environment. Sadly,
in the past decades the wildlife and the forests of Tibet have been almost
totally destroyed by the Chinese. The effects on Tibet's delicate environment
have been devastating. What little is left in Tibet must be protected and
efforts must be made to restore the environment to its balanced state.

China uses Tibet for the production of nuclear weapons and may also
have started dumping nuclear waste in Tibet. Not only does China plan to
dispose of its own nuclear waste but also that of other countries, who have
already agreed to pay Peking to dispose of their toxic materials.

The dangers present are obvious. Not only living generations, but future
generations are threatened by China's lack of concern for Tibet's unique
and delicate environment.

5

Negotiations on the future status of Tibet and the relationship between the
Tibetan and Chinese people should be started in earnest. [italics added]

We wish to approach this subject in a reasonable and realistic way, in a
spirit of frankness and conciliation and with a view to finding a solution
that is in the long term interest of all: the Tibetans, the Chinese, and all other
peoples concerned. Tibetans and Chinese are distinct peoples, each with
their own country, history, culture, language, and way of life. Differences
among people must be recognized and respected. They need not, however,
form obstacles to genuine co-operation where this is in the mutual benefit

of both peoples. It is my sincere belief that if the concerned parties were to meet and discuss their future with an open mind and a sincere desire to find a satisfactory and just solution, a breakthrough could be achieved. We must all exert ourselves to be reasonable and wise, and to meet in a spirit of frankness and understanding.

Let me end on a personal note. I wish to thank you for the concern and support which you and so many of your colleagues and fellow citizens have expressed for the plight of oppressed people everywhere. The fact that you have publicly shown your sympathy for us Tibetans, has already had a positive impact on the lives of our people inside Tibet. I ask for your continued support in this critical time in our country's history.

Thank you.

Framework for Sino-Tibetan Negotiations

We are living today in a very interdependent world. One nation's problems can no longer be solved by itself. Without a sense of universal responsibility our very survival is in danger. I have, therefore, always believed in the need for better understanding, closer co-operation and greater respect among the various nations of the world. The European Parliament is an inspiring example. Out of the chaos of war, those who were once enemies have, in a single generation, learned to co-exist and to co-operate. I am, therefore, particularly pleased and honoured to address the gathering at the European Parliament.

As you know, my own country—Tibet—is undergoing a very difficult period. The Tibetans—particularly those who live under Chinese occupation—yearn for freedom and justice and a self-determined future, so that they are able to fully preserve their unique identity and live in peace with their neighbours.

For over a thousand years we Tibetans have adhered to spiritual and environmental values in order to maintain the delicate balance of life across the high plateau on which we live. Inspired by the Buddha's message of non-violence and compassion and protected by our mountains, we sought to respect every form of life and to abandon war as an instrument of national policy.

Our history, dating back more than two thousand years, has been one of independence. At no time since the founding of our nation in 127 BC, have we Tibetans conceded our sovereignty to a foreign power. As with all nations, Tibet experienced periods in which our neighbours, Mongol, Manchu, Chinese, British and the Gorkhas of Nepal sought to establish influence over us. These eras have been brief and the Tibetan people have never accepted them as constituting a loss of our national sovereignty. In fact, there have been occasions when Tibetan rulers conquered vast areas of China and other neighbouring states. This, however, does not mean that we Tibetans can lay claim to these territories.

In 1949 the People's Republic of China forcibly invaded Tibet. Since that time Tibet has endured the darkest period in its history. More than a million of our people have died as a result of the occupation. Thousands of monasteries were reduced to ruins. A generation has grown up deprived of education, economic opportunity, and a sense of its own national character. Though the current Chinese leadership has implemented certain reforms, it is also promoting a massive population transfer onto the Tibetan plateau. This policy has already reduced the six million Tibetans to a minority. Speaking for all Tibetans, I must sadly inform you, our tragedy continues.

I have always urged my people not to resort to violence in their effort to redress their suffering. Yet I believe all people have the moral right to peacefully protest injustice. Unfortunately, the demonstrations in Tibet have been violently suppressed by the Chinese police and military. I will continue to counsel for non-violence, but unless China forsakes the brutal methods it employs, Tibetans cannot be responsible for a further deterioration in the situation.

Every Tibetan hopes and prays for the full restoration of our nation's independence. Thousands of our people have sacrificed their lives and our whole nation has suffered in this struggle. Even in recent months, Tibetans have bravely sacrificed their lives to achieve this precious goal. On the other hand, the Chinese totally fail to recognize the Tibetan people's aspirations and continue to pursue a policy of brutal suppression.

I have thought for a long time on how to achieve a realistic solution to my nation's plight. My cabinet and I solicited the opinion of many friends and concerned persons. As a result, on September 21, 1987, at the Congressional Human Rights Caucus in Washington, D.C., I announced a Five Point Peace Plan for Tibet. In it I called for the conversion of Tibet into a zone of peace, a sanctuary in which humanity and nature can live together in harmony. I also called for respect for human rights and democratic ideals, environmental protection, and a halt to the Chinese population transfer into Tibet.

The fifth point of the Peace Plan called for earnest negotiations between the Tibetans and the Chinese. We have, therefore, taken the initiative to formulate some thoughts which, we hope, may serve as a basis for resolving the issue of Tibet. I would like to take this opportunity to inform the distinguished gathering here of the main points of our thinking.

The whole of Tibet known as Cholka-Sum (U-Tsang, Kham, and Amdo) should become a self-governing democratic entity founded on law by agreement of the people for the common good and the protection of themselves and their environment, in association with the People's Republic of China.

The Government of the People's Republic of China could remain responsible for Tibet's foreign policy. The Government of Tibet should, however, develop and maintain relations, through its own Foreign Affairs Bureau, in the fields of commerce, education, culture, religion, tourism, science, sports, and other non-political activities. Tibet should join international organizations concerned with such activities.

The Government of Tibet should be founded on a constitution or basic law. The basic law should provide for a democratic system of government entrusted with the task of ensuring economic equality, social justice and protection of the environment. This means that the Government of Tibet will have the right to decide on all affairs relating to Tibet and the Tibetans.

As individual freedom is the real source and potential of any society's development, the Government of Tibet would seek to ensure this freedom by full adherence to the Universal Declaration of Human Rights including the rights to speech, assembly, and religion. Because religion constitutes the source of Tibet's national identity, and spiritual values lie at the very heart of Tibet's rich culture, it would be the special duty of the Government of Tibet to safeguard and develop its practice.

The government should be comprised of a popularly elected Chief Executive, a bi-cameral legislative, branch, [sic] and an independent judicial system. Its seat should be in Lhasa.

The social and economic system of Tibet should be determined in accordance with the wishes of the Tibetan people, bearing in mind especially the need to raise the standard of living of the entire population.

The Government of Tibet would pass strict laws to protect wildlife and plant life. The exploitation of natural resources would be carefully regulated. The manufacture, testing, and stockpiling of nuclear weapons and other armaments must be prohibited, as well as the use of nuclear power and other technologies which produce hazardous waste. It would be the Government of Tibet's goal to transform Tibet into our planet's largest natural preserve.

A regional peace conference should be called to ensure that Tibet becomes a genuine sanctuary of peace through demilitarization. Until such a peace conference can be convened and demilitarization and neutralization achieved, China could have the right to maintain a restricted number of military installations in Tibet. These must be solely for defence purposes.

In order to create an atmosphere of trust conducive to fruitful negotiations, the Chinese Government should cease its human rights violations in Tibet and abandon its policy of transferring Chinese to Tibet.

These are the thoughts we have in mind. I am aware that many Tibetans will be disappointed by the moderate stand they represent. Undoubtedly, there will be much discussion in the coming months within our own community, both in Tibet and in exile. This, however, is an essential and invaluable part of any process of change. I believe these thoughts represent the most realistic means by which to re-establish Tibet's separate identity and restore the fundamental right to the Tibetan people while accommodating China's own interests. I would like to emphasize, however, that whatever the outcome of the negotiations with the Chinese may be, the Tibetan people themselves must be the ultimate deciding authority. Therefore, any proposal will contain a comprehensive procedural plan to ascertain the wishes of the Tibetan people in a nationwide referendum.

I would like to take this opportunity to state that I do not wish to take any active part in the Government of Tibet. Nevertheless, I will continue to work as much as I can for the well-being and happiness of the Tibetan people as long as it is necessary.

We are ready to present a proposal to the Government of the People's Republic of China based on the thoughts I have presented. A negotiating team representing the Tibetan government has been selected. We are prepared to meet with the Chinese to discuss details of such a proposal aimed at achieving an equitable solution.

We are encouraged by the keen interest being shown in our situation by a growing number of governments and political leaders, including former President Jimmy Carter of the United States. We are encouraged by the recent changes in China which have brought about a new group of leadership, more pragmatic and liberal.

We urge the Chinese Government and leadership to give serious and substantive consideration to ideas I have described. Only dialogue and a willingness to look with honesty and clarity at the reality of Tibet can lead to a viable solution. We wish to conduct discussions with the Chinese Government bearing in mind the larger interests of humanity. Our proposal will therefore be made in a spirit of conciliation and we hope that the Chinese will respond accordingly.

My country's unique history and profound spiritual heritage render it ideally suited for fulfilling the role of a sanctuary of peace at the heart of Asia, its historic status as a neutral buffer state, contributing to the stability of the entire continent, can be restored. Peace and security for Asia as well as for the world at large can be enhanced. In the future, Tibet need no longer be an occupied land, oppressed by force, unproductive, and scarred by suffering. It can become a free haven where humanity and nature live in harmonious balance; a creative model for the resolution of tensions afflicting many areas throughout the world.

The Chinese leadership needs to realize that colonial rule over occupied territories is today anachronistic. A genuine union or association can only come about voluntarily, when there is satisfactory benefit to all the parties concerned. The European Community is a clear example of this. On the other hand, even one country or community can break into two or more entities when there is a lack of trust or benefit, and when force is used as the principal means of rule.

I would like to end by making a special appeal to the honorable members of the European Parliament and through them to their respective constituencies to extend their support to our efforts. A resolution of the Tibetan problem within the framework that we propose will not only be for the mutual benefit of the Tibetan and Chinese people but will also contribute to regional and global peace and stability. I thank you for providing me the opportunity to share my thoughts with you.

(Speech by H.H. the Dalai Lama at the European Parliament, Strasbourg, June 15, 1988).

Appendix IV

Nobel Peace Laureate Joint Declaration, November 6, 1998*

WE, THE UNDERSIGNED, have gathered in Charlottesville to participate in a conference presented by the University of Virginia and the Institute for Asian Democracy on human rights, conflict, and reconciliation. We wish to use this opportunity to reaffirm our missions to the international community.

Whereas, the children of the world are oftentimes victims of conflict and require protection, we must establish safe havens for children of war and advance the cause of children's rights;

Whereas, the vast majority of arms sales are to non-democratic governments and scarce resources are devoted to education, housing, and health, we call upon all nations to adopt the International Code of Conduct on Arms Transfers and to dedicate their resources to erasing the gap between the world's rich minority and its poor majority;

Whereas, in order to find a peaceful resolution to the Tibet issue, we urge that the Chinese government enter into negotiations that will serve the interests of the Tibetan and Chinese peoples. Also, that these negotiations be conducted expeditiously, as an indication of China's good will and sincere intent;

* Jeffrey Hopkins (ed.), *The Art of Peace: Nobel Peace Laureates Discuss Human Rights and Conflict Resolution,* Ithaca, New York: Snow Lion Publications, 2000, pp. 227–9.

Whereas, the U.N. General Assembly has adopted resolutions calling for upholding the will of the Burmese people as expressed in the 1990 elections and further calls for the State Peace and Development Council to enter into a substantive political dialogue with Aung San Suu Kyi and representatives of ethnic groups as the best means of promoting national reconciliation and democracy, we urge that the U.N. resolution be implemented fully;

Whereas, the dignity of the indigenous peoples of the world continues to be marginalized, we must accept and respect other peoples, communities, and cultures, and integrate the mosaic languages, traditions, and peoples into the community of nations;

Whereas, the world community has responded to the global landmine crisis with the Mine Ban Treaty, already signed by 133 governments and ratified by 49, we call upon the signatory states to ratify and non-signatories to join as soon as possible and all governments to expand their commitment to mine clearance and victim assistance;

We resolve that, it is our hope that this declaration will advance not only our own initiatives but bring about a more peaceful world. Moreover, we urge the international community to seek new ways of promoting justice, reconciliation, and peace in societies making the transition from repression to democracy and from conflict to civil societies under the rule of law.

Betty Williams, Northern Ireland (1976)

Archbishop Desmond Tutu, South Africa (1984)

President Oscar Arias Sánchez, Costa Rica (1987)

His Holiness the Dalai Lama, Tibet (1989)

Harn Yawnghwe, participating on behalf of Aung San Suu Kyi, Burma (1991)

Rigoberta Menchú Tum, Guatemala (1992)

José Ramos-Horta, East Timor (1996)

Jody Williams, United States (1997)

Bobby Muller, United States (1997), for the International Campaign to Ban Landmines.

Appendix V

Table of the 14 Dalai Lamas*

1.	Gendun Drup	1391–1474
2.	Gendun Gyatso	1476–1542
3.	Sonam Gyatso	1543–1588
4.	Yonten Gyatso	1589–1616
5.	Ngawang Losang Gyatso	1617–1682
6.	Tsangyang Gyatso	1683–1703
7.	Kelsang Gyatso	1708–1757
8.	Jampel Gyatso	1758–1804
9.	Lungtog Gyatso	1805–1815
10.	Tsultrim Gyatso	1816–1837
11.	Khedrup Gyatso	1838–1855
12.	Trinle Gyatso	1856–1875
13.	Tubten Gyatso	1876–1933
14.	Tenzin Gyatso	1935–

* Gill Farrer-Halls, *The World of the Dalai Lama: An Inside Look at His Life, His People, and His Vision,* Wheaton, Illinois: Quest Books, 1998, p. 61.

Appendix VI

Universal Declaration of Human Rights*
Adopted and Proclaimed by General
Assembly Resolution 217 A (III) of
10 December 1948

On December 10, 1948 the General Assembly of the United Nations adopted and proclaimed the Universal Declaration of Human Rights the full text of which appears in the following pages. Following this historic act the Assembly called upon all Member countries to publicize the text of the Declaration and 'to cause it to be disseminated, displayed, read and expounded principally in schools and other educational institutions, without distinction based on the political status of countries or territories.'

Preamble

Whereas recognition of the inherent dignity and of the equal and inalienable rights of all members of the human family is the foundation of freedom, justice and peace in the world,

Whereas disregard and contempt for human rights have resulted in barbarous acts which have outraged the conscience of mankind, and the advent of a world in which human beings shall enjoy freedom of speech and belief and freedom from fear and want has been proclaimed as the highest aspirations of the common people,

Whereas it is essential, if man is not to be compelled to have recourse, as a last resort, to rebellion against tyranny and oppression, that human rights should be protected by the rule of law,

* 'Universal Declaration of Human Rights', *www.un.org/overview/rights.html*

Whereas it is essential to promote the development of friendly relations between nations,

Whereas the people of the United Nations have in the Charter reaffirmed their faith in fundamental human rights, in the dignity and worth of the human person and in the equal rights of men and women and have determined to promote social progress and better standards of life in larger freedom,

Whereas Member States have pledged themselves to achieve, in cooperation with the United Nations, the promotion of universal respect for and observance of human rights and fundamental freedoms,

Whereas a common understanding of these rights and freedoms is of the greatest importance for the full realization of this pledge,

NOW, THEREFORE, THE GENERAL ASSEMBLY proclaims THIS UNIVERSAL DECLARATION OF HUMAN RIGHTS as a common standard of achievement for all peoples and all nations, to the end that every individual and every organ of society, keeping this Declaration constantly in mind, shall strive by teaching and education to promote respect for these rights and freedoms and by progressive measures, national and international, to secure their universal and effective recognition and observance, both among the peoples of Member States themselves and among the peoples for territories under their jurisdiction.

Article 1

All human beings are born free and equal in dignity and rights. They are endowed with reason and conscience and should act towards one another in a spirit of brotherhood.

Article 2

Everyone is entitled to all rights and freedoms set forth in this Declaration, without distinction of any kind, such as race, colour, sex, language, religion, political or other opinion, national or social origin, property, birth or other status.

Furthermore, no distinction shall be made on the basis of the political, jurisdictional or international status of the country or territory to which a person belongs, whether it be independent, trust, non-self-governing or under any other limitation of sovereignty.

Article 3

Everyone has the right to life, liberty, and security of person.

Article 4

No one shall be held in slavery or servitude; slavery and the slave trade shall be prohibited in all their forms.

Article 5

No one shall be subjected to torture or to cruel, inhuman or degrading treatment or punishment.

Article 6

Everyone has the right to recognition every where as a person before the law.

Article 7

All are equal before the law and are entitled without any discrimination to equal protection of the law. All are entitled to equal protection against any discrimination in violation of this Declaration and against any incitement to such discrimination.

Article 8

Everyone has the right to an effective remedy by the competent national tribunals for acts violating the fundamental rights granted him by the constitution or by law.

Article 9

No one shall be subjected to arbitrary arrest, detention, or exile.

Article 10

Everyone is entitled in full equality to a fair and public hearing by an independent and impartial tribunal, in the determination of his rights and obligations and of any criminal charge against him.

Article 11

Everyone charged with a penal offence has the right to be presumed innocent until proved guilty according to law in a public trial at which he has had all the guarantees necessary for his defence.

No one shall be held guilty of any penal offence of account of any act or omission which did not constitute a penal offence, under national or international law, at the time when it was committed. Nor shall a heavier penalty be imposed than the one that was applicable at the time the penal offence was committed.

Article 12

No one shall be subjected to arbitrary interference with his privacy, family, home, or correspondence, nor to attacks upon his honour and reputation. Everyone has the right to the protection of the law against such interference or attacks.

Article 13

Everyone has the right to freedom of movement and residence within the borders of each State.

Everyone has the right to leave any country, including his own, and to return to his country.

Article 14

Everyone has the right to seek and to enjoy in other countries asylum from persecution.

This right may not be invoked in the case of prosecutions genuinely arising from non-political crimes or from acts contrary to the purposes and principles of the United Nations.

Article 15

Everyone has the right to a nationality.

No one shall be arbitrarily deprived of his nationality nor denied the right to change his nationality.

Article 16

Men and women of full age, without any limitation due to race, nationality, or religion, have the right to marry and to found a family. They are entitled to equal rights as to marriage, during marriage, and at its dissolution.

Marriage shall be entered into only with the free and full consent of the intending spouses.

The family is the natural and fundamental group unit of society and is entitled to protection by society and the State.

Article 17

Everyone has the right to own property alone as well as in association with others.

No one shall be arbitrarily deprived of his property.

Article 18

Everyone has the right to freedom of thought, conscience, and religion: this right includes freedom to change his religion or belief, and freedom, either alone or in community with others in public or private, to manifest his religion or belief in teaching, practice, worship, and observance.

Article 19

Everyone has the right to freedom of opinion and expression; this right includes freedom to hold opinions without interference and to seek, receive, and impart information and ideas through any media and regardless of frontiers.

Article 20

Everyone has the right to freedom of peaceful assembly and association.

No one may be compelled to belong to an association.

Article 21

Everyone has the right to take part in the government of his country, directly or through freely chosen representatives.

Everyone has the right to equal access to public service in his country.

The will of the people shall be the basis of the authority of government; this will shall be expressed in periodic and genuine elections which shall be by universal and equal suffrage and shall be held by secret vote or by equivalent free voting procedures.

Article 22

Everyone, as a member of society, has the right to social security and is entitled to realization, through national effort and international co-operation and in accordance with the organization and resources or each State, of the economic, social, and cultural rights indispensable for his dignity and the free development of his personality.

Article 23

Everyone has the right to work, to free choice of employment, to just and favourable conditions of work and to protection against unemployment.

Everyone, without any discrimination, has the right to equal pay for equal work.

Everyone who works has the right to just and favourable remuneration ensuring for himself and his family an existence worthy of human dignity, and supplemented, if necessary, by other means of social protection.

Everyone has the right to form and to join trade unions for the protection of his interests.

Article 24

Everyone has the right to rest and leisure, including reasonable limitation of working hours and periodic holidays with pay.

Article 25

Everyone has the right to a standard of living adequate for the health and well-being of himself and of his family, including food, clothing, housing and medical care, and necessary social services, and the right to security in the event of unemployment, sickness, disability, widowhood, old age, or other lack of livelihood in circumstances beyond his control.

Motherhood and childhood are entitled to special care and assistance. All children, whether born in or out of wedlock, shall enjoy the same social protection.

Article 26

Everyone has the right to education. Education shall be free, at least in the elementary and fundamental stages. Elementary education shall be compulsory. Technical and professional education shall be made generally available and higher education shall be equally accessible to all on the basis of merit.

Education shall be directed to the full development of the human personality and to the strengthening of respect for human rights and fundamental freedoms. It shall promote understanding, tolerance, and friendship among all nations, racial or religious groups, and shall further the activities of the United Nations for the maintenance of peace.

Parents have a prior right to choose the kind of education that shall be given to their children.

Article 27

Everyone has the right freely to participate in the cultural life of the community, to enjoy the arts and share in scientific advancement and its benefits.

Everyone has the right to the protection of the moral and material interests resulting from any scientific, literary or artistic production of which he is the author.

Article 28

Everyone is entitled to a social and international order in which the rights and freedoms set forth in this Declaration can be fully realized.

Article 29

Everyone has duties to the community in which alone the free and full development of his personality is possible.

In the exercise of his rights and freedoms, everyone shall be subjected only to such limitations as are determined by law solely for the purpose of securing due recognition and respect for the rights and freedoms of others and of meeting the just requirements of morality, public order, and the general welfare in a democratic society.

These rights and freedoms may in no case be exercised contrary to the purpose and principles of the United Nations.

Article 30

Nothing in this Declaration may be interpreted as implying for any State, group, or person any right to engage in any activity or to perform any act aimed at the destruction of any of the rights and freedoms set forth herein.

Glossary

Bodhichitta	Arising of the awakening mind.
Bodhisattva	A being who has decided to bring all beings to enlightenment and is following the path of enlightenment. A sublime bodhisattva is one who has attained one of the ten bodhisattva levels.
Bhikshu	Fully ordained Buddhist monk.
Buddha	One who is enlightened. One who has dispelled the darkness of the two obscurations (of negative emotions and conceptual views) and developed the two kinds of omniscience (knowing the nature of phenomena and knowing the multiplicity of phenomena).
Buddha Shakyamuni	The historical Buddha, born as Siddhartha of the Shakya clan in India two thousand five hundred years ago.
Caste	System describing Hindu hereditary social class.
Chenresig	(Sanskrit *Avalokiteshvara*). The Bodhisattva embodying the compassion of all the Buddhas. The Dalai Lama is believed by his people to be an incarnation of Chenresig.
Deity yoga	A Vajrayana practice centered on a deity that represents one's own potential for enlightenment. The deity can be male or female, peaceful or wrathful, and is chosen according to the practitioner's nature. Deity yoga is a swift means to transform one's ordinary, deluded perceptions into wisdom.
Dharamsala/ McLeod Ganj	The area in India in the State of Himachal Pradesh where the Dalai Lama and Tibetan refugees have settled.
Dharma	This term has many different meanings. In the present context, it is synonymous with Buddhadharma and designates all the

teachings of the Buddha, the Buddhas, and the enlightened masters. According to Buddhist tradition, these teachings reveal the path to awakening. The Dharma has two main aspects: the transmission Dharma, that is, the words that serve as a support for the teachings; and the Dharma of spiritual realization resulting from authentic spiritual practice.

Eightfold path

The Nobel Eight-fold Path consists of eight steps which are: (1) Right faith (*samyag drsti*), (2) right resolve (*sankalpa*), (3) right speech (*vak*), (4) right action (*karmanta*), (5) right living (*ajiva*), (6) right effort (*vyayama*), (7) right thought (*smrti*) and (8) right concentration (*samadhi*). Buddha's ethical 'middle path' is like the 'golden mean' of Aristotle. Self-indulgence and self-mortification are equally ruled out. In his very first Sermon at Saranatha he said: 'There are two extremes, O monks, from which he who leads a religious life must abstain. One is life of pleasure, devoted to desire and enjoyment: that is base, ignoble, unspiritual, unworthy, unreal. The other is a life of mortification: it is gloomy, unworthy, unreal. The Perfect One, O monks, is removed from both these extremes and has discovered the way which lies between them, The Middle Way which enlightens the eyes, enlightens the mind, which leads to rest, to knowledge, to enlightenment, to *Nirvana*.

This is the Noble Eight-fold Path contained in the Fourth Noble Truth.

The Four Noble Truths

The Four Noble Truths (*arya satya*) are:

(a) There is suffering (*duhkha)*.

(b) There is cause of suffering (*duhkha-samudaya*).

(c) There is cessation of suffering (*duhkha-nirodha*).

(d) There is a way leading to this cessation of suffering (*duhkha-nirodha-gamini pratipat*).

There is an ethical and spiritual path by following which misery may be removed and liberation attained. This is the Noble Eight-fold path.

Emotions

(Negative, conflicting, or afflictive; in Sanskrit *klesha*). Mental phenomena that assail the body and mind and lead to harmful actions, creating a state of mental torment.

Emptiness	(Or voidness or *shunyata*). The realization of emptiness is a key practice of Mahayana Buddhism.
Geshe (in Tibetan *dgebshes*)	This literally means 'spiritual friend'. The title 'Geshe' designates a Doctorate of Philosophy in the monastic system.
Karma	A fundamental principle of Indian religions based on the conception of human life as a link in a chain of lives, each life being determined by acts accomplished in a previous life.
Lama	(Meaning in Sanskrit *guru*). Literally 'heavy' or 'loaded' (with qualities). Designates a person who is capable of leading others to spiritual realization; teacher.
Mahayana	The Great Vehicle, or the Vehicle of the Bodhisattvas. It is great because its aim is full Buddhahood for all beings.
Mind	In the Tibetan Buddhist context, the mind is not a real entity but a succession of moments of consciousness that we perceive as a continuity. The ultimate nature of the mind has two inseparable aspects: emptiness (*shunyata*), its essence; and luminosity, the nature of its cognitive faculties.
Nagarjuna	(First–Second century). Indian Buddhist master who expounded the Middle Way (*Madhyamaka*) teachings.
Nirvana	The state of deliverance from suffering or *samsara*.
Right	'That which results in happiness.'
Samsara	The world of suffering and ignorance created by karma; also called cyclic existence.
Sangha	The community of Dharma practitioners, from ordinary beings to Bodhisattvas.
Vipashyana	Clear insight meditation.
Vinaya	That portion of the Buddhist canon containing the teachings on monastic discipline.
Wisdom	The ability to understand correctly, usually with the particular sense of understanding emptiness.
Wrong	That which results in sufferings. Anything that produces an unpleasant or painful effect.

Bibliography

This Bibliography is divided into primary and secondary sources. The Primary Bibliography includes the following:

A.i. Books by The Dalai Lama;

A.ii. Articles by The Dalai Lama;

A.iii. Books on The Dalai Lama (includes books figuring The Dalai Lama's writings and interviews with him; Publications from Dharamsala and related Tibet Publications);

A.iv. Articles and interviews in journals with/on The Dalai Lama (includes journals published from Dharamsala and related Tibet journals published in Dharamsala and elsewhere);

B. Articles by/on/with The Dalai Lama in newspapers and periodicals;

C. Internet sources on The Dalai Lama.

It is not possible to mention the authorship of The XIV Dalai Lama in a standard bibliographical format, since different works cite his name differently. For example he is mentioned as H.H. The Dalai Lama; H.H. The Dalai Lama of Tibet, Tenzin Gyatso; H.H. XIV Dalai Lama; His Holiness Tenzin Gyatso The Fourteenth Dalai Lama; His Holiness the Dalai Lama; His Holiness The XIV Dalai Lama; His Holiness The XIV Dalai Lama of Tibet; His Holiness, The Dalai Lama of Tibet; Tenzin Gyatso the Fourteenth Dalai Lama; Tenzin Gyatso, His Holiness the 14th Dalai Lama; Tenzin Gyatso, His Holiness the Dalai Lama; The Dalai Lama; The Fourteenth Dalai Lama His Holiness Tenzin Gyatso—as can be discerned from sections A.i. and A.ii.

The Secondary Bibliography includes the following: books, articles, newspapers/periodicals, internet sources, and unpublished theses.

Primary Sources

A.i

Books by The Dalai Lama

Dialogues on Universal Responsibility and Education With His Holiness The Dalai Lama and Others: Workshop Papers in Print, Dharamsala: Library of Tibetan Works and Archives, 1995.

H.H. The Dalai Lama of Tibet, Tenzin Gyatso, *The Dalai Lama at Harvard: Lectures On the Buddhist Path to Peace,* edited and trans. by Jeffrey Hopkins, Ithaca, USA: Snow Lion Publications, 1988.

H.H. The Dalai Lama, *Worlds in Harmony: Dialogues on Compassionate Action,* New Delhi: Full Circle, 1998.

Healing Emotions: Conversations with the Dalai Lama on Mindfulness, Emotions and Health, edited by Daniel Goleman, Boston: Shambhala, 1997.

His Holiness Tenzin Gyatso The Fourteenth Dalai Lama, *A Human Approach to World Peace,* London: Wisdom Publications, 1984.

His Holiness The Dalai Lama with Ouaki, Fabien, *Imagine All the People: A Conversation with the Dalai Lama on Money, Politics, and Life as it could Be,* Boston: Wisdom Publications, 1999.

His Holiness The Dalai Lama, *Beyond Dogma: The Challenge of the Modern World,* edited by Marianne Dresser, trans. Alison Anderson, New Delhi: Rupa and Co., (1996) 1997.

———, *Five Point Peace Plan for Tibet: Strasbourg, Proposal,* June 15, 1988, Dharamsala (H.P.): Office of Information and International Relations, Central Tibetan Secretariat, Gangchen Kyishong, n.d.

———, *Spiritual Advice for Buddhists and Christians,* edited by Donald W. Mitchell, New Delhi: New Editions Publishing House, (1998) 1999.

His Holiness the Dalai Lama, *Speeches Statements Articles Interviews: 1987 to June 1995,* Dharamsala: The Department of Information and International Relations, Central Tibetan Administration, Gangchen Kyishong, 1995.

———, *The Heart of Compassion: A Dalai Lama Reader,* Delhi: Full Circle, 1997.

His Holiness the XIV Dalai Lama, *On the Environment: Collected Statements,* Dharamsala: Department of Information and International Relations, Central Tibetan Administration of His Holiness the XIV Dalai Lama, 1995.

His Holiness The Dalai Lama and Carrière, Jean-Claude, *The Power of Buddhism,* Dublin: Newleaf, (1994) 1996.

His Holiness The XIV Dalai Lama, *Path For Spiritual Practice,* New Delhi: Tushita Mahayana Meditation Centre, 1997.

His Holiness, The Dalai Lama of Tibet, *My Land and My People,* New Delhi: Srishti Publishers and Distributors, (1962) 1997.

Tenzin Gyatso His Holiness the Dalai Lama, *Ancient Wisdom, Modern World: Ethics for the New Millennium,* London: Abacus, (1999) 2000.

Tenzin Gyatso, The Fourteenth Dalai Lama, *Universal Responsibility and the Good Heart,* Dharamsala: Library of Tibetan Works and Archives, 1980.

Tenzin Gyatso the Fourteenth Dalai Lama, *Compassion and the Individual,* Boston: Wisdom Publications, (1991), Reprinted 1992.

_____, *The Global Community and the Need for Universal Responsibility,* Boston: Wisdom Publications, 1992.

The Dalai Lama, A Policy of Kindness: An Anthology of Writings By and About the Dalai Lama, edited and compiled by Piburn, Sidney, Delhi: Motilal Banarsidass Publishers Pvt. Ltd., (1990) 1997.

The Dalai Lama, *Freedom In Exile: An Autobiography of the Dalai Lama of Tibet,* London: Abacus, (1990) 1998.

_____, *Message,* Brochure issued on the World Festival of Sacred Music: A Global Quest for Unison, New Delhi: Tibet House, September 4, 1998.

_____, *The Four Noble Truths,* New Delhi: HarperCollins Publishers India, (1997) 1998.

_____, *The Power of Compassion: A Collection of Lectures by His Holiness the XIV Dalai Lama,* trans. by Jinpa Geshe Thupten, New Delhi: HarperCollins Publishers India Pvt. Ltd., (1995) 1998.

The Fourteenth Dalai Lama His Holiness Tenzin Gyatso, *Kindness, Clarity, and Insight,* edited by Hopkins, Jeffrey, and Elizabeth Napper, trans. by Jeffrey Hopkins, New York: Snow Lion Publications, 1984.

The Political Philosophy of His Holiness the XIV Dalai Lama, edited by Shiromany, A.A., New Delhi: Tibetan Parliamentary and Policy Research Centre and Friedrich Naumann Stiftung, 1998.

The Spirit of Tibet: Universal Heritage, Selected Speeches and Writings of H.H. The Dalai Lama XIV, edited by Shiromany, A.A., New Delhi: Tibetan Parliamentary and Policy Research Centre/Allied Publishers Limited, 1995.

The Spirit of Tibet, Vision for Human Liberation: Selected Speeches and Writings of H.H. The XIV Dalai Lama, edited by Shiromany, A.A., New Delhi: Tibetan Parliamentary and Policy Research Centre in Association with Vikas Publishing House, 1996.

A.ii

Articles/Chapters by The Dalai Lama

'China Cannot Escape from Truth', *Tibetan Review,* (Delhi), vol. XXXVI, no. 4, April 2000, pp. 16–17.

'Dalai Lama Cautions in New China Contact', *Tibetan Review*, (Delhi), January 2001, pp. 7–8.

'Dalai Lama on Modern Progress and Ancient Wisdom', *Tibetan Review*, (Delhi), January 2001, p. 15.

'Dalai Lama Says Democracy is Inevitable', *Tibetan Review*, (Delhi), November 2000, p. 10.

H.H. the Dalai Lama, 'Address to Parliament', *The Middle Way: Journal of the Buddhist Society*, (London), vol. 71, no. 3, November 1996, pp. 178–82.

———, 'Address to the Buddhist Society', *The Middle Way: Journal of the Buddhist Society*, (London), vol. 71, no. 3, November 1996, pp. 147–50.

———, 'Universal Responsibility and Human Rights', *Tibetan Review*, (Delhi), vol. XXIV, no. 6, June 1989, pp. 18–19.

H.H. XIV Dalai Lama, 'Meeting-Points in Science and Spirituality', *Tibetan Review*, (Delhi) vol. XVIII, no. 10, October 1983, pp. 12–14.

'His Holiness The Dalai Lama on the Forty-Second Anniversary of Tibetan National Uprising Day 10 March 2001', *Tibetan Bulletin: The Official Journal of the Tibetan Administration*, (Department of Information and International Relations, Gangchen Kyishong, Dharamsala), vol. 5, issue 2, March-June 2001, pp. 18–19.

His Holiness the Dalai Lama, 'A Universal Religion: Kindness for Mankind', *Adarsha: Tibetan Nyingma Buddhist Review*, (Lisboa, Portugal), no.5, autono N-5, 1997, pp. 6–7.

———, 'Turning the Three Wheels of the Dharma', *Tibet House Bulletin*, (New Delhi), vol. 17, no. 2, November 2000, p. 1–4.

His Holiness The Dalai Lama, 'Asian Values and Democracy', *Tibetan Bulletin: The Official Journal of the Tibetan Administration*, (Department of Information and International Relations, Gangchen Kyishong, Dharamsala), vol. 3, Issue 1, January-February 1999, pp. 19–20.

His Holiness the Dalai Lama, 'China and the Future of Tibet,' *Common Voice: Journal of the Allied Committee of the People of Eastern Turkestan, Mongolia, Manchuria and Tibet Presently Under China*, (Gangchen Kyishong: Dharamsala), vol. II, 1992, p. 1–6.

His Holiness The Dalai Lama, 'I Believe …,' *Tibetan Bulletin: The Official Journal of the Tibetan Administration*, (Department of Information and International Relations, Gangchen Kyishong, Dharamsala), vol. 3, issue 1, January–February 1999, p. 29.

———, 'Introduction to the Buddhist Tantric Tradition', *Tibet House Bulletin*, (New Delhi), vol. 14, no. 2, November 1998, pp. 1, 3, and 7.

His Holiness the Dalai Lama, 'Solving the Tibet Problem Needs a Soft Landing, Not a Hard Crash', *Tibetan Bulletin: The Official Journal of the Tibetan*

Administration, (Department of Information and International Relations, Gangchen Kyishong, Dharamsala), September-December 1995, pp. 32–3.

His Holiness The Dalai Lama, 'Statement of His Holiness The Dalai Lama on the 38th Anniversary of Tibetan National Uprising Day–March 10, 1997', *Adarsha: Tibetan Nyingma Buddhist Review,* (Lisboa, Portugal), no. 3/4, January–June, 1997, pp. 6–7.

His Holiness the Dalai Lama, 'The Four Seals in Buddhism', Tushita's XIV Dharma Celebration, (New Delhi: Tushita Mahayana Meditation Centre), 28th January, 2001.

_____, 'Tibet's Case for Self-Determination', *Tibetan Bulletin: The Official Journal of the Tibetan Administration,* (Department of Information and International Relations, Gangchen Kyishong, Dharamsala), May-June 1991, pp. 8–9.

_____, 'What is Buddhism?', *Adarsha: Tibetan Nyigma Buddhist Review,* (Lisboa, Portugal), no. 2, October–December, 1996, pp. 6–7.

His Holiness the Dalai Lama's Millennium Peace Summit Message,' *Tibetan Bulletin: The Official Journal of the Tibetan Administration,* (Department of Information and International Relations, Gangchen Kyishong, Dharamsala), vol. 4, issue 4, September-December 2000, p. 21.

His Holiness the XIV Dalai Lama of Tibet, 'An Ethical Approach to Environmental Protection', in Nancy Nash (ed.), *Tree of Life: Buddhism and Protection of Nature, with a Declaration on Environmental Ethics from His Holiness The Dalai Lama,* Manchester, U.K.: Alliance of Religions and Conservation, (1987) 2nd edn, 1999, p. 15.

His Holiness The XIV Dalai Lama, 'Misconceptions and Realities of the Tibetan Issue', *Tibetan Review,* (Delhi), vol. XII, no. 10, October 1977, pp. 11–13.

His Holiness the XIV Dalai Lama. 'Spiritual Contributions to Social Progress', *Tibetan Review* (Delhi), vol. XVI, no. II, November 1981, pp. 18–19.

His Holiness XIV Dalai Lama, 'Place of Ethics and Morality in Politics', *Tibetan Review,* (Delhi), vol. XIV, no. 7, July 1979, pp. 15–16.

His Holiness's Address on Education,' *Sherig News: Quarterly Newsletter of the Department of Education,* (Gangchen Kyishong, Dharamsala), vol. 3, no. 3, Winter 1999, pp. 1–4.

'International Pressure Best Bet to Get China Talking,' *Tibetan Review,* (Delhi), vol. XXXV, no. 4, April 2000, pp. 21–22.

'Morals for the New Millennium: The Dalai Lama Prescribes "Secular Ethics" for the Ailments of the 21st Century', *Tibetan Bulletin: The Official Journal of the Tibetan Administration,* (Department of Information and International Relations, Gangchen Kyishong, Dharamsala), vol. 4, issue 1, January-April 2000, p. 5.

Statement of His Holiness The Dalai Lama on the 38th Anniversary of Tibetan National Uprising Day', *Tibetan Bulletin: The Official Journal of the Tibetan Administration,* (Department of Information and International Relations, Gangchen Kyishong, Dharamsala), March-April 1997, pp. 5–6.

Statement of His Holiness the Dalai Lama on the 40th Anniversary of the Tibetan National Uprising Day', *Rangzen: The Magazine of the Tibetan Youth Congress,* (McLeod Ganj: Dharamsala), vol. XXIV, no.1/2, Spring/Summer 1999, pp. 8–10.

Tenzin Gyatso, His Holiness the 14th Dalai Lama, 'What Can Religion Contribute to Mankind,' *Chöyang: The Voice of Tibetan Religion and Culture,* (Council for Religious and Cultural Affairs, Gangchen Kyishong, Dharamsala), vol. 1, no. 2, 1987, pp. 2–5.

Tenzin Gyatso, The Fourteenth Dalai Lama, 'An Ethical Approach to Environmental Protection', in Petra K. Kelly, Gert Bastian and Pat Aiello (eds), *The Anguish of Tibet,* Berkeley, California: Parallax Press, 1991, p. 238.

The Dalai Lama, 'Conflicts Based on Religious Differences Are Sad, Futile,' *Tibetan Review,* (Delhi), vol. XXX, no. 2, February 1995, pp. 17–18.

———, 'Eschew Violence', *Tibet Foundation Newsletter,* (London), no. 31, February 2001, p. 3.

———, 'Your Success Gives us Hope', *Tibetan Review,* (Delhi), vol. XXVI, no. II, November 1991, pp. 11–12.

A.iii
Books on The Dalai Lama
Includes works figuring The Dalai Lama's writings and interviews with him, Dharamsala Publications, and related Tibet Publications

Blais, Genevieve M.S.W., *The Dalai Lama: A Beginner's Guide,* London: Hodder and Stoughton, 2000.

Bunson, Mathew E., *The Dalai Lama's Book of Wisdom,* London: Rider, 1997.

———, *China in Tibet, Striking Hard Against Human Rights: Executive Summary, 1997 Annual Report: Human Rights Violations in Tibet,* Dharamsala: Tibetan Centre for Human Rights and Democracy, 1997.

———, *Closing the Doors: Religious Repression in Tibet,* Gangchen Kyishong, Dharamsala: Tibetan Centre for Human Rights and Democracy, n.d.

Bunson, Mathew E., *China's Current Policy in Tibet: Life-and-Death Struggle to Crush an Ancient Civilization, A Report Compiled and Published by the Department of Information and International Relations,* Central Tibetan Administration, Gangchen Kyishong, Dharamsala, September 29, 2000.

Bunson, Mathew E., *Creeds of Our Times*, Delhi: Full Circle Publishing and the Foundation for Universal Responsibility of His Holiness the Dalai Lama, 2000.

Chapela, Leonard R., 'Economic Institutions of Buddhist Tibet,' *The Tibet Journal*, (Library of Tibetan Works and Archives, Gangchen Kyishong, Dharamsala), vol. XVII, no. 3, Autumn 1992, pp. 2–40.

Demilitarization of the Tibetan Plateau: An Environmental Necessity, Dharamsala: Environment and Development Desk, Department of Information and International Relations, 2000.

Dialogues on Universal Responsibility and Education, Dharamsala: Library of Tibetan Works and Archives, 1995.

Discovery, Recognition and Enthronement of the 14th Dalai Lama, Dharamsala: Library of Tibetan Works and Archives, 2000.

Executive Summary, Human Rights Violations in 1998, Tibet: Crackdown on Humanity, Gangchen Kyishong, Dharamsala: Tibetan Centre for Human Rights and Democracy, n.d.

Facts About Tibet, Dharamsala: Sixth Central Executive Committee, Tibetan Youth Congress, n.d.

Farrer-Halls, Gills, *The World of The Dalai Lama: An Inside Look at His Life, His People, and His Vision,* Wheaton, Illinois: Quest Books, 1998.

Franz, Michael R., *Rule by Incarnation: Tibetan Buddhism and its Role in Society and State,* Colorado: Westview Press, 1982.

Goodman, Michael Harris, *The Last Dalai Lama: A Biography,* Boston: Shambhala, 1986.

Harrer, Heinrich, *Return to Tibet*, London: Weidenfeld and Nicolson, 1984.

Hicks, Roger, and Ngakpa Chogyam, *Great Ocean: An Authorized Biography of the Buddhist Monk Tenzin Gyatso His Holiness the Fourteenth Dalai Lama,* London: Penguin Books, (1984) 1990.

His Holiness the 14th Dalai Lama of Tibet: Dedicated to His Holiness the 14th Dalai Lama on the Occasion of the 60th Anniversary of His Enthronement and the 50th Anniversary of His Assuming Political Power of Tibet, Compiled by the Department of Information and International Relations, Published by the Committee for the 60th Enthronement Anniversary Celebration of the 50th Anniversary of his Holiness the Dalai Lama Assuming State Responsibility, December 2000.

Hopkins, Jeffrey, (ed.), *The Art of Peace: Nobel Peace Laureates Discuss Human Rights and Conflict, and Resolution,* Ithaca, New York: Snow Lion Publications, 2000.

Ingram, Catherine, *In the Footsteps of Gandhi,* Berkeley, California: Parallax Press, 1990.

Interim Report, Consecration of the Statue of Lord Buddha and the International Conference on Ecological Responsibility: A Dialogue with Buddhism 30ᵗʰ Sept to 4ᵗʰ Oct. 1993, Organized by Tibet House, Delhi: Cultural Centre of H.H. the Dalai Lama, November 1993.

International Resolutions and Recognitions on Tibet, The Department of Information and International Relations, Central Tibetan Administration, Gangchen Kyishong, Dharamsala, (1989) 1994.

Kranti, Vijay, *Dalai Lama The Nobel Peace Laureate Speaks: Based on First-Hand Interviews and Exclusive Photographs of H.H. Tenzin Gyatso, The 14th Dalai Lama of Tibet*, New Delhi: Centrasia Publishing Group, 1990.

Levenson, Claude B., *Symbols of Buddhism,* Paris: Editions Assouline, 1996.

_____, *The Dalai Lama: A Biography,* trans. Stephen Cox, Bombay: Oxford University Press, 1989.

Malik, Inder L., *Dalai Lama's of Tibet: Succession of Births*, New Delhi: Uppal Publishing House, 1984.

Michael, Franz, *Rule by Incarnation: Tibetan Buddhism and Its Role in Society and State*, Boulder, Colorado: Westview Press, 1982.

Mitra, Swati, (ed.), *Walking with the Buddha: Buddhist Pilgrimages in India,* New Delhi: Eicher Goodearth Limited, 1999.

Mullin, Glenn H., (ed. and trans.), Sidney Piburn, Anne Kandt, and Christine Cox, (eds), *Selected Works of the Dalai Lama III: Essence of Refined Gold,* Ithaca, New York: Snow Lion Publications, Inc., (1982) 2ⁿᵈ edn 1985.

Nash, Nancy, (ed.), *Tree of Life, Buddhism and Protection of Nature: With a Declaration on Environmental Ethics from His Holiness The Dalai Lama,* Manchester, United Kingdom: Alliance of Religions and Conservation, (1987) 2ⁿᵈ edn 1999.

Nobel Peace Prize Award Ceremony 1989: Speeches, Dharamsala: Office of Information and International Relations, n.d.

Present Conditions in Tibet, Gangchen Kyishong, Dharamsala, Office of Information and International Relations, 1990.

Rahul, Ram, *The Dalai Lama: The Institution*, New Delhi: Vikas Publishing House Pvt. Ltd., 1995.

Religion, Nature and Survival: The Inter-Religious Conference Convened on 25ᵗʰ November, 1989 at the India International Centre, (New Delhi), Inter-Religion Forum for Communal Harmony, Tibet House, New Delhi, (1991) 1992.

Rowell, Galen, *The Dalai Lama: My Tibet*, London: Thames and Hudson, 1990.

Second International Conference of Tibet Support Groups, Germany, June 14–17 1996: A Report, Convened by Tibetan Government-in-Exile In Co-operation with Friedrich Naumann Stiftung, n.d.

Sherring, Charles A., *Western Tibet and the British Borderland, The Sacred Country of Hindus and Buddhists: With an Account of the Government, Religions and Customs of its People,* Delhi: Asian Educational Services, (1906) 1993.

South East Asia, Human Rights: NGO Seminar on Tibet, Gangchen Kyishong, Dharamsala: Tibetan Centre for Human Rights and Democracy, 1998.

Tewari, Ramesh Chandra, and Krishna Nath, (eds), *Universal Responsibility: A Felicitation Volume in Honour of His Holiness the Fourteenth Dalai Lama, Tenzin Gyatso, on His Sixtieth Birthday,* New Delhi: Foundation for Universal Responsibility of His Holiness The Dalai Lama and A 'N' B Publishers, 1996.

The Legal Status of Tibet: Three Studies by Leading Jurists, Dharamsala: Office of Information and International Relations, 1989.

Tibet, Crackdown On Humanity: Annual Report 1998, Human Rights Violation in Tibet, Dharamsala: Tibetan Centre for Human Rights and Democracy, January 1999.

The Tibetan Administration at Dharamsala, Gangchen Kyishong, Dharamsala: The Office of Information and International Relations, Central Tibetan Secretariat, November 1988.

Tibet's Environment A Crucial Issue, Gangchen Kyishong, Dharamsala: Environment and Development Desk, Department of Information and International Relations, Central Tibetan Administration, 1998.

Tibet: Environment and Development Issues 1992, Dharamsala: Department of Information and International Relations, Central Tibetan Administration, 1992.

Tibet's Parliament In Exile, New Delhi: Tibetan Parliamentary and Policy Research Centre, 1996.

Tibet, Saving a People From Annihilation: Proceedings of the Second World Parliamentarians Convention on Tibet, Vilnius, Lithuania, 26–28 May 1995, Dharamsala: All Party Indian Parliamentary Forum for Tibet, 1997.

Tsering, Diki, *Dalai Lama, My Son: A Mother's Story,* edited and introduced by Khedroob Thondup, New Delhi: Penguin Books, 2000.

Tsomo, Tsering, and Shankar Sharan, (eds), *Tibet Since the Asian Relations Conference,* New Delhi: Tibetan Parliamentary and Policy Research Centre, 1998.

Tsomo, Tsering, (ed.), *Environment and Development: Annual Newsletter 1993–94,* Dharamsala: Environment and Development Desk, Department of Information and International Relations, Central Tibetan Administration, Gangchen Kyishong, 1994.

The Nobel Peace Prize And The Dalai Lama, edited and compiled by Piburn, Sidney, New York: Snow Lion Publications, 1990.

Weber, Renée, *Dialogues with Scientists and Sages: The Search for Unity,* London and New York: Routledge and Kegan Paul, (1986) Reprinted 1987.

A.iv
Articles and interviews in journals with/on The Dalai Lama (Includes journals published from Dharamsala and related Tibet journals published in Dharamsala and elsewhere)

'A Struggle of a Nation', *Tibetan Bulletin: The Official Journal of the Tibetan Administration,* (Department of Information and International Relations, Gangchen Kyishong, Dharamsala), vol. V, issue 1, January-February 2001, pp. 16–19.

'A Tale of Cultural Genocide', *Tibetan Bulletin: The Official Journal of the Tibetan Administration,* (Department of Information and International Relations, Gangchen Kyishong, Dharamsala), July–August 2000, pp. 6–10.

Ackerly, John, 'Tibet, Gandhi and King: The Merits of Non-violent Resistance', *Tibetan Review* (Delhi) XXIII, no. 8, August 1988, pp. 15–18.

'An Appeal', *Rangzen: The Magazine of the Tibetan Youth Congress,* (McLeod Ganj: Dharamsala), vol. XXII, no. 1, Spring 1997, p. 9.

Bharati, Agehananda, 'Tibetan Buddhism in America: The Late Seventies', *The Tibet Journal,* (Library of Tibetan Works and Archives, Gangchen Kyishong, Dharamsala), vol. 4, no. 2, Summer 1979, pp. 3–11.

Caroe, Olaf, 'Tibet and the Dalai Lama', *The Tibet Journal,* (Library of Tibetan Works and Archives Gangchen Kyishong, Dharamsala), vol.II, no. 4, Winter 1977, p. 11.

'Celebration, Reflection and Commitment', *Rangzen: The Magazine of the Tibetan Youth Congress,* (McLeod Ganj, Dharamsala), vol. XXVII, no.3, Autumn 2000, p. 3.

'China Silences UN Human Rights Body, Again', *Tibetan Bulletin: The Official Journal of the Tibetan Administration,* (Department of Information and International Relations, Gangchen Kyishong, Dharamsala), vol. 4, issue 2, May–June 2000, p. 30.

'Dalai Lama Against Hatred Towards Chinese', *Tibetan Review,* (Delhi), vol. XXXV, no. 5, May 2000, p. 14.

'Dalai Lama Prefers Secular Democratic Tibet', *Tibetan Review,* (Delhi), vol. XXXV, no. 3, March 2000, p. 8.

'Dalai Lama Desires Apolitical Role', *Tibetan Review,* (Delhi), vol. XXXIV, no. 9, September 1999, pp. 10–11.

Dhondup, Tashi, 'Independence First, Democracy Secondary', *Tibetan Review,* (Delhi), November 2000, pp. 23–4.

Dolma, Ani Jangchub, 'Planting the Seeds of Peace in Northern Ireland', *Mandala,* (California), March 2000, p. 74.

Dupuis, Oliver, 'Pacifism is not Nonviolence: Activating the Tibetan Struggle Through Worldwide Satyagraha', *Tibetan Review,* (Delhi), vol. XXXI, no. 7, July 1997, p. 19.

'A Question of Survival', *March: Magazine of the Delhi Tibetan Youth Congress,* (Delhi), vol. XXI, November 1999, pp. 4–5.

Farouqui, Ather, 'Practising Non-violence', *Thirdworld,* (Karachi), July 1990, pp. 37–45.

French, Patrick, 'Evolving Patterns of Tibetan Resistance', *Tibetan Bulletin: The Official Journal of the Tibetan Administration,* (Department of Information and International Relations, Gangchen Kyishong, Dharamsala), vol. 4, issue 3, July–August 2000, pp. 27–8.

Godfrey, Paul, 'Satyagraha as an Option in the Tibetan Struggle', *Tibetan Bulletin: The Official Journal of the Tibetan Administration,* (Department of Information and International Relations, Gangchen Kyishong, Dharamsala), May–June 1996, p. 33.

Goldstein, Melvyn C., and Paljor Tsarong, 'Tibetan Buddhist Monasticism: Social Psychological and Cultural Implications', *The Tibet Journal,* (Dharamsala, Library of Tibetan Works and Archives, Gangchen Kyishong, Dharamsala), vol. 10, 1985, pp. 14–31.

Herzer, Eva, 'Aspect of Autonomy: A Study in Autonomous Arrangements Around the World', *Tibetan Bulletin: The Official Journal of the Tibetan Administration,* (Department of Information and International Relations, Gangchen Kyishong, Dharamsala), vol. 4, issue 3, July–August 2000, pp. 14–19.

Huber, Toni, 'Traditional Environmental Protectionism in Tibet Reconsidered', *The Tibet Journal,* (Library of Tibetan Works and Archives, Gangchen Kyishong, Dharamsala), vol. XVI, no. 3, Autumn 1991, pp. 63–77.

Huitzi, 'The Institution of the Dalai Lamas in Question', *Lungta,* (Geneva, Switzerland), no. 7, August 1993, pp. 24–31.

Hyde-Chambers, Fredric R., 'The Dalai Lama and the People of Tibet', *The Middle Way: Journal of the Buddhist Society,* (London), vol. 7, no. 1, May 1996, pp. 3–13.

Kennedy Jr., John F., 'I am Optimistic, the Dalai Lama Speaks', *Tibetan Bulletin,* (Department of Information and International Relations, Gangchen Kyishong, Dharamsala), January–February 1998, pp. 20–2.

Klieger, P. Christian, 'The Institution of The Dalai Lama as a Symbolic Matrix,' *The Tibet Journal,* (Library of Tibetan Works and Archives, Gangchen Kyishong, Dharamsala), vol. XVI, no.1, Spring 1991, pp. 96–107.

Kyab, Amnyé, 'What the "Middle Way Approach" Isn't', *Tibetan Review,* (Delhi), vol. XXXIII, no. 5, May 1998, p. 15.

Lhundup, L. Pema, 'Tibet, China and U.N.', *March: The Magazine of the Delhi Tibetan Youth Congress,* (Delhi), vol. XXI, November 1999, pp. 12–13.

Martin, Chris and Robert W. Ankerson Junior, (eds), 'Mind and Life—I,' *Chöyang: The Voice of Tibetan Religion and Culture,* (Council for Religious and Cultural Affairs, Gangchen Kyishong, Dharamsala), (special issue), 1991, pp. 152–68. .

McGirk, Tim, 'The Dalai Lama on his frustration with Beijing', *Tibetan Bulletin,* (Department of Information and International Relations, Central Tibetan Administration, Gangchen Kyishong, Dharamsala), vol. 3, issue 2, March–April 1999, pp. 20–1.

'Media in The News Age Tibetans', *Rangzen: The Magazine of the Tibetan Youth Congress,* (McLeod Ganj, Dharamsala), vol. XXV, no. 2, Summer 2000, p. 23.

Mullens, James G., 'Action is Still Tibet's Best Strategy,' *Tibetan Review,* (Delhi) vol. XXXII, no. 7, July 1997, pp. 18–19.

_____, 'Buddhism and the West', *Tibetan Review,* (Delhi), vol. XVI, no.2, February 1981, pp. 8–14.

Mullin, Glenn H., 'Tibetan Buddhism and the Dalai Lama Office', *Tibetan Review,* (Delhi), vol. XX, no.4, April 1985, pp. 11–15.

_____, 'Tibetan Buddhism and the Dalai Lama Office', *Tibetan Review,* (Delhi), vol. XX, no. 3, March 1985, pp. 10–17.

_____, 'Three Letters from the Seventh Dalai Lama', *Tibetan Review,* (Delhi), vol. XVI, no. 3, March 1981, pp. 9–12.

_____, 'The U.S. Tour: A Traditional Perspective', *The Tibet Journal,* (Library of Tibetan Works and Archives, Gangchen Kyishong, Dharamsala), vol. V, no.1&2, Spring/Summer 1980, pp. 69–77.

Nashold, James, 'The Meeting of East and West: The Dalai Lama's First Trip to the United States', *The Tibet Journal,* (Library of Tibetan Works and Archives, Gangchen Kyishong, Dharamsala), no. 1 & 2, vol. V, Spring/Summer, 1980, pp. 34–41.

Norberg-Hodge, Helena, 'Learning from Ladakh', *Tibetan Bulletin: The Official Journal of the Tibetan Administration,* (Department of Information and International Relations, Gangchen Kyishong, Dharamsala), September–October 1991, pp. 14–16.

Norbu, Dawa T., 'Self-Determination: The Satisfactory Solution', *Tibetan Bulletin: The Official Journal of the Tibetan Administration,* (Department of Information and International Relations, Gangchen Kyishong, Dharamsala), May–June 1998, pp. 24–8.

_____, 'What Tibet Did in 2100 years', *Tibetan Review,* (Delhi), March 1993, pp. 8–9.

Norbu, Jamyang, 'Rangzen Charter, Supplement: Confusion in the Direction of the Freedom Struggle', *March: Magazine of the Delhi Tibetan Youth Congress,* (Delhi), vol. XXI, November 1999, pp. 13–19.

————, 'Non-Violence or Non-Action: Some Gandhian Truths About the Tibetan Peace Movement', *Tibetan Review,* (Delhi), vol. XXXII, no. 9, September 1997, pp, 18–21.

Norbu, Tseten, 'Where Are the Conditions for Holding A Referendum', *Tibetan Review,* (Delhi), vol. XXXII, no. 10, October 1997, pp. 20–1.

Pallis, Marco, 'The Dalai Lama: His Function, His Associates, His Rebirth', *The Middle Way: Journal of the Buddhist Society,* (London), vol. 71, no. 1, May 1996, pp. 25–36.

'Parents Forced to Bring Back Their Children from India', *Human Rights Update,* (Dharamsala: Tibetan Centre for Human Rights and Democracy), vol. III, no. 20, October 31, 1998.

Phuntsok, Tsewang, 'Self-Determination: A Case for Tibet', *Tibetan Bulletin: The Official Journal of the Tibetan Administration,* (Department of Information and International Relations, Gangchen Kyishong, Dharamsala), vol. 4, issue 3, July–August 2000, pp. 20–3.

Rigzin, Tsepak, and Francesca Hamilton, 'Buddhism and Meat Eating', *Tibetan Review,* (Delhi), vol. XVII, no. 9, September 1983, pp. 8–11.

Schwartz, Ronald D., 'Evolving Pattern of Tibetan Resistance', *Tibetan Bulletin, The Official Journal of the Tibetan Administration,* (Department of Information and International Relations, Gangchen Kyishong, Dharamsala), vol. 4, issue 3, July–August 2000, pp. 29–30.

Sen Geeti and Rajiv Mehrotra, 'Laughter and Compassion: His Holiness Tenzin Gyatso the XIVth Dalai Lama of Tibet in Conversation with Geeti Sen and Rajiv Mehrotra', *India International Centre Quarterly,* (Delhi), vol. 18, no. 4, Winter 1991, pp. 107–27.

Shakbapa, Wangchuk Derek, 'Referendum: Independence is the Key to Tibet's Survival', *Tibetan Review,* (Delhi), vol. XXXII, no. 6, June 1997, pp. 19–20.

Sheel, R.N. Rahul, 'The Institution of the Dalai Lama', *The Tibet Journal,* (Library of Tibetan Works and Archives, Gangchen Kyishong, Dharamsala), vol. XIV, no. 3, Autumn 1989, pp. 19–32.

Singer, Wendy, 'The Dalai Lama's Many Tibetan Landscapes', *The Kenyon Review,* vol. XXV, no. 3/4, Summer/Fall 2003, pp. 233–56.

Singh, A.J., 'Interview with the Dalai Lama: "God is your Business, Karma is my Business"', *The Tibet Journal,* (The Library of Tibetan Works and Archives Gangchen Kyishong, Dharamsala), vol. II, no.3, Autumn 1977, pp. 8–12.

Sivaraksa, Sulak, 'Sustainable Communities: A Thai Buddhist Perspective', *Tibet House Bulletin*, (New Delhi), vol. 15 and 16, no. 2 and 1, November 1999 and May 2000, pp. 1 and 3.

'Snubs and Sensitivities—The Millennium World Peace Summit', *Tibetan Bulletin*, (Department of Information and International Relations, Central Tibetan Administration, Dharamsala), vol. 4, issue 4, September–December 2000, pp. 19–20.

'Strasbourg Unrolls the Red Carpet for the Dalai Lama: Freedom Struggle to Continue so Long as China Does Not Negotiate', *Tibetan Review* (Delhi), vol., XXXI, no. 12, December 1996, pp. 10–14.

Snyder, Louise Rachel, 'Laughing with the Dalai Lama', *Tibetan Bulletin*, (Gangchen Kyishong, Department of Information and International Relations, Dharamsala), vol. 3, no. 6, November–December 1999, pp. 20–2.

Taksham, Lobsang Sengay, 'Human Rights and Universality: Asian Excuse and Contradictions', *Tibetan Review*, (Delhi), vol. XXX, no. 2, February 1995, pp. 12–16.

The Tibet Journal, (Gangchen Kyishong, Dharamsala, Library of Tibetan Works and Archives), vol. V, no.1 and 2, Spring/Summer 1980.

Thinley, Pema, 'Democracy is an Integral Part of the Tibetan Freedom Struggle', *Tibetan Bulletin: The Official Journal of the Tibetan Administration*, (Department of Information and International Relations, Gangchen Kyishong, Dharamsala), May–June 1996, 11–13.

'Tibet at Chinese Conference', *Rangzen: The Magazine of the Tibetan Youth Congress*, (McLeod Ganj: Dharamsala), vol. XXIV, no. 1/2, Spring/Summer 1999, p. 12.

Tulku, Sharpa, and Alex Turner, 'Missing the Point of Buddhism: Old Confusions Resurface in a New Book', *Tibetan Review*, (Delhi), vol. XXX, no. 6, June 1995 pp. 12–15.

Wadlow, René, 'Dialogue Among Civilizations: The Universal and the Specific', *Tibetan Review*, (Delhi), November 2000, p. 22.

Wangkhang, Tsering D, 'Can 100,000 Exiles Decide for Six Million in Tibet?', *Tibetan Review*, (Delhi), vol. XXXII, no. 8, August 1997, p. 13.

Wardle, Heather, 'Learning From Ladakh', *Tibetan Bulletin: The Official Journal of the Tibetan Administration*, (Department of Information and International Relations, Gangchen Kyishong, Dharamsala), September–October 1991, pp. 14–16.

Yeshi, Kim, 'The Tibetan Buddhist View of the Environment', *Chöyang I*, (Council for Religious and Cultural Affairs, Gangchen Kyishong, Dharamsala), 1991, pp. 264–9.

B.
Newspapers/Periodicals
Including Interviews with the Dalai Lama

Addy, Premen, 'A Light Unto The Nations', *The Statesman*, (New Delhi), 5 January 1997.

Aron, Sunita, 'Can Dalai Lama do what Others Couldn't?', *Hindustan Times*, (Mumbai), 18 January 2004.

Bakshi, Rajni, 'Exploring the Mind', *The Hindu*, (New Delhi), 7 January 2001.

Bartwal, Hemendra Singh, 'Dalai New Honest Broker on Ayodhya', *The Hindu* (New Delhi), January 9, 2004.

Bhatt, Jagdish, 'Dalai Lama Rules Out Talks to End in Impasse', *Times of India*, (New Delhi), 20 December 1995.

Bhushan, Bharat, 'Craig Can Help Build Mutual Trust: Dalai', *The Hindustan Times*, (New Delhi), 16 November 1997.

———, 'I'm Not Seeking Independence from China: Dalai', *The Hindustan Times*, (New Delhi), 15 November 1997.

———, 'Building Bridges with Chinese Pro-democracy Activists: Tibet in Focus 1', *The Hindustan Times*, (New Delhi), 14 November 1997.

Chanda, Sudipto, 'Just a Lama Praying for Patience', *The Statesman*, (New Delhi), 5 January 1997.

Chopra, Parveen, and Swati Chopra, (in an interview with His Holiness the Dalai Lama), 'We are Born to be Happy,' *Life Positive* (New Delhi), vol. 6, issue 6, August 2001, pp. 20–34.

Clifton, Tony, 'A Life in Exile', *Newsweek*, (New York), vol. CXXX, no. 15, 13 October 1997, pp. 48–51.

'Compassion is the Key to Happiness', *The Hindustan Times* (New Delhi), 31 January 2000.

'Dalai Lama for Strict Religious Practices', *The Hindu*, (New Delhi), 17 November 1999.

'Dalai Lama's Offer', *Tibetan Review*, (Delhi), vol. XIV, no. 7, July 1979, p. 16. See also *Tribune*, (Chandigarh), 4 July 1979.

Dewatshang, Kunga Samten, 'Escape from Lhasa', *the Asian Age*, (New Delhi), 19 April 1988.

Ganguly, Meenakshi, 'The Dalai Lama: "It's Time to Prepare New Leaders"', *Time*, (Hong Kong), 17 July 2000, pp. 22–3.

———, 'Paying the Ultimate Price', *Time*, (Hong Kong), 20 April 1998, p. 25.

Gittings, John, 'One Country, Two Systems—Mark-II?', *The Guardian*, (London), 14 April 1998.

Gittings, John, 'Tibet Bombing Confirms Worst Fears of Dalai Lama', *The Guardian,* (London), 1 January 1997.

Hazarika, Sanjoy, 'Faith Endures: Dalai Lama Speaks, Laughs and Ponders', *The Statesman,* (New Delhi), 9 April 2000.

'"Hinduism and Buddhism are Twins": Dalai Lama', *The Indian Express,* (New Delhi), 10 April 2001.

Kranti, Vijay, 'Refugee, Monk and Statesman', *Mainstream,* (New Delhi), vol. XXXIII, no. 33, July 8, 1995, p. 9–34.

Liu, Melinda, 'China's Balkan Crisis', *Newsweek,* (New York), 19 April 1999, pp. 34–6.

Malhotra, Jyoti, 'Dalai at CII Summit Ruffles Chinese Feathers', *The Indian Express,* (New Delhi), 9 January 1999.

McGirk, Tim, '"I am Ready to Talk Any Time": The Dalai Lama on His Frustrations with Beijing', *Time,* (Hong Kong), vol. 153, no. 2, 18 January 1999, p. 21.

Mohan, C. Raja, 'Dalai Lama for Autonomy Within China: Focus on Tibet-2', *The Hindu,* (New Delhi), 15 November 1997.

_____, 'Tibetans Hope for New Negotiations with China: Focus on Tibet-1', *The Hindu,* (New Delhi), 14 November 1997.

Ogden, Christopher, 'Talking Softly, Without the Big Stick: Sensitive to China's Distrust, the US and the Dalai Lama Keep Talks Low-Key', *Time,* (Hong Kong), vol. 152, no. 20, 23 November 1998, p. 32.

Pandey, Maneesh, 'Better Sino-Indian Ties Might Help Resolve Tibet Issue: Q&A\ Dawa Norbu', *The Times of India,* (New Delhi), 26 August 1998.

Poole, Teresa, 'Dalai Lama set for Autonomy Route to China: Drops Independence demand for Tibet to restart talks with Beijing', *The Hindustan Times,* (New Delhi), 11 November 1998.

Sarin, Jaideep, 'Tibetan Youth Militancy on the Rise', *The Hindustan Times,* (New Delhi), 2 January 1996.

Saxena, Shobhan, 'UN Draws Flak as Dalai Lama, Tutu to Skip Peace Summit,' *Indian Express,* (Delhi), 28 August 2000.

Sengupta, Ramananda, 'Some Plain Speak, At Last', *Outlook,* (New Delhi), 11 May 1988, pp. 27–8.

Singh Kanwaldeep, 'Dalai Preaches Ethics to Corporate Captains', *The Times of India,* (New Delhi), 9 January 1999.

Subramanian, N.V., 'The Situation in Tibet is Grave: The Dalai Lama on the New Panchen Lama, Chinese Policies and His Professed Middle Path,' *Sunday* (Calcutta), 7–13 January 1996, pp. 12–16.

'Tibetans Worried About Dalai's China Overture', *Asian Age,* (New Delhi), 1 November 1998.

C.
Select Internet Sources on The Dalai Lama

His Holiness the Dalai Lama, 'Universal Responsibility: Key to Human Survival', *http://www.ahrchk.net/hrsolid/mainfile.php/1999vol09no03/829/?print=yes*

'The Dalai Lama: on human value', *http://www.news.utoronto.ca/bin6/thoughts/040510-35.asp*

The Dalai Lama. 'Human Rights and Universal Responsibility' *http://www.tibet.com/DL/vienna.html*

'The 14ᵗʰ Dalai Lama—Nobel Lecture, December 11, 1989', *http://nobelprize.org/peace/laureates/1989/lama-lecture.html*

Philip Russell Brown, 'Socially Engaged Buddhism', *http://www.buddhanet.net/filelib/genbud/eng_bud.txt*

www.tibet.com

www.tibet.org

www.tchrd.org

Secondary Sources
Books

Almond, Brenda, *Introducing Applied Ethics*, Oxford: Blackwell Publishers Ltd, 1995.

Alott, Philip, *Eunomia* (New Order for a New World), Oxford: Oxford University Press, 1990.

Attfield, Robin, and Andrew Belsey, (eds), *Philosophy and the Natural Environment: Royal Institute of Philosophy Supplement*: 36, Cambridge: Cambridge University Press, 1994.

_____, Attfield, Robin, and Kathereine Dell, (eds), *Values, Conflict and the Environment*, Aldershot: Avebury, 1996.

Badiner, Allan Hunt, (ed.), *Dharma Gaia: A Harvest of Essays in Buddhism and Ecology*. Berkeley, California: Parallax Press, 1990.

Baier, Annette, *A Progress on Sentiments: Reflections on Hume's Treatise*, Cambridge: Harvard University Press, 1992.

_____, *Moral Prejudices*, Cambridge: Harvard University Press, 1994.

Banerjee, N.V, *Buddhism and Marxism: A Study in Humanism*, New Delhi: Orient Longman, 1978.

Batchelor, Martine, and Kerry Brown, (eds), *Buddhism and Ecology*, London and New York: Cassell Publishers Limited, 1992.

Burgess, Heidi, and Guy M. Burgess, *Encyclopedia of Conflict Resolution*, Santa Barbara, California: ABC-CLIO, Inc., 1997.

Burhenne, Wolfgang E., and Will A. Irwin, *The World Charter for Nature,* Berlin: Erich Schmidt Verlag GmbH, 1983.

Callicott, J. Baird, and Roger T. Ames, (eds), *Nature in Asian Traditions of Thought: Essays in Environmental Philosophy,* Delhi: Sri Satguru Publications, (1989) 1991.

Carman, John, and Mark Juergensmeyer, *A Bibliographic Guide to the Comparative Study of Ethics,* Cambridge: Cambridge University Press, 1991.

Carr, Brian, and Indira Mahalingam, (eds), *Companion Encyclopedia of Asian Philosophy,* London: Routledge, 1997.

Chakrishar, Thupten N., *Anything For Tibet: My Beloved Country,* New Delhi: Paljor Publications, 1999.

Chapple, Cristopher Key, *Nonviolence to Animals, Earth, and Self in Asian Traditions,* Delhi: Sri Satguru Publications, (1993) 1995.

Chhemed, Rigzin Lama, *Dhammapada: Dalai Lama Tibeto-Indological Studies Series,* vol. IV, Sarnath: Central Institute of Higher Tibetan Studies, 1982.

Clarke, J.J., *Nature in Question: An Anthology of Ideas and Arguments,* London: Earthscan Publications, 1993.

Collingwood, R., *The Idea of Nature,* London: Oxford University Press, 1960.

David, Phys. T.W., *Dialogues of the Buddha:* Part I, London: Luzac, 1969.

De Silva, Padmasiri, *Value Orientations and Nation Building,* Colombo, Sri Lanka: Lake House Investment Ltd., 1976.

Desai, Valji Govindji, (ed. & trans.), *the Diary of Mahadev Desai:* vol. 1, Yeravda-Pact Eve, 1932, Ahmedabad: Navjivan Publishing House, 1953.

Deutsch, Eliot, (ed.), *Culture and Modernity: East-West Philosophic Perspectives,* Delhi: Motilal Banarsidass Publishers Private Limited, (1991) 1994.

Devall, Bill, and George Sessions, *Deep Ecology: Living as if Nature Mattered,* Layton, UT: Gibbs Smith, 1985.

Dewan, M.L., *Towards a Sustainable Society: Perceptions,* New Delhi: Clarion Books, 1995.

Doboom Tulku Lama, *The Buddhist Path to Enlightenment: Tibetan Buddhist Philosophy and Practice,* California: Point Loma Publications, 1996.

Donnet, Pierre-Antoine, *Tibet: Survival in Question,* trans. Tica Broch, Delhi: Oxford University Press, 1994.

Dwivedi, O.P., *Environmental Ethics: Our Dharma to the Environment,* New Delhi: Sanchar Publishing House, 1994.

Edwards, Paul, (ed.), *The Encyclopedia of Philosophy,* vol. VI, New York: Cromwell Collier and Macmillan Inc., 1967.

Ennals, David and Frederick Hyde-Chambers, *Tibet in China: An International Alert Report,* (London), August 1988.

Eppsteiner, Fred, (ed.), *The Path of Compassion: Writings on Socially Engaged Buddhism,* Berkeley, California: Parallax Press, (1985) rev. edn 1988.

Fisher, Mary Pat, *Living Religions,* Upper Saddle River, N.J.: Prentice Hall, (1991) second ed. 1994.

Frankel, Joseph, *International Relations in a Changing World,* Oxford: Oxford University Press, (1979) 1981.

Gandhi, M.K., (ed.), *Young India,* (Weekly Paper) Ahmedabad: Navjivan Publishing House, 1919–1931.

_____, *Hind Swaraj or Indian Home Rule,* Ahmedabad: Navjivan Publishing House, 1938.

_____, *Ashram Observances in Action,* trans. from Gujarati by Valji Govindji Desai , Ahmedabad: Navjivan Publishing House, (1932) 1955.

_____, *Hind Swaraj or Indian Home Rule,* Ahmedabad: Navjivan Publishing House, 1962.

_____, *Satyagraha in South Africa,* Ahmedabad: Navjivan Publishing House, 1950.

_____, *An Autobiography Or The Story of My Experiments with Truth,* trans. from the original in Gujarati by Mahadev Desai, Ahmedabad: Navjivan Publishing House, (1927) 1972.

_____, *All Men are Brothers,* Krishna, Kriplani, (ed.) New York: Columbia University Press, 1958 (1980).

Glazier, Stephen D., (ed.), *Anthropology of Religion,* Westport, Connecticut: Greenwood Press, 1997.

Goldstein-Kyaga, Katrin, (ed.), *Nonviolence in Asia: The Art of Dying or a Road to Change,* Sweden: Stockholm University, 1999.

Goldstein, Melvyn, and Bell, Cynthia, *Nomads of Western Tibet,* Berkeley and Los Angeles: University of California Press, 1990.

Gormley, W. Paul, *Human Rights and Environment: The Need for International Co-operation,* Leydon: A.W. Sijthoff, 1976.

Gudmunsen, Chris, *Wittgenstein and Buddhism,* London: The Macmillan Press Ltd., 1977.

Guha, Ramachandra, *Environmentalism: A Global History,* Delhi: Oxford University Press, 2000.

Gunesekera, Romesh, *Reef,* London: Granta Books, 1994.

Harrer, Heinrich, *Return to Tibet,* London: Weidenfeld and Nicolson, 1984.

Harris, Ian, 'How Environmentalist is Buddhism?' *Religion,* vol. 21, April 1991, pp. 101–14.

Harvey, Peter, *An Introduction to Buddhist Ethics,* Cambridge, U.K.: Cambridge University Press, 2000.

Hazra, Kanai Lal, *Royal Patronage of Buddhism in Ancient India*, Delhi: D.K. Publications, 1984.

Hingorani, Anand T., and Ganga A. Hingorani, *The Encyclopaedia of Gandhian Thoughts*, New Delhi: Publications Department, All India Congress Committee (I), 1985.

Hobbes, Thomas, *Leviathan*, edited by Michael Oakeshott, New York: Collier Books, 1962.

Horner, I.B., (trans. from the Pali), *The Collection of Middle Length Sayings (Majjhima Nikāya), vol. I: The First Fifty Discourses (Mūlapannāsa)*, London: The Pali Text Society, 1976.

_____, *Early Buddhism and The Taking of Life*, Kandy, Sri Lanka: The Wheel Publication no. 104, Buddhist Publication Society, 1967.

Huntington, Samuel P., *The Third Wave: Democratization in the Late Twentieth Century*, Norman and London: University of Oklahoma Press, 1992.

_____, *The Clash of Civilizations And the Remaking of World Order*, New Delhi: Penguin Books, (1996) 1997.

Ibish, Yusuf, and Heana Marculescu, *Contemplation and Action in World Religions*, Houston: Rothko Chapel, 1978.

Iyer, Raghavan, (ed.), *The Dhammapada with Udanvarga*, New York: Concord Grove Press, 1986.

Iyer, Raghavan, *The Moral and Political Thought of Mahatma Gandhi*, London: Concord Grove Press, 1983.

Jackson, Roger R., and John J. Makransky, (eds), *Buddhist Theology: Critical Reflections by Contemporary Buddhist Scholars*, Surrey: Curzon, 2000.

Janus, Robert J., 'Tibet', *The World Book Encyclopedia*, vol. 19, Chicago: World Book Inc., 1994.

Jones, Ken, *Beyond Optimism: A Buddhist Political Ecology*, Oxford: Carpenter Publishing, 1993, reviewed by Diana Winton in *Turning Wheel*, (Berkeley, C.A.), Summer 1996, p. 29.

_____, *The Social Face of Buddhism: An Approach to Political and Social Activism*, London: Wisdom Publications, 1989.

_____, *Buddhism and Social Action: An Explanation*, Kandy: Buddhist Publication Society, 1981.

Kalupahana, David J., *Ethics In Early Buddhism*, Honolulu: University of Hawai'i Press, 1995.

Kateb, George, *Hannah Arendt: Politics, Conscience, Evil*, Oxford (Oxfordshire): Martin Robertson, 1984.

Kearney, Richard, *Modern Movements in European Philosophy*, Manchester: Manchester University Press, 1987.

Keown, Damien, *Contemporary Buddhist Ethics*, Richmond, Surrey: Curzon Press, 2000.

Keown, Damien, *Buddhism and Bioethics*, London: St. Martin's Press, 1995.

_____, *The Nature of Buddhist Ethics*, London: Macmillan, 1992.

Keown, Damien, et al, (eds), *Buddhism and Human Rights*, Surrey: Curzon, 1998.

Khoshoo, T.N., *Mahatma Gandhi: An Apostle of Applied Human Ecology*, New Delhi: Tata Energy Research Institute, 1995.

Kingdon, Ward F., *The Mystery Rivers of Tibet*, Philadelphia: Lippincott, 1923.

_____, *The Riddle of Tsangpo Gorges*, London: Arnold, 1926.

Kirthisinghe, Buddhadasa P., *Buddhist Concepts: Old and New*, Delhi: Sri Satguru Publications, 1983.

Kleinman, Arthur, Veena Das, and Margaret Lock, (eds), *Social Suffering*, Berkeley: University of California Press, 1996.

Klieger, P. Christiaan, *Tibetan Nationalism*, Meerut: Archana Publications, 1992.

Kotler, Arnold, (ed.), *Engaged Buddhist Reader: Ten Years of Engaged Buddhist Publishing*, Berkeley, California: Parallax Press, 1996.

Kraft, Kenneth, (ed.), *Inner Peace, World Peace: Essays on Buddhism and Nonviolence*, Albany: State University of New York Press, 1992.

Kumar, Anand, *Tibet: A Sourcebook*, New Delhi: Radiant Publishers, 1995.

Kumar, Satish, (ed.), *The Schumacher Lectures*, New York: Harper Colophon Books, 1981.

Lamb, Alistair, *Britain and Chinese Central Asia*, London: Routledge and Kegan Paul, 1960.

Laptev, I., *The World of Man and the World of Nature*, Moscow: Soviet Publishers, (1978) 1979.

Lazar, Edward, (ed.), *Tibet: The Issue is Independence: Tibetans in Exile Address the Key Tibetan Issue the World Avoids*, Delhi: Full Circle, 1988.

Leach, Edmund, *Custom Law and Terrorist Violence*, Edinburgh: Edinburgh University Press, 1977.

Levinson, David, (series ed.), *Aggression and Conflict: A Cross Cultural Encyclopedia*, Santa Barbara, California: ABC-CLIO, 1994.

Levi-Strauss, Claude, *Race and History*, Paris: UNESCO, 1952.

Lexicon Universal Encyclopedia: Vol. 6, New York: Lexicon Publications, Inc., 1980.

Lopez Jr., Donald S., *Modern Buddhism: Readings for the Unenlightened*, London: Penguin Books, 2002.

_____, *Prisoners of Shangrila*, Chicago: University of Chicago Press, 1998.

Lopez Jr., Donald S., and Steven C. Rockfeller, (eds), *The Christ and the Bodhisattva*, Albany: State University of New York Press, 1987.

Martin, Julia, (ed.), *Ecological Responsibility, A Dialogue with Buddhism: A Collection of Essays and Talks,* (Sambhota Series V), New Delhi: Tibet House, 1997.

Mascaro, J., *The Dharmapada,* London: Penguin, 1973.

_____, and S., McFarlane, 'Buddhism', in E. Lazlo and J.Y. Yoo, (eds), *World Encyclopedia of Peace* vol. 1, Oxford: Pergamon Press, pp. 97–103.

Michael, Franz, *Rule by Incarnation: Tibetan Buddhism and its Role in Society and State,* Boulder: Westview Press, 1982.

Morgan, Peggy, and Clive Lawton, (eds), *Ethical Issues in Six Religious Traditions,* Edinburgh: Edinburgh University Press, 1996.

Murphy, Dervla, *Tibetan Foothold,* London: Flamingo, (1966) 2000.

Nagpal, Tanvi, and Camilla Foltz, (eds), *Choosing Our Future: Visions of a Sustainable World* as cited in *World Resources Institute: Publications 1999* (Washington, D.C.: World Resources Institute), 1999, p. 32.

Nash, Roderick Frazer, *The Rights of Nature: A History of Environmental Ethics,* Madison, Wisconsin: The University of Wisconsin Press, 1989.

Norbu, Dawa T., *Tibet: The Road Ahead,* London: Rider, 1998.

Norbu, Namkhai, *The Necklace of gZi: A Cultural History of Tibet,* Dharamsala: Narthang Publications, (1981) 1989.

Parekh, Bhikhu, *Colonialism, Tradition and Reform: An Analysis of Gandhi's Political Discourse,* Sage: New Delhi, 1989.

Pauling, Linus, (honorary Editor-in-Chief) and Erwin Lazlo and Jong Youl Yoo (eds), *World Encyclopedia of Peace,* vol. 1, Oxford: Pergamon Press, 1986.

Pereira, L.P.N., *Buddhism and Human Rights: A Buddhist Commentary on the Universal Declaration of Human Rights,* Colombo: Karunaratne and Sons, 1991.

Prebish, Charles S (ed.), *Buddhism: A Modern Perspective,* London: The Pennsylvania State University Press, 1975.

Puri, Rashmi-Sudha, *Gandhi on War and Peace,* New York: Praeger, 1987.

Queen, Christopher S., (ed.), *Engaged Buddhism in the West,* Boston: Wisdom Publications, 2000.

Queen, Christopher S. and Sallie B. King, (eds), *Engaged Buddhism: Buddhist Liberation Movements in Asia,* Albany: State University of New York Press, 1996.

Radhakrishnan, S., *Recovery of Faith,* New Delhi: HarperCollins *Publishers* India, 1997.

_____, *The Dhammapada: With Introductory Essays, Pali Text, English Translation and Notes,* Madras: Oxford University Press, (1950) 1984.

Rahul, Ram, *The Government and Politics of Tibet,* Delhi: Vikas Publications, 1969.

Rai, Lal Deosa, *Human Rights in the Hindu-Buddhist Tradition,* Jaipur: Nirala Publications, 1995.

Rapaport, Anatole, *Fights, Games and Debates*, Michigan: University of Michigan Press, 1960.

Ratnapala, Nandasena, *Crime and Punishment in the Buddhist Tradition*, New Delhi: Mittal Publications, 1993.

Ray, Himanshu Prabha, *Monastery and Guild: Commerce Under the Sâtvâhanas*, Delhi: Oxford University Press, 1986.

Raz, Joseph, (ed.), *Authority*, Oxford: Basil Blackwell, 1990.

Regan, Stephen, (ed.), *The Eagleton Reader*, Oxford: Blackwell Publishers, 1998.

Richardson, Hugh, *Tibet and Its History*, Boston: Shambhala, 1984 second edition.

Rudolph, Suzanne Hoeber, and James Piscatori, *Transnational Religion and Fading States*, Colorado: Westview Press, 1997.

Russell, Bertrand, *Political Ideals*, London: Routledge, 1997.

⸺ and H., Saddhatissa, (trans.), *The Sutta-Nipâta*, London: Curzon Press, 1985.

Sabine, George H., *A History of Political Thought*, London: George G. Harrap & Co. Ltd., 1937.

Said, Abdul Aziz, 'Pursuing Human Dignity', in Abdul Aziz Said, ed., *Human Rights and World Order*, New Brunswick, New Jersey: Transaction Books, 1978, pp. 1–21.

Samdhong, Rimpoche, (ed.), *Selected Writings and Speeches: A Collection of Selected Writings and Speeches on Buddhism and Tibetan Culture*, Sarnath, Varanasi: Alumni of Central Institute of Higher Tibetan Studies, 1999.

⸺, *Tibet: A Future Vision*, New Delhi: Tibetan Parliamentary and Policy Research Centre, 1997.

Sarkisyanz, E., *Buddhist Backgrounds of Burmese Revolution*, The Hague: Martinus Nijhoff, 1965.

Schopenhauer, A., *On the Basis of Morality*, trans. E.F.J. Payne, Indianapolis: Bobbs-Merrill, 1965.

Schumacher, E.F., *Small is Beautiful: A Study of Economics as if People Mattered*, London: Vintage, 1993.

Schweitzer, Albert, *Indian Thought and its Development*, trans. Charles E.B. Russell, New York: Henry Holt, 1936.

Shakya, Tsering, *The Dragon in the Land of Snows: A History of Modern Tibet Since 1947*, London: Pimlico, 1999.

Sharma, Chandradhar, *A Critical Survey of Indian Philosophy*, Delhi: Motilal Banarasidass Publishers Pvt. Ltd., (1960) reprinted 1991.

Sharma, S.K., and Usha Sharma, (eds), *Encyclopaedia of Tibet*, vol. 5, New Delhi: Anmol Publications Pvt. Ltd., 1996.

Sharma, Swaran Lata, *Tibet: Self-Determination in Politics Among Nations*, New Delhi: Criterion Publications, 1988.

Shiva, Vandana, 'Recovering the Real Meaning of Sustainability', in David E. Cooper, and Joy A. Palmer, (eds), *The Environment in Question: Ethics and Global Issues,* London: Routledge, 1992.

Singh, Birinder Pal, *Problem of Violence: Themes in Literature,* Shimla: Indian Institute of Advanced Study, 1999.

Sivaraksa, Sulak, *Siam in Crisis,* Bangkok: Thai Inter-Religious Commission for Development (TICD), 2533/(1980), Second edition 1990.

Sivaraksa, Sulak, (hon. ed.), Pipob Udomittipong, and Chris Walker, (eds), *Socially Engaged Buddhism For the New Millennium: Essays in Honour of The Ven. Phra Dhammapitaka (Bhikkhu P.A. Payutto) On his 60th birthday Anniversary,* Bangkok: Sathikoses-Nagapradipa Foundation and Foundation for Children, 12 May 2542 (1999).

Sizemore, Russell F. and Donald K. Swearer, (eds), *Ethics, Wealth and Salvation: A Study of Buddhist Social Ethics,* Columbia: University of South Carolina Press, 1990.

Smith Jr., Warren W., *Tibetan Nation: A History of Tibetan Nationalism and Sino-Tibetan Relations,* Colorado: Westview Press, Inc., 1996.

Sondhi, M.L. 'The Return of Tibet to World Politics', in Petra Kelly, Gert Bastian and Pat Aiello (eds), *The Anguish of Tibet,* Berkeley, California: Parallax Press, 1991, pp. 265–9.

Steiner, Henry J. and Philip Alston, *International Human Rights in Context: Law, Politics, Morals,* Oxford: Clarendon Press, 1996 (second reprint).

Suzuki, Daisetz Teitaro, (trans. from *Sanskrit*), *The Lankavatara Sutra: A Mahayana Text,* London: Routledge and Kegan Paul, (1932) 1978.

Symonides, Janusz, (ed.), *Human Rights: New Dimensions and Challenges,* Aldershot, England: Dartmouth publishing Company Limited/Ashgate Publishing Limited, Jointly with Paris: United Nations Educational, Scientific and Cultural Organization, 1998.

Tambiah, S.J., *World Conqueror and World Renouncer,* Cambridge, England: Cambridge University Press, 1976.

Tendulkar, D.G., *Mahatma: Life of Mohandas Karamchand Gandhi,* (8 vols.), vol.IV, 1934–1938, Bombay: Vithalbhai K. Jhaveri and D.G. Tendulkar, July 1952.

——, *Mahatma: Life of Mohandas Karamchand Gandhi,* (8 vols.), vol.VIII, 1947–1948, Bombay: Vithalbhai K. Jhaveri and D.G. Tendulkar, 30 January 1954.

Thapar, Romila, *Aśoka and the Decline of the Mauryas,* Oxford: Oxford University Press, 1961.

Thich Nhat, Hanh, *Love in Action: Essays on Non-Violent Social Change,* Berkeley: Parallax Press, 1993.

——, *Being Peace,* London: Rider; New York: University of New York Press, 1987.

Thich Nhat, Hanh, *Interbeing: Fourteen Guidelines for Engaged Buddhism*, Berkeley: Parallax Press, 1987.

Toulmin, S., and J. Goodfield, *The Fabric of the Heavens*, Harmondsworth: Penguin, 1963.

Tronto, Joan, *Moral Boundaries: A Political Argument for an Ethic of Care*, New York: Routledge, 1993

Tucker, Mary Evelyn, and Duncan Ryuken Williams, (eds), *Buddhism and Ecology: The Interconnectedness of Dharma and Deeds*, Harvard: Harvard Centre for the Study of World Religions, 1997.

Universal Declaration of Human Rights, United Nations Department of Public Information, November 1988.

Ursul, A.D., (ed.), *Philosophy and the Ecological Problems of Civilization*, trans. H. Cambell Creighton, Moscow: Progress Publishers, 1983.

Waddell, L. Austine, *Tibetan Buddhism: With its Mystic Cults, Symbolism and Mythology, and in its Relation to Indian Buddhism,* New York: Dover Publications, Inc., 1972.

Wayman, A. (trans. from Tibetan), *The Ethics of Tibet: The Bodhisattva Section of Tsong-Kha-Pa's Lam Rim Chen Mo*, Albany: State University of New York Press, 1991.

Weber, Max, *The Religion of India: The Sociology of Hinduism and Buddhism,* New York: The Free Press, 1958.

Williams, Duncan Ryuken, *Buddhism and Ecology: The Interconnection of Dharma and Deeds.* Cambridge, MA: Harvard University Center for the Study of World Religions, 1997.

Wuthnow, Robert, (ed.), *The Encyclopaedia of Politics and Religion,* vol. I and II, London: Routledge, 1998.

Williams, Duncan Ryuken and, Christopher S. Queen, *American Buddhism: Methods and Findings, in Recent Scholarship*, Richmond, Surrey: Curzon Press, 1999.

Xinru Liu, *Ancient India and Ancient China: Trade and Religious Exchanges AD 1–600*, Delhi: Oxford University Press, 1994.

Yu Ying-Shih, 'Han Foreign Relations', in *The Cambridge History of China*, vol. 1, Cambridge: University Press, 1986.

Zelliot, Eleanor, *From Untouchable to Dalit: Essays on the Ambedkar Movement*, New Delhi: Manohar, 1992.

Articles

Bhattacharjea, Mira Sinha, 'Self-determination for the Tibetan People: A Political Argument', *China Report*, (New Delhi), vol. 32, no. 4, 1996, 353–61.

Bhikkhu, Santikaro, 'Planting Rice Together: Socially Engaged Monks in Thailand', *Turning Wheel*, (Berkeley, California), Summer 1996, pp. 16–20.

Boruah, Bijoy H., 'Comments on the Note Entitled "The Idea of Human Rights" by Mrinal Miri', *Journal of Indian Council of Philosophical Research*, (New Delhi), vol. XVII, no. 2, January–April 2000, pp. 163–5.

'Broadly Engaging,' *Dharma Life*, (Birmingham, U.K.), vol. 16, summer 2001, pp. 50–4.

Cheney, Jim and Anthony Weston, 'Environmental Ethics as Environmental Etiquette: Toward on Ethics-Based Epistemology', *Environmental Ethics*, (Denton, Tx.: The Center for Environmental Philosophy and the University of North Texas), vol. 21, no. 2, Summer 1999, pp. 115–34.

Drucker, Claudia, 'Hanna Arendt on the Need for a Public Debate on Science', *Environment Ethics*, (Texas, USA), vol. 20, no. 3, Fall 1998, pp. 305–16.

Freeman, Michael, 'Human Rights, Asian Values, and the Clash of Civilizations', *Issues and Studies*, (National Chengchi University, Taipei), 34, No. 10, October 1998, pp. 48–78.

Gandhi, M.K., 'Religion Vs. No Religion,' *Harijan: A Journal of Applied Gandhism*, (1933–1955 in nineteen volumes), vol. X, 1946, New York: Garland Publishing, Inc., 1973, p. 172.

Herzer, Eva, 'The Law of Force or the Force of Law?: A Case Study of Tibet', *Turning Wheel: Journal of the Buddhist Peace Fellowship*, (Berkeley, C.A.), Summer 2000, pp. 26–8.

Horigan, Damien, 'Buddhist Perspectives On the Death Penalty,' *Turning Wheel: Journal of the Buddhist Peace Fellowship*, (Berkeley, CA), Winter 1999, pp. 16–19.

Huntington, Samuel, 'The Clash of Civilizations?' *Foreign Affairs*, (New York), vol. 72, 1993, pp. 22–49.

India International Centre Quarterly, (New Delhi), vol. 26 and 27, November 4 and 1, Spring 2000 incorporating Winter 1999.

James, Simon P., 'Thing-Centered Holism in Buddhism, Heidegger, and Deep Ecology', *Environmental Ethics*, (Denton, Texas: The Center for Environmental Philosophy and the University of North Texas), vol. 22, no. 4, Winter 2000, pp. 359–75.

Jan, Hung-Yi, 'Interaction Between Mainland China and the UN Human Rights Regime', *Issues and Studies*, (National Chengchi University, Taipei), vol. 34, no.11/12, November/December 1998, pp. 56–89.

Joshi, H.M., 'Violence—Gandhian Technique of Resisting Violence', *Journal of the Oriental Institute*, (Baroda: Oriental Institute), nos. 1–2, vol. XLIII, September–December 1993, pp. 67–90.

Keith, Linda Camp, 'The United Nations International Covenant on Civil and Political Rights: Does it Make a Difference in Human Rights Behaviour,' *Journal of Peace Research*, (New Delhi: Sage Publications), vol. 36, no. 1, 1999, pp. 95–118.

Kraft, Kenneth, 'The Wheel of Engaged Buddhism: A New Map of the Path,' *Shambhala Sun*, (Boulder, California), November 1999, p. 24.

Lal, Vinay, 'Gandhi and the Ecological Vision of Life: Thinking Beyond Deep Ecology', *Environmental Ethics*, (Denton, Tx.: The Centre for Environmental Philosophy and the University of North Texas), vol. 22, no. 2, Summer 2000, pp. 149–69.

Lubis, T. Mulya, 'Human Rights Standard Setting in Asia: Problems and Prospects', *The Indonesian Quarterly*, (Jakarta), vol. XXI, no. 1, First Quarter 1993, pp. 25–37.

Methta, Geeta, 'Gandhi's Integral Humanism', *Gandhi Marg: Quarterly Journal of Gandhi Peace Foundation*, (New Delhi), vol. 21, no. 2, July–September 1999, pp. 221–6.

Miri, Mrinal, 'A Note on the Idea of Human Rights', *Journal of Indian Council of Philosophical Research*, (New Delhi), vol. XVII, no. 2, January–April 2000, pp. 159–63.

Myokyo-ni, Venerable, 'Living Buddhism: Part I', *The Middle Way: Journal of Buddhist Society*, (London), vol. 74, no. 1, May 1999, pp. 2–11.

Nathan, Andrew J., 'Human Rights in Chinese Foreign Policy', *The China Quarterly*, (SOAS, London), no. 139, September 1994, pp. 622–35.

'Norwegian Nobel Committee: The 1989 Nobel Peace Prize', *The Middle Way: Journal of the Buddhist Society*, (London), vol. 71, no. 1, May 1996, pp. 14–24.

Nussbaum, Martha, 'Compassion: The Basic Social Emotion,' *Social Philosophy and Policy*, vol. 13, no. 1, 1996, pp. 27–58.

Parayil, Govindan, 'Sustainable Development: The Fallacy of a Normatively-Neutral Development Paradigm', *Journal of Applied Philosophy*, (Oxford), vol. 15, no. 2, 1998, pp. 179–94.

Pensa, Corrado, 'A Buddhist View of Ecology: Interdependence, Emptiness and Compassion', *Journal of Dharma*, (Bangalore: India), vol. XXVI, no.1, January–March 2001, pp. 36–46.

Redetop, Paul, 'The Emerging Discipline of Conflict Resolution Studies', *Peace Journal: The Canadian Journal of Peace Studies*, (Manitoba, Canada), vol. 31, no.1, February 1999, pp. 76–88.

Rogers, Ben, 'The Nature of Value and the Value of Nature: A Philosophical Overview', *International Affairs*, (Royal Institute of International Affairs: Oxford), vol. 76, no. 2, 2000, pp. 315–23.

Sautman, Barry, 'Tibet: Myths and Realities', *Current History*, (Philadelphia, USA), vol. 100, no. 647, September 2001, pp. 278–83.

Swearer, Donald K, 'Buddhism and Ecology: Challenge and Promise', *Earth Ethics*, (Washington, DC, USA), vol. 10, no. 1, Fall 1998, pp. 19–22.

Thompson, Janna, 'Environment as Heritage', *Environmental Ethics*, (Denton, Texas: The Centre for Environmental Philosophy and the University of North Texas), vol. 22, no. 3, Fall 2000, pp. 241–58.

Udomittipong, Pipob, 'Tibet: Report from Dharamsala', *Seeds of Peace*, (Bangkok), vol. 14, no. 3, 2541, (1998), pp. 9–11.

'UN meeting on Ecology and the Role of Religion', *News*, (Harvard: Harvard University Centre for the Study of World Religion), vol. 6, no. 1, fall 1998, p. 1 and 3.

Vyas, Nitin J., 'Vitality and Viability of Buddhism Today', *Journal of the Oriental Institute*, (Vadodara: Oriental Institute, M.S. University of Baroda), vol. XLIV, no. 1–4, September 1994–June 1995, pp. 53–8.

Walter, Michael L., 'The Spiritual Ecology of Tibet', *Himalayan Research Bulletin*, (Seattle, USA), vol. XII, nos. 1–2, 1992, p. 127.

Williams, Duncan Ryuken, and Christopher S. Queen, 'American Buddhism: Methods and Findings in Recent Scholarships', *Japanese Journal of Religious Studies*, (Nagoya, Japan), vol. 27, nos. 1–2, Spring 2000, pp. 143–6.

Winston, Diana, 'Universal Education: On the Frontier of Socially Engaged Buddhism', *Turning Wheel: Journal of Buddhist Peace Foundation*, (Berkeley, California), Summer 1999, pp. 14–18.

Newspapers/Periodicals

'A Message of Undeniable Importance', *The Hindu*, (Delhi), 11 December 1998.

'A Survey of Human-Rights Law: The World is Watching', *The Economist*, (London), 5 December 1998, pp. 8–10.

Bunting, Madeleine, 'Holy New Alliance', *The Guardian*, (London), 1 September 1999.

'China Plans to Bring Radioactive Waste', United News of India (UNI), 28 September 1998.

'Controversies and Culture', *The Economist*, (London), 5 December 1988, pp. 8–10.

'Dalai Lama Seeks International Help for Panchen Lama', *The Times of India*, (New Delhi), 2 December 1995.

Earth Ethics: Evolving Values for an Earth Community, (Washington, DC, USA), vol. 10, no. 1, Fall 1998, pp. 1–31.

'Environment, Religion Must Go Hand-in-hand', *The Hindustan Times*, (New Delhi), 6 June 2000.

'Floods: Dam Breach in Tibet, China "Hushed" It Up', *The Indian Express*, (New Delhi), 11 July 2000.

Ganguly, Meenakshi, 'Paying the Ultimate Price', *Time*, (Hong Kong), 20 April 1998, p. 25.

Hilton, Isabel, 'Looking for the Lama', *The Guardian*, (London), 15 September 1999.

Iyer, Pico, 'China's Buddha Complex: For Beijing Nothing is Sacred', *The New York Times*, (New York), 3 December 1995 as cited in *The Panchen Lama Lineage: How Reincarnation is Being Reinvented as a Political Tool*, Gangchen Kyishong, Dharamsala: The Department of Information and International Relations, Central Tibetan Administration, (1995) 1996, p. 90.

_____, 'The Panchen Lama, A Tiny Pawn in the Sino-Tibetan Endgame', *Asian Age*, (New Delhi), 8 December 1996.

McGirk, 'Tibetan Nun's Himalayan Odyssey', *The Hindustan Times*, (New Delhi), 16 February 1994.

Madsen, Stig Toft, 'Globalization, Demystification and Schism in Tibetan Buddhism', *Economic and Political Weekly*, (Mumbai), July 23, 1994, pp. 1926–8.

Monahan, Jerome, 'Beyond the Basics', *Guardian Education*, (London), Tuesday 11 April 2000, p. 62.

Narula, Sunil, 'Some Plainspeak, At Last: Tibet, and Beijing's Military Aid to Pakistan Dominate the Chinese Army Chief's Visit to India', *Outlook*, (New Delhi), 11 May 1998, pp. 26–7.

Norbu, Dawa, 'The Middle Way: Tibetan Buffer Between India and China', *The Statesman*, (New Delhi), 18 September 1999.

Phadnis, Aditi, and Paromita Mukherjee, 'The Third Force: The Karmapa and his Significance', *Sunday*, (Calcutta), 17–23 December 1995, p. 22.

Ram, N., 'India Can Help Develop Tibet–Lin Bo, Deputy Division Chief, Development and Planning Commission, TAR', *Frontline*, (Chennai), vol. 17, no. 18, 2–15 September 2000, pp. 128–9.

_____, 'Of Development in a Prefecture–Lobsang Cheuda, Vice Governor, Shannan Prefecture Government', *Frontline*, (Chennai), vol. 17, no. 18, 2–15 September 2000, pp. 126–8.

_____, 'On a Performing System of Democratic Centralism–Song Helping, Vice-Governor of Lhasa Municipal Government', *Frontline*, (Chennai), vol. 17, no. 18, 2–15 September 2000, pp. 124–6.

_____, 'Tibet-A Reality Check', *Frontline*, (Chennai), vol. 17, no. 18, 2–15 September 2000, pp. 4–23.

Rhode, William, 'In Search of Nirvana', *Sunday,* (Delhi), 7–13 May 1995, pp. 54–6.

———, 'In Search of Nirvana: What Accounts for the Renewed Interest is Buddhism?', *Sunday,* (Calcutta), 7–13 May 1995, pp. 45–56.

Sabet, Katia, 'In Faith Does Home Beckon', *The Statesman,* (New Delhi), 5 January 1997.

Shakya, Tsering, 'Solving the Tibetan Problem', *Time,* (Hong Kong), 17 July 2000, p. 25.

Singh, Shubha, 'Beijing Talks on Tibet', *The Pioneer,* (New Delhi), 21 July 1993.

Sorabjee, Soli J., 'Why Human Right are Universal', *Indian Express,* (New Delhi), 10 December 1999.

Swamy, Subramaniam, 'Sino-Indian Relations Through the Tibet Prism', *Frontline,* (Chennai), vol. 17, no. 18, 2–15 September 2000, pp. 24–9.

Thapa, Vijay Jung, 'Tibetan's in Exile: Politics Rattles Tradition', *India Today,* (New Delhi), 31 December 1995, pp. 90–3.

'The Human Rights Law Survey,' *The Economist,* (London), 5 December 1988.

'The Mosquito Strategy', *The Hindustan Times,* (New Delhi), 16 November 1997.

Thukral, Gobind, 'Free Tibet Drive May Get a Boost', *The Hindustan Times,* (New Delhi), 9 December 1995.

———, 'Where Are the Big Powers: Tibetans', *The Hindustan Times,* (New Delhi), 5 December 1995.

'Tibetan YC Assails China', *The Times of India,* (New Delhi), 1 December 1995.

'Tibetans Storm China Consul, Set Fire to Flags', *The Asian Age,* (New Delhi), 8 January 1999.

Trikha, N.K., 'Tibetans: A Democratic Transformation', *The Hindustan Times,* (New Delhi), 18 March 1996.

'UN Prevents Dalai Lama From Speaking', *Asian Age,* (New Delhi), 5 March 2001.

Wehrfritz, George, and Russell Watson, 'Why Tibet Matters,' *Newsweek,* (New York), vol. CXXX, no. 15, 13 October 1997, pp. 15–17.

Weiskopf, Michael, 'China Reportedly Agrees to Store Western Nuclear Wastes', *The Washington Post,* (Washington, D.C.) 18 February 1984.

Internet Sources

Brown, Philip Russell, 'Socially Engaged Buddhism: A Buddhist Practice for West', *http://www.buddhanet.net/filelib/genbud/eng_bud.txt*

'The Dalai Lama: on human value,' *http://www.news.utoronto.ca/bin6/thoughts/040510-36.asp*

'Universal Declaration of Human Rights,' *http/www.un.org/Overview/rights.html*

Thesis

Rajesh M.N.,'*Role of Gompa in Traditional Tibetan Society: A Thematic Study*',
    Unpublished Doctoral Thesis, JNU, 1998.

Index